"Dr Rachel Hoare has generously provided practitioners with a brilliant book that captures how expressive arts are essential in supporting adolescents challenged by traumatic stress. Articulately written, it is groundbreaking in scope and breadth and provides practitioners with numerous practical, informative, and inspirational guidelines and strategies. This volume is a 'must read' for anyone who works with traumatic stress and elevates the role of expressive arts (movement, sound, image, enactment, and narrative) to its essential place as a psychotherapeutic intervention for refugees and anyone who has survived crises."

Cathy Malchiodi, *PhD, LPCC, LPAT, REAT, author of* Trauma and Expressive Arts Therapy: Brain, Body, and Imagination in the Healing Process *and* Handbook of Expressive Arts Therapy

"This book offers a comprehensive framework that is universally applicable to professionals, groups, and institutions working with children and youth refugees worldwide. The case stories validate the relevant steps and professional guidance for refugees' recovery from traumatic experiences.

Amidst the turmoil and upheaval the world has witnessed, children and young people have been uprooted and scarred by violent conflict. This book stands as a guiding compass, directing us to the healing power of the arts when delivered with care and precision. The extensive research, practice, and lived experience serve as beacons, illuminating the path to bridging knowledge and practice gaps. This book is a 'well' for wellbeing, providing reassurance and guidance for humanitarian work! I strongly recommend it."

Kunle Adewale, *founder, Global Arts in Medicine Fellowship*

"This book is a well-structured, accessible, and encouraging guide for all professionals who want to reflect on and improve their work with refugee adolescents.

Dr Hoare guides the reader towards an essential understanding of the impact of forced migration and traumatic experiences on adolescent brain development and the development of key therapeutic skills and values. She offers insightful, clearly illustrated methods of incorporating expressive arts techniques into diverse psycho-social support settings.

Indispensable reading for anyone supporting refugee adolescents!"

Jessica Farnan, *manager, Youth and Education Service for Refugees and Migrants, Dublin, Ireland*

Psychological Support for Refugee Adolescents

Psychological Support for Refugee Adolescents demonstrates the therapeutic powers of the expressive arts to address the specific needs of adolescent refugees in a trauma-informed and culturally sensitive manner.

Bridging the gaps in guidance on support for refugee adolescents, this essential resource integrates neuroscience, trauma theory, and creative interventions and provides tools for readers to use in both clinical and non-clinical settings. Chapters are organised into sections tailored to support the professionals involved in caring for adolescent refugees, including both psychotherapists and non-psychotherapists, with practical advice that is accessible across disciplines. Through richly detailed case studies featuring diverse refugee experiences, this book demonstrates how creative modalities, including visual arts, music, movement, and embodied practices, can be expertly tailored to honour cultural contexts while also addressing trauma symptoms, sleep disturbances, isolation, and other challenges.

An essential read for any professional involved in support for adolescent refugees, this book will also be of interest to arts and expressive therapists and mental health practitioners more broadly. The online support material for this book includes downloadable and photocopiable activities tailored for application to both psychotherapeutic and more general wellbeing support, aiding readers in their work with refugee adolescents.

Rachel Hoare is an assistant professor in the School of Languages, Literatures and Cultures at Trinity College Dublin, where she founded the Research Centre for Forced Migration Studies. She is also a faculty member at the Children's Therapy Centre in Mullingar, Ireland, and works with the Irish Child and Family Agency as a part-time expressive arts child and adolescent psychotherapist, supporting unaccompanied asylum-seeking adolescents.

Psychological Support for Refugee Adolescents

An Expressive Arts Approach to Wellbeing and Trauma Recovery

Rachel Hoare

Routledge
Taylor & Francis Group

LONDON AND NEW YORK

Cover Credit: Ellen Sanders

First published 2026
by Routledge
4 Park Square, Milton Park, Abingdon, Oxon OX14 4RN

and by Routledge
605 Third Avenue, New York, NY 10158

Routledge is an imprint of the Taylor & Francis Group, an informa business

British Library Cataloguing-in-Publication Data
A catalogue record for this book is available from the British Library

ISBN: 978-1-032-55306-1 (hbk)
ISBN: 978-1-032-55305-4 (pbk)
ISBN: 978-1-003-43003-2 (ebk)

DOI: 10.4324/9781003430032

Typeset in Times New Roman
by Deanta Global Publishing Services, Chennai, India

Access the Support Material: www.routledge.com/9781032553054

For the refugee adolescents whose stories I have been privileged to witness, who embody the true meaning of strength through their extraordinary stories of courage, resilience, and healing, and for those who walk with them, offering empathy and connection during difficult journeys.

For my husband Nev and our children Alannah, Tom, Harry, and Charlie, whose journeys into adulthood constantly challenge and inspire me. To my parents, step-parents, grandparents, and aunties who have taught me the importance of humanity, compassion, inclusion, and acceptance.

To my sisters Gill and Chim, and to Val, Lorraine and Julie, all amazing women who supported me through my own turbulent adolescence and beyond. To Gags, Fran, Ali, and Miriam, who continue to celebrate my enduring teenage spirit.

Contents

Foreword

In the context of increasing numbers of individuals being forcibly displaced world-wide, the securitisation of asylum regimes, and rising anti-refugee sentiment, the wellbeing of refugee adolescents is of core concern. Whether alone or with family members, refugee adolescents face multiple challenges, both as refugees and as adolescents who are on the threshold of adulthood. These challenges relate to the complexity of their lives across time and borders: their lives prior to leaving their countries of origin, during their migration journeys, and in the countries where they begin to rebuild their lives and where they look to the future. Their experiences across time and space, within an ever-changing societal and political landscape, intersect with one another, thus adding to the complexity of their situations. While working with refugees can be a deeply rewarding experience, it also poses many difficulties and dilemmas for practitioners. This is why this book is so important.

Grounded in theory, research evidence, and clinical practice, *Psychological Support for Refugee Adolescents: An Expressive Arts Approach to Wellbeing and Trauma Recovery* is an invaluable resource. It will provide practitioners across multiple fields of practice with knowledge, skills, and useful tools to respond in ways that honour the individual young person with whom they work, while recognising the complexity of the societal, cultural, and political contexts in which they have lived and are now living. All too frequently, refugees are depicted in singular ways: as people fleeing persecution, with all other aspects of their identity remaining hidden, unrecognised and unspoken about. Researchers and practitioners alike are prone to this, with sometimes very little acknowledgement of the multiple intersecting identities of displaced people, of which their identity as a refugee is just one.

The fact that this book specifically focuses on refugee youth as both refugees *and* adolescents, situated within their broader ecological context, is of vital importance. Through the case studies which introduce us to young people with diverse experiences – Chima, Natalia, Daahir, Nabeel, Anastasiya, Omar, Ovie, Mira, Hassan, and Aran – the theory is brought to life, resulting in the reader gaining huge insight into the very varied lived experiences of refugee adolescents as they navigate life in exile. In a world where people of refugee backgrounds are frequently stereotyped and dehumanised, this focus on human stories of individual young people is an inspiring feature, which highlights not only the adversity faced by the young people in question but also honours the everyday, ordinary aspects of their lives as sons and daughters, as brothers and sisters, as teenagers, as friends. Yet despite this attention to the individual lived realities of young refugees, the book also consistently attends to the broader political and societal contexts in which refugee adolescents are situated. For instance, the discussion of Natalia's experiences highlights how European temporary protection policies have created a two-tier system that privileges certain refugee groups while others face lengthy asylum processes, demonstrating how macro-level policies directly impact individual refugee trajectories and opportunities for integration. All too often, interventions by practitioners can be individualised in their focus, with a lack of attention to the broader context. This book, rooted in Bronfenbrenner's ecological systems theory, is different in this regard.

The book is both comprehensive and accessible, packed with research evidence and practice wisdom. As such, it will be an immensely helpful resource for a range of professionals working with refugee adolescents, both unaccompanied refugee young people and those displaced with their families. It charts the migration trajectory from pre-migration experiences through to post-migration; discusses stress, trauma, and brain development; provides key information and research evidence in relation to mental health and stigma, with continuous attention to cultural considerations. It outlines what a trauma-informed, therapeutic approach might look like, identifying kindness and patience as key, and highlights the vital importance of attending to our own biases in the context of the development of empathic relationships, where bearing witness to distress is possible. Importantly, rather than focusing only on mental distress and vulnerability, the book attends to resilience and capacity, with a particular focus on how practitioners might support refugee adolescents to develop adaptive coping skills. The chapters on expressive arts provide a wealth of information on key expressive arts modalities – visual arts, music, drama, dance/movement, and therapeutic writing – thus enabling practitioners with and without clinical experience to learn about diverse ways to work with adolescents. The often-neglected area of working with interpreters is also comprehensively and thoughtfully discussed. In addition, the book encourages a very considered and reflective approach to practice and importantly addresses the key issue of self-care for practitioners working in this field.

While all of the chapters incorporate examples from practice – a key strength of the book – the detailed case studies are particularly helpful. Not only will they help practitioners across a range of disciplines to develop considerable insight into the experiences of refugee adolescents, but they also provide nuanced information about the approach a practitioner might take. The case studies very helpfully distinguish between interventions suited to psychotherapists and those suited to other professionals working with refugee adolescents.

For example, we learn that Laura, a social care worker, in working with Daahir, an unaccompanied minor, pays particular attention to the pronunciation of his name and acknowledges his use of multiple names, and how she works collaboratively with Daahir to create a digital mental health toolkit, with detailed information about its content. We also learn about Mohammed, a psychotherapist working with Omar, who thoughtfully uses football as a 'transcultural portal' for trauma processing, employing both physical play and symbolic representation through sand tray work to help Omar safely explore his experiences of displacement while reconnecting with aspects of his identity and building new social connections.

While the growing number of displaced refugees globally can be overwhelming to those working in this area and, of course, to people of refugee background themselves, and while political solutions at a global level are needed to address inequality, conflict, climate change, and displacement, individual professionals have a significant role to play. The support that professionals across a range of disciplines provide to refugee adolescents has the potential to have a considerable positive impact not only on the wellbeing and life trajectory of the young people in question but also on their families and on the individuals, groups, and communities with which they interact now and in the future. Each individual professional working with this cohort has a role to play, and this book is a very welcome and timely contribution to support them in doing so.

Muireann Ní Raghallaigh
Associate Professor of Social Work
UniversityCollege Dublin

Preface

As an expressive arts child and adolescent psychotherapist working with refugee adolescents, I have witnessed first-hand how opportunities for healing extend far beyond the therapy room. While psychotherapy offers the primary clinical framework for transformation through the expressive arts, these creative approaches – including visual arts, movement, music, and storytelling – can also foster healing when thoughtfully incorporated into classrooms, foster homes, residential settings, community spaces, and all contexts where refugee adolescents spend their time. This insight has inspired this book.

Drawing from clinical experience, academic research, and the stories shared by the refugee adolescents themselves, this book serves two audiences: clinicians seeking to deepen their practice and non-clinical professionals whose paths cross with refugee adolescents: educators, social workers, social care workers, foster carers, youth workers, healthcare professionals, legal advocates, and community volunteers. Every person who offers even a moment of connection plays a vital role in these young people's healing and integration journeys. A school caretaker, a training centre receptionist, and a residential centre night porter are among those who have been specifically named by the refugee adolescents I work with as significant figures in their lives.

What connects us all is the need to engage in trauma-informed ways that honour both trauma experiences and cultural identities. The expressive arts approaches shared here can be adapted across settings, creating healing possibilities whether you are a trained psychotherapist or someone of equal importance in a young person's recovery journey.

This book showcases the unique contributions each of us can make while strengthening our collective capacity to support these remarkable young people as they navigate their path towards healing.

Acknowledgements

Laura, your boundless creativity and sense of fun are a joy to all who are lucky enough to come into your orbit. Your contributions are reflected on every page through the clinical supervision, guidance, and friendship you have so generously and selflessly shared. Your supervision is always profoundly supportive, offering wisdom that extends far beyond different approaches and techniques into the heart of what it means as a human to deeply connect with another's experience.

Norma, thank you for your wisdom and experience in clinical supervision. Your work integrating human rights principles into psychotherapy continues to inspire me, and I find myself returning to your insights time and again as a touchstone for my own practice.

Eileen, and all at the Children's Therapy Centre in Ireland, thank you for inspiring me and setting me on this incredible journey.

My thanks to all of my wonderful friends and colleagues, too numerous to mention, who have encouraged me along the way and always believed in me. You will never know how important your support and belief have been.

My heartfelt thanks to Ellen Sanders, my wonderful niece and illustrator, whose creativity, patience, and courage know no bounds. Ellen instinctively knew what was needed, and her illustrations bring the stories to life in beautiful ways.

At Routledge, I am indebted to Lauren Redhead and Grace McDonnell for their invaluable support throughout the manuscript development process and to Ayushi Awasthi for her excellent editorial support. I would also like to convey my appreciation to Siobhan Denham for her meticulous copy-editing, carried out with infinite patience and sensitivity.

Finally, I gratefully acknowledge funding for the copy-editing process from the Trinity College Trinity Trust fund. This fund provides grant support for a wide variety of College projects where funding is unavailable from mainstream resources. The Trinity Trust, primarily supported by the Trinity Affinity Credit Card Programme, enables vital academic initiatives that enhance Trinity's unique educational experience. For more information about the Trinity Trust and the Trinity Affinity credit card that supports it, please visit www.tcd.ie/alumni/services /affinity-credit-card.

Introduction

In a world where forced displacement has reached unprecedented levels, children and adolescents bear a disproportionate burden of this global crisis. By late 2023, the cumulative global total of displaced children and adolescents had reached 47.2 million worldwide (UNICEF 2024), and the need for effective, culturally responsive approaches to support these young people has become increasingly urgent. This book addresses this critical need. It offers a comprehensive framework for using the expressive arts to support adolescent refugees navigating the complex challenges of forced displacement while simultaneously experiencing the developmental transition from childhood to adulthood.

Researchers have described this experience as a 'double burden' – young people must simultaneously navigate the formative tasks of adolescence, such as identity development, establishing independence and building meaningful relationships, while also processing the profound disruptions and traumatic experiences of displacement, including cultural dislocation, interrupted education, severed community ties, and often exposure to violence and persecution. This complex interplay creates specific psychological needs often not addressed by traditional approaches to support. Language barriers, cultural differences, and the impact of trauma on verbal expression can all limit the effectiveness of conventional talk-based approaches (Bonz et al. 2019).

The expressive arts – drawing, movement, music, drama, storytelling, and more – offer powerful alternatives. These creative modalities provide non-verbal pathways for processing experiences, expressing emotions, and building connections. When skilfully integrated into trauma-informed practice, they create opportunities for healing that transcend cultural and linguistic barriers while honouring the resilience and cultural identities of refugee youth.

This book is grounded in both clinical experience and research evidence, bridging theory and practice through detailed case studies that demonstrate how expressive arts can be adapted across diverse settings and professional roles. From residential care workers to teachers, social workers to psychotherapists, professionals in

DOI: 10.4324/9781003430032-1

various capacities will find practical strategies to enhance their work with refugee adolescents.

Informed by ecological perspectives on human development (Bronfenbrenner et al. 2006), the book recognises that adolescent refugee experiences are shaped by multiple interconnected environments – from immediate family relationships and friendships to broader cultural contexts. This framework helps practitioners understand how creative activities can address needs across different ecological layers, creating more holistic and effective support. The structure and progression of the book are fundamentally shaped by this ecological perspective.

The chapters evolve in a carefully structured sequence. Early chapters establish the theoretical foundations, exploring the impact of forced displacement on adolescent development, the neurobiological effects of trauma on the developing brain, and culturally diverse understandings of mental health and healing. These foundational concepts provide the context for understanding why expressive arts approaches are particularly valuable for this population.

Subsequent chapters introduce a trauma-informed framework that distinguishes between approaches appropriate for all practitioners and those requiring specialised psychotherapy training. This practical distinction ensures that professionals across various settings can implement supportive practices within their scope of expertise while recognising when more specialised approaches may be needed.

The heart of the book lies in its detailed case studies, where composite narratives based on real clinical experiences demonstrate creative approaches to addressing common challenges faced by refugee adolescents. Each case study illustrates different aspects of expressive arts practice, from using football-themed activities to develop social connections, to employing visual arts for processing trauma, to supporting sleep disturbances through creative rituals and dream work. Throughout these narratives, a consistent message emerges: the expressive arts offer pathways to healing that honour cultural diversity, build on existing strengths, and create opportunities for genuine connection across differences. Rather than imposing Western psychological frameworks, these approaches invite refugee adolescents to express and process their experiences in ways that feel meaningful and authentic to them.

The final chapters provide practical guidance for implementing these approaches, including working effectively with interpreters and supporting the wellbeing of practitioners through creative self-care practices. A comprehensive activity locator helps readers quickly find specific techniques for addressing common needs, making the book a valuable reference tool for ongoing practice.

This book comes at a critical moment when forced displacement continues to disrupt the lives of millions of young people worldwide. While the challenges facing refugee adolescents are profound, so too is their capacity for resilience and growth when provided with appropriate support. The expressive arts, with their emphasis on creativity, embodiment, and cultural expression, offer powerful resources for nurturing this resilience.

As you read, you will encounter stories of transformation – moments that might appear unremarkable yet hold profound significance. Through creative engagement, even brief activities can open doorways to expression, connection, and healing that might otherwise remain closed. You will see how simple activities like drawing, movement, or storytelling can create safe spaces for processing difficult experiences and rebuilding a sense of identity and belonging in a new environment.

Beyond specific techniques, this book offers a philosophy of practice – one that respects the unique journey of each adolescent refugee while recognising common patterns and needs. It emphasises the importance of cultural humility, trauma sensitivity, and a strengths-based approach that views refugee adolescents not as victims of circumstance but as active participants in their own healing and growth.

Whether you are new to working with refugee adolescent populations or bring years of experience, this book invites you to expand your repertoire of creative approaches while deepening your understanding of the dynamic intersection between trauma, culture, development, and resilience. By integrating expressive arts into your practice, you can create more responsive, engaging, and effective support for adolescent refugees navigating the challenging journey of displacement and adaptation.

This is not merely a book about techniques; it is an invitation to reimagine how we support adolescent refugees at the intersection of displacement and development. Through the expressive arts, we can create spaces where they are truly seen, heard, and supported in reclaiming their voices, rebuilding their lives, and realising their potential in new contexts. In doing so, we honour both their profound challenges and their remarkable capacity for healing and growth.

References

Bonz, A, del Carmen Casas, S and Arslanbek, A. 2019. 'Conflict and displacement: Finding the space for creativity'. In A Bonz and A. A. del Carmen Casas, *Art therapy practices for resilient youth*, 337–359. Routledge.

Bronfenbrenner, U and Morris, P. 2006. 'The bioecological model of human development'. In R A Lerner, *Handbook of child psychology: Theoretical models of human development*, 793–828. John Wiley & Sons.

UNICEF. 2024. *Child displacement.* New York: Unicef.

Chapter 1

The Impact of the Adolescent Migration Trajectory

Introduction

Adolescents who are displaced from their homeland are also moving from child-hood to adulthood, which means that they must navigate multiple challenges related to this developmental transition while living through forced displace-ment. This chapter explores the experiences of the pre-flight, flight, and post-flight (including the reconciliation of home and host cultures in new identity formation), stages of forced displacement through the eyes of Chima and Natalia, two adolescents from different countries who experienced forced displacement to the same European country. In order to protect the identities of real individuals, Chima and Natalia are composite characters who represent a variety of experi-ences and convey the shared challenges and resilience of the adolescent refugees I have worked with.

This exploration draws on the ecological model of human development frame-work detailed by psychologist Urie Bronfenbrenner (1979) and its subsequent iterations leading to the bioecological model (Bronfenbrenner and Morris 2006), as a way of developing an understanding of the variables and factors which affect adolescent experiences of, and adaptation to, living in a conflict zone, fleeing that conflict zone and resettling in another country.

For Chima and Natalia, respectively, these variables included factors which increased the risk of psychological distress, developmental disruption, and mala-daptive coping patterns such as the daily stressors of living in a conflict situation or the negative impact of growing up with a primary caregiver who had mental health difficulties, as well as those which bestowed some protection such as close friendships and community and faith-based supports. Experiences of reconcil-ing host and home country identities through social, educational, cultural, lin-guistic, and family adaptation are also explored through their adolescent eyes. Bronfenbrenner's framework helps us to understand the dynamic ways in which social environments influence adolescent's adaptive responses to the extreme adversities of war.

DOI: 10.4324/9781003430032-2

International Context

According to UNHCR estimates, conflict, violence, and other crises left a record 47 million children and adolescents displaced from their homes at the end of 2024, which is the highest number recorded since World War II (UNHCR 2024). Estimates of the numbers of children and adolescents on the move are frequently based on census data and are often not disaggregated by age, making it very difficult to identify a statistically precise number of adolescent refugees (International Data Alliance for Children on the Move 2023). However, those European countries which do have more detailed statistics, such as Greece, Malta, Bulgaria, and Italy, document large numbers of adolescent refugees amongst those accompanied by family members as well as those who are unaccompanied by a family member or legal guardian, with a prevalence of older adolescents (15–17 years) amongst the latter (UNICEF 2023).

Adolescents who are forcibly displaced from their homeland and moving to a new country are also moving from childhood to adulthood. This experience has been described as a 'double mourning' (Volkan 2018) or a 'double burden' (Tefferi 2007), and these young people can struggle to find their place in these two new 'in-between' worlds. Displacement places significant psychological stress on all those who are forced to flee their homes, and the migration trajectory is often described in terms of the stages of pre-flight, flight, and post-flight (Oldroyd et al. 2021). In this chapter, we are guided by the further division by Papadopoulos (2002:26) of the pre-flight stage into the time before the violence ('anticipation') and the actual violence ('devastating events'). In addition to the immediate post-flight experiences, the reconciliation of home and host cultures in new identity formation is also explored as part of this stage.

Both accompanied and unaccompanied adolescents are considered a high-risk group at all stages. They may face pressure to join armed groups or be exposed to high levels of violence and sexual abuse during the pre-flight stage (Rousseau and Gagnon 2020). For unaccompanied adolescents, the lack of safety or protection during the journey to exile together with the overwhelming loss of family and friends is felt acutely at this developmental stage. Furthermore, both groups often face increased suffering through their living conditions and treatment in host countries (Fazel and Betancourt 2018; Papadopoulos 2002).

This chapter explores the experiences of displaced adolescents during these three stages through the eyes of Chima, a 15-year-old male, who travelled to the host country alone from a country in Africa, and 16-year-old Natalia, who travelled with her mother from a country in Eastern Europe. This exploration draws on the socio-ecological framework developed and refined by psychologist Urie Bronfenbrenner as a way of recognising that individuals influence and are impacted by a complex range of intersected social influences and interactions at the individual, interpersonal, organisational, and community levels (Bronfenbrenner 1979; Bronfenbrenner and Morris 2006). Although there is broad consensus that this theory accounts for the complexity of child and adolescent development and is universally applicable, difficulties of implementation due to the complexity of all factors being potentially mutually and systematically influential have also been highlighted, and new ways of approaching implementation have been proposed (Elliott and Davis 2020).

In the context of the refugee adolescent this framework facilitates understanding of how the adolescent social environment shapes their experiences of, and responses to the stages of forced migration, focusing on the impact of exposure to daily stressors and potentially traumatic events, the effects of risk and protective factors, and the responses to social adaptation and integration opportunities (Bennouna et al. 2020). In this framework, the *microsystem* is the displaced adolescent's most proximal level of influence, which includes settings such as the family, the reception centre, the school, and the place of worship. The *mesosystem* refers to points of connection between two or more of the adolescent's settings, such as the influence of friends on the place of worship or of the family on the school. The *exosystem* encompasses contextual influences that are not experienced directly by the adolescent but that have an indirect impact on their experiences and may include the asylum status of the parent(s) and their social networks. The *macrosystem* comprises the organisation and structure of a society, such as their migration policies, housing situation, and dominant belief systems, and the *chronosystem* comprises environmental changes over time, such as having to flee one's country of origin and life transitions such as adolescence. Figure 1.1 provides a visual representation of Bronfenbrenner's ecological systems theory applied to adolescent refugees, illustrating how various factors at different ecological levels interact to influence the adaptation and resilience of young people like Chima and Natalia during forced displacement.

Adolescent Experiences of the Three Stages of Forced Migration

Although Bronfenbrenner's conceptualisation of the chronosystem is particularly pertinent to the refugee adolescent, Hayes (2020) argues that consideration within this system of the impact on refugee adolescent mental health of the time spent in temporary resettlement contexts is often lacking in research into the experiences of forced displacement. This lack of research is even more evident at the intersection between the length of time which has passed since displacement and the transition to adolescence. The transition to adolescence is conceptualised in a seminal paper by Graber and Brooks-Gunn (1996), as essentially a universal transitional period which has key moments or 'turning points.' They argue that turning points which occur in the context of this transitional period are more likely to result in longer-lasting psychosocial changes than those which occur during non-transitional periods. The pre-flight, flight, and post-flight experiences of refugees (Oldroyd et al. 2021) can be conceptualised as turning points within this transitional period.

The division of the pre-flight stage by Papadopoulos (2002:26) into the 'anticipation' and 'devastating events' phases is especially salient during the adolescent developmental period, given the high level of plasticity of the adolescent brain. This plasticity makes it extremely susceptible to emotional responses to the rapidly changing socio-political situations which are part of the macrosystems of adolescent refugees (Frydenberg 2019). More specifically, impulse control, planning, and decision-making are largely frontal cortex functions of the brain which mature during adolescence (Burton et al. 2014) and which carry very important functions throughout both phases of pre-flight, as well as the flight and post-flight stages of forced migration. Chapter 2 provides a more detailed exploration of the impact of stress on the adolescent developing brain.

The scale, nature, and persistence of the impact of these experiences during adolescence also depend on differences in personality, life experiences, coping styles, and resilience, which will have been shaped by adolescent refugee interactions with their environment (their microsystem) during childhood. These experiences and their responses to them will help determine the extent to which they are able to manage the adversity which comes from having to flee their homes (Lahad et al. 2013). The sections that follow are therefore positioned at the intersection of the developmental phase of adolescence and forced migration and conceptualise the three stages of forced migration as turning points in the refugee adolescent experience within the socio-ecological framework.

Introducing Chima and Natalia and their Risk and Protective Factors

Although the experiences of Chima and Natalia in their respective home countries were very different, they can both be better understood by drawing on Bronfenbrenner's socio-ecological framework to conceptualise how their families and communities shape their experiences of, and responses to, the situations of armed conflict and forced migration in their countries (see Figure 1.1). By using this perspective, it is possible to identify the factors which increase risk and those which bestow some protection for adolescents who have been forced to flee their homelands. However, it is also important to remember that the same factor can increase risk in one context and bestow protection in another, thus illustrating the importance of considering the complex interplay between individual, relationship, community, and societal factors. For example, Catani (2018) points out that violence in the family (the microsystem) may increase for some during times of war, thereby constituting a risk factor (Sriskandarajah et al. 2015), whereas for others the family may serve as a protective factor by providing nurturing care (Dubow et al. 2012).

Chima had been living in a situation of ongoing conflict in an African country for his entire life (his chronosystem). A number of people in his community had been killed, and many family members had been internally displaced. As an adolescent living in a chronosystem with so many risks to his wellbeing and survival, Chima found it impossible to rely on any adult to protect him when he was in danger (Masten and Narayan 2012), and being unable to prevent himself or his

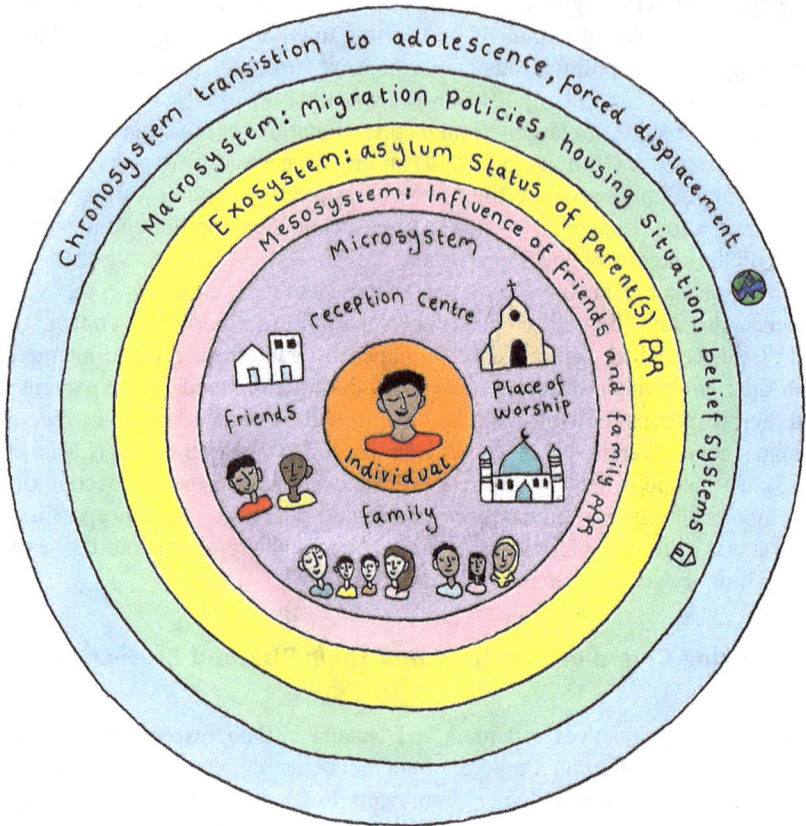

Figure 1.1 Bronfenbrenner's Ecological Systems Model applied to Refugee Adolescent Development.

family members from being hurt, humiliated, or killed had left him feeling powerless (Sleijpen et al. 2016). The daily stressors of living in a conflict situation, which included not knowing where the next meal was coming from, not being able to access regular education, being exposed to physical and emotional abuse from combatants on both sides of the conflict, and not knowing when the next attack on his community was going to happen, can have long-term damaging effects on mental health and psychosocial wellbeing, compromise coping and increase vulnerability to the impact of traumatic stress (Miller and Rasmussed 2010). These stressors were everyday realities for Chima. Furthermore, as he reached adolescence and the violence escalated, Chima was fearful that he would be forced to join a rebel group of fighters, as several of his friends had been forced to join this group.

Chima's protective factors were mainly interpersonal and community-based and can be conceptualised through the microsystems in which he participates and the mesosystem that links them. He lived in a close-knit community with his extended family where life was experienced and decisions made collectively, where everyone worked for the community and where people engaged in collective coping by relying on one another for emotional, economic, and social support. Chima reached out to his parents and friends for support. As a Muslim, he engaged in collective faith-based practices and experienced and marked celebrations and loss within this microsystem which interlinked with school, peers, and family within his mesosystem. Chima also drew on his individual protective factor of resilience which included the embodiment of 'adaptive fatalism' conceptualised by Atari-Khan et al. (2021), as an acceptance that the future was uncertain and out of his control.

Natalia, on the other hand, had never experienced any armed conflict in her country. Although she had heard many stories from her mother and her grandmother about growing up under a repressive regime (therefore comprising part of Natalia's macrosystem), she had not experienced this herself. It is however important to note that there is growing evidence that trauma can be passed between generations through impacting on DNA and gene function (Ryan et al. 2016), and that living in conditions of war, conflict, and oppression have been identified as stress-inducing triggers for such epigenetic modifications (Raza et al. 2023). It was therefore important to be curious about the impact that this may have had on Natalia and to explore it with her during therapy.

Natalia's main risk factors stemmed from growing up with a clinically depressed mother who struggled to provide consistent, responsive care during her infancy and childhood (her microsystem). Natalia's insecure attachment to her mother shaped the formation of Natalia's internal working model, a lifelong template for preconceptions of the value, reliability, and expectations of relationships (Bowlby 1988; Holmes and Slade 2018) and is also likely to have contributed to the anxiety, fear, and low self-esteem which have an important impact on her quality of life (Sunderland 2016). A study by Qouta et al. (2007),of psychological distress among Palestinian adolescents living in a combat zone, found a negative correlation between non-responsive and non-attuned mothering and adolescent resilience. Punamaki et al. (1997) found that war-exposed children who had loving and non-rejecting primary caregivers were more creative and efficient in problem solving than those who exhibited insecure attachment patterns.

However, it is also important to point out that although early attachment relationships shape the lens through which children view later relationships, peer groups, friendships, extended family, teachers, and mentors can mitigate the negative effects of early relationship experiences (Yan Lee and Lok 2012). For Natalia, her protective factors were based around her microsystems which consisted of support being available during times of need from her grandmother and her close friendship network, together with her positive orientation to school, and her regular participation in dance classes.

Natalia often stayed with her local grandmother, whose nurturing care mitigated the impact of her mother's lack of responsiveness during childhood. Natalia had travelled alone as a teen to study English, so she was familiar with the country and its culture. She developed coping skills from therapy before the war and knew that connecting with friends, staying active, doing chores, and watching specific film clips helped her cope.

Pre-flight: Anticipation and Devastating Events

Adolescents in conflict zones face extreme socio-political instability and violence during their transition to adolescence, leading to a lasting psychological impact (Shaar 2013). Chima found the distinction between anticipation and devastating turning points less shocking than Natalia, as he lived in ongoing conflict, his every-day reality (his chronosystem). His father's opposition to the regime put the entire family at risk. Chima felt constantly anxious and in a constant state of high alert during the anticipation phase. The attack on his village (devastating events) forced him to flee suddenly, like in Natalia's case. He was 14 at the time.

For Natalia, the instability of the anticipation phase played out in the media and especially via platforms like Telegram and Instagram. Although this can be con-ceptualised in relation to her mesosystem, as these digital platforms interact with other microsystems such as home, work, friends, and school, it is also important to note that social media is embedded in all levels of Bronfenbrenner's multi-layered ecology from immediate to more abstracted contextual forces (McHale et al. 2009). Natalia described being in a constant state of high alert and feeling very anxious all of the time when rumours and the signs of an imminent invasion began to circulate on social media. She was 15 years old at the time and felt unheard as her mother and grandmother dismissed her war fears, while social media overload disrupted her sleep

When the war actually started (the devastating events), Natalia, her mother, her grandmother, and her grandmother's dog stayed in their basement for 48 hours, and she describes feeling terrified at hearing the constant shelling. When a friend offered to bring them to the border of their country so that they could leave, Natalia's grandmother refused to leave her dog, and Natalia was distraught at the prospect of leaving them both behind. Natalia recalls the arguments that went on for 24 hours around her grandmother not leaving and describes the deep sadness she felt at having to leave the person she felt closest to in her life when the decision was finally made for herself and her mother to leave.

Flight

Chima fled with his cousin and uncle when violence erupted in their village while his younger sisters worked in the fields and his father was trading in another village, leaving Chima fearful for his family's safety and unaware of their whereabouts. Chima's mother had died when he was about 12. After three days of trekking, Chima's cousin and uncle were captured by government forces, while Chima man-aged to escape. He hid in a mosque for months, aided by the religious leader, until a smuggler safely took him to another African country, where he stayed illegally for about six months. Negative attitudes towards displaced populations affected Chima's daily life, restricting his access to services and freedom for fear of being reported to the authorities.

Chima felt terrified and constantly on high alert, which led him to keep doors open and never turn his back to them. He received no news of his family and struggled to feel hope for the future. He consistently felt low and unable to experience emotions. At the end of this period, Chima was flown to a European host country. He had never flown before and recalled feeling frightened and alone during take-off, findingthe flight away from Africa and into the unknown extremely upsetting. He claimed asylum as a separated child at 15 upon arriving in the host country.

Natalia and her mother were driven 16 hours to the border in a small car. Natalia recounted her terror at checkpoints, witnessing border guards violently drag young men from their cars to beat them. She recalled her disgust at the border guards' language, which she grew up speaking, and vowed never to speak it again. Natalia and her mother crossed the border into a safe neighbouring country, where they received warm clothes and food and stayed for three days at a community centre while waiting to be relocated. Natalia felt relieved to be safe but was sad to leave her grandmother and dog behind. The country's macrosystem, with its shared border, history, and similar norms and culture, led to a favourable response to Natalia, her mother, and others fleeing the neighbouring country.

Natalia constantly checked her phone for updates on their region and became very fearful when there was no news forthcoming. Her grandmother did not have a phone, so Natalia was relying on other people around her grandmother to keep her informed. Natalia also felt an obligation to constantly check on her behalf, as she was worried that she had no access to news about what was going on. After three days of staying in the community centre and with heightened anxiety and fear for her grandmother and her dog, Natalia and her mother were allocated a flight to the host country.

Post-flight

Fleeing individuals face traumatic events before and during flight, and often suffer further from their treatment and living conditions in host countries (Fazel and Betancourt 2018; Papadopoulos 2002). Upon arrival, Chima was questioned by immigration staff and, as an unaccompanied minor, was taken to the social work department for an initial assessment of his immediate protection, health, and faith-based needs. A care plan was developed, and Chima was taken to a registered children's short-term residential intake unit. A detailed social work risk and needs assessment over several weeks allowed for careful matching with a foster family placement.

Chima reported being treated with kindness by the authorities from the moment he arrived in the host country to the time, three weeks later, when he arrived at his new foster placement. He highlighted his relief when the social worker provided a prayer mat and a Qur'an. He spent his first night in a short-term unit with other young people from various countries. Although he reported feeling disoriented and confused by the different cultural practices he encountered, he said that he drew some comfort from knowing that there were others in the same situation as himself. He felt safe with the welcoming residential unit staff. Chima was extremely worried about his family, with whom he had been out of contact since separating from his uncle and cousin.

After three weeks, a foster mother was found for Chima, and he moved to another part of the city. His social worker helped him apply to the Irish Red Cross *Restoring Family Links Service* to find his family. Chima also started his educational journey in the host country in the *Youth and Education Service for Refugees and Migrants* (Youth and Education Service 2021), where he learned English, Maths, Computer literacy, and engaged in classes about Irish culture. His social worker began the asylum application process with a short preliminary interview. Chima, his social worker and lawyer, completed the asylum questionnaire, then waited 18 months for his interview, during which time he became anxious and withdrawn, fearing that his application would be refused, and he would be returned home.

The first year was especially difficult for Chima due to concerns for his family's safety. After a year, the Red Cross informed him that his father and sisters were alive and had fled to safety, but there was still no news of his uncle and cousin. Chima felt hopeful for the first time upon learning his father and sisters were alive.

Chima was granted refugee status two years after arriving in the host country. As he was still under 18 at this point, he was able to apply for family reunification for his father and his sisters. Three and a half years after Chima had first landed in the host country, his father and sisters arrived, and he said that it was only at this point that he could start feeling any emotions again. He described how 'his heart started to thaw' as soon as he saw them at the airport, and after so long he again knew what it was to feel happiness. After they had been there for a month or so, Chima talked candidly about the challenges of finding appropriate accommodation for them as well as the pressure and frustrations he experienced of being their cultural and language broker (Lazarevic 2017). He expressed gratitude for the host country's sanctuary and praised his social care worker's support for him and his family.

Natalia's situation in the host country differed from Chima's for two main reasons. First, unlike Chima, she had arrived with her mother and was therefore likely to have access to greater levels of support (Bean et al. 2007), and second she was granted automatic temporary protection through the European temporary protection visa scheme, the first of its kind to be introduced in the history of the European Union (Nare et al. 2022). The main advantages of this were the expeditious process and the automatic granting of the right to work and study embedded in the macrosystem, both of which eased Natalia's transition and integration into the host country. However, this process has highlighted the inconsistency of

European migration policies and their differential application in different member states. People from Natalia's country of origin were granted the right to work and participate in the receiving societies without having to endure the lengthy asylum processes experienced by all other people seeking asylum, although the hospitality arrangements are still provisional. It is hoped that the preferential treatment received by refugees from Natalia's country and the critical analyses of these treatments (see Bajaj and Cody Stanford 2022; Kienast et al. 2022) will inform practice for future groups of refugees regardless of their national origins.

Natalia and her mother were taken from the airport to an asylum support hub, where they were registered and stayed for three nights while more permanent accommodation was secured. They were given a double ensuite room in a hotel. There were set meal times and activities such as English classes organised for them. Natalia described feeling a sense of relief that they were safe which was accompanied by great sadness at having left her grandmother and her dog behind as well as a huge sense of overwhelm at not knowing what the future would hold. She described the emptiness she felt about her future and being able to continue her education. She also reported being very nervous about having to be in one room with her mother, with whom relations had been very strained before the invasion.

During the first few weeks, Natalia reported many arguments between them as well as frustration at having to act as her language and cultural broker, given her greater familiarity with these aspects of life in the host country (Trickett and Jones 2007). She was also becoming increasingly frustrated with the fact that no one was allowed to cook in the centre and that the meal times were tightly controlled, and she found the food bland and unhealthy. However, Natalia was then offered the opportunity to continue her education and also managed to find herself a part-time job, so her mood began to improve as being busy helped her to cope.

Reconciling Host and Home Country Identities (Acculturation)

The reconciliation and integration of host and home country identities is a critical aspect of the post-flight stage. It was very important for Chima to retain his cultural customs and languages, but he was also keen to improve his English and to learn about the cultural norms of his new home. He was able to re-engage with his interrupted education within a few weeks of arriving when he enrolled in the *Youth and Education Service for Refugees and Migrant* education programme where new students were accepted at any stage of the academic year to facilitate swift and flexible education access. In addition, his foster carer linked him in with the local football club where he was able to develop relationships with adolescents from the host and many other countries and hone the skills learned in the streets of his home country, thereby demonstrating the importance of sport as a vehicle for refugee youth integration (Ha and Lyras 2013; Hoare 2024).

The local mosque was a vital source of comfort, community, and solidarity for Chima in his microsystem, especially as he described missing the community aspect of practising his religion in his home country. Upon arriving at his foster placement, he described how he thought that people were unfriendly in the neighbourhood, as no one spoke to one another. Chima had always seen himself in relation to others – as being part of a community – and he struggled at first with recognising himself as an individual. When he transitioned into mainstream education after three months in the access programme, he was introduced to a peer mentor who helped him to navigate the school system which he described as being extremely helpful, as school in the host country was so different from schooling in his home country. Peer mentoring within the school system has been shown to facilitate social integration and promote academic and school engagement, with mentors acting as cultural and system translators and interpreters (Lazarevic 2017). In relation to personal identity, Chima talked about identifying very strongly with his African home country but also pointed out some similarities between the two cultures, including the importance of family and a shared sense of humour.

Whereas Chima had accepted that a permanent return to his home country was extremely unlikely in the future, Natalia believed that her stay would be temporary, which meant that she was not especially interested in actively integrating into the local community. Indeed, all of the people in the hotel where she was living were from the same country. However, once Natalia engaged in education and work with people from the host country, and when she found herself still in the host country one year later, she gradually started to accept that her stay might be longer than originally expected and started to plan for further education in the country. She re-engaged with her love of dancing by starting to learn the traditional dancing of the host country. As there was less cultural distance between her country of origin and the host country than for Chima, the expectations of teachers, healthcare professionals, and other professionals supporting Natalia in relation to her capacity for integration and acceptance by the host community were higher (Alisic and Kartal 2019).

These accounts show that the daily activities in each phase of forced migration for the refugee adolescent both influence and are influenced by the multi-layered ecology within which their lives are embedded. This ranges from their core environment and interactions with parents, peer group and school (microsystems) to the interactions between the microsystems such as cultural brokering for the parents by the refugee adolescent in the healthcare context (mesosystem) to the larger political, economic, legal, and cultural contexts of the larger society (macrosystems), the effect of parental depression (exosystem) and the external factors of war and conflict leading to the major life transition of having to flee their country of origin during their transition to adolescence (chronosystem).

To understand more fully the impact of potentially traumatic experiences on adolescent refugees, it is also important to examine the development of the human brain during adolescence. Chapter 2 will present an accessible synthesis of current knowledge on the development of the adolescent brain and the impact of different stressors in the forced migration context.

References

Alisic, E and Kartal, D. 2019. 'The role of trauma and cultural distance in refugee integration'. In S Kehoe and E Heilinger, *Responsibility for Refugee and Migrant Integration*, 113–131. De Gruyter.

Atari-Khan, R, Covington, A, Gerstein, L, Herz, H, Varner, B, Brasfield, C, Shurigar, B, et al. 2021. 'Concepts of resilience among trauma-exposed Syrian refugees'. *The Counseling Psychologist, 49*(2): 233–268. doi:10.1177/0011000020970522.

Bajaj, S and Cody Stanford, F. 2022. 'The Ukrainian refugee crisis and the pathology of racism'. *British Medical Journal, 376*: 1–2.

Bean, T, Derlyn, I, Eurelings-Bontekoe, E, Broekaert, E and Spinhoven, P. 2007. 'Comparing psychological distress, traumatic stress reactions and experiences of unaccompanied refugee minors with experiences of adolescents accompanied by parents'. *The Journal of Nervous and Mental Disease, 195*(4): 288–297. doi:10.1097/01.nmd.0000243751.49499.93.

Bennouna, C, Stark, L and Wessells, M. 2020. 'Children and adolescents in conflict and displacement'. In S Song and P Ventevogel, *Child, adolescent and family refugee mental health*, 54–96. Springer.

Bowlby, J. 1988. *A secure base: Parent-child attachment and healthy human development.* Basic Books.

Bronfenbrenner, U. 1979. *The ecology of human development.* The President and Fellows of Harvard College.

Bronfenbrenner, U and Morris, P A. 2006. 'The bioecological model of human development'. In R M Lerner and W Damon, *Handbook of child psychology: Theoretical models of human development*, 793–828. John Wiley & Sons.

Burton, M, Pavord, E and Williams, B. 2014. *An introduction to child and adolescent mental health.* Sage Publications Ltd.

Catani, C. 2018. 'Mental health of children living in war zones: A risk and protection perspective'. *World Psychiatry, 17*(1): 104–105.

Dubow, E, Huesmann, L, Boxer, P and Landau, S. 2012. 'Exposure to political conflict and violence and post-traumatic stress in Middle East youth: Protective factors'. *Journal of Clinical Child and Adolescent Psychology, 41*(6): 402–416.

Elliott, S and Davis, J. 2020. 'Challenging taken-for-granted ideas in early childhood education: A critique of Bronfenbrenner's ecological systems theory in the age of post-humanism'. In K Cutter-Mackenzie-Knowles, K Malone and E Barratt Hacking, *Research handbook on childhood nature*, 1119–1154. Springer.

Fazel, M and Betancourt, T. 2018. 'Preventive mental health interventions for refugee children and adolescents in high-income settings'. *The Lancet Child and Adolescent Health, 2*(2): 121–132.

Frydenberg, F. 2019. *Adolescent coping: Promoting resilience and wellbeing.* 3rd edn. Routledge Taylor and Francis Group.

Graber, J and Brooks-Gunn, J. 1996. 'Transitions and turning points: Navigating the passage from childhood through adolescence'. *Developmental Psychology, 32*(4):768–776.

Ha, J-P and Lyras, A. 2013. 'Sport for refugee youth in new society: The role of'. *South African Journal for Research in Sport, Physical Education and Recreation, 35*(2):121–140.

Hayes, S. 2020. 'Commentary: Deepening understanding of refugee children and adolescents using Bronfenbrenner's bioecological and PPCT models – A Commentary on Arakelyan and Ager'. *The Journal of Child Psychiatry and Psychology, 62*(5): 510–513.

Hoare, R. 2024. 'Friendship is crucial for refugee children – here's how to talk to your child about being welcoming'. *Conversations*. https://theconversation.com/friendship-is-crucial-for-refugee-children-heres-how-to-talk-to-your-child-about-being-welcoming-220718?utm_source=clipboard&utm_medium=bylinecopy_url_button

Holmes, J and Slade, J. 2018. *Attachment in therapeutic practice*. Sage Publications Ltd.

International Data Alliance for Children on the Move. 2023. *Missing from the story: The urgent need for better data to protect children on the move.* IDAC.

Kienast, J, Feith Tan, N and Vedsted-Hansen, J. 2022. 'Preferential, differential or discriminatory? EU protection arrangements for persons displaced from Ukraine'. In S Carrera and M Ineli-Ciger, *EU responses to the large-scale refugee displacement from Ukraine*, 383–400. European University Institute.

Lahad, M, Shacham, M and Ayalon, O. 2013. *The 'Basic PH' model of coping and resiliency.* Jessica Kingsley.

Lazarevic, V. 2017. 'Effects of cultural brokering on individual wellbeing and family dynamics among immigrant youth'. *Journal of Adolescence*, 55: 77–87. doi:10.1016/j.adolescence.2016.12.010.

Masten, A and Narayan, A. 2012. 'Child development in the context of disaster, war and terrorism: Pathways of risk and resilience'. *Annual Review of Psychology*, 63: 227–257.

McHale, S, Dotterer, A and Kim, J-Y. 2009. 'An ecological perspective on the media and youth development'. *American Behavioral Science*: 1186–1203. doi:10.1177/0002764209331541.

Miller, K E and Rasmussed, A. 2010. 'War exposure, daily stressors, and mental health in conflict and post-conflict settings: Bridging the divide between trauma-focused and psychosocial frameworks'. *Social Science and Medicine*, 70(1): 7–16.

Nare, L, Abdelhady, D and Irastorza, N. 2022. 'What can we learn from the reception of Ukrainian Refugees'. *Nordic Journal of Migration Research*, 12(3): 255–258.

Oldroyd, J, Kabir, A, Dzakpasu, F, Mahmud, H, Rana, J and Islam, R. 2021. 'The experiences of children and adolescents undergoing forced separation from their parents during migration: A systematic review'. *Health and Social Care in the Community*, 29(4): 888–898.

Papadopoulos, R. 2002. *Therapeutic care for refugees: No place like home.* Tavistock Clinic Series.

Punamaki, R, Qouta, S and El Sarraj, E. 1997. 'Models of traumatic experiences and children's psychological adjustment: The role of perceived parenting, children's resources and activity'. *Child Development*, 68: 718–728.

Qouta, S, P Raija-Leena, E Montgomery, and E El Sarraj. 2007. 'Predictors of psychological distress and positive resources among Palestinian adolescents: Trauma, child, and mothering characteristics'. *Child Abuse and Neglect* 31: 699–717.

Raza, Z, Hussein, S, Foster, V, Wall, J, Coffey, P, Martin, J and Gomes, R. 2023. 'Exposure to war and conflict: The individual and inherited epigenetic effects on health, with a focus on post-traumatic stress disorder'. *Frontiers in Epidemiology*: 1–14.

Rousseau, C and Gagnon, M. 2020. 'Intervening to address the impact of stress and trauma on refugee children and adolescents resettled in high-income countries'. In S Song and P Ventevogel, *Child, adolescent and family refugee mental health*, 290–316. Springer.

Ryan, J, Chaudieu, C, Ancelin, M and Saffery, R. 2016. 'Biological underpinnings of trauma and post-traumatic stress disorder: Focusing on genets and epigenetics'. *Epigenomics*, 8(11): 1553–1569.

Shaar, K H. 2013. 'Post-traumatic stress disorder in adolescents in Lebanon as wars gained in ferocity: A systematic review'. *Journal of Public Health Research*, 2(17):99–105.

Sleijpen, M, Boeije, H, Kleber, R and Mooren, T. 2016. 'Between power and powerlessness: A meta-ethnography of sources of resilience in young refugees'. *Ethnicity and Health*, *21*(2): 158–180. doi:10.1080/13557858.

Sriskandarajah V, Neuner, F and Catani, C. 2015. 'Parental care protects traumatized Sri Lankan traumatised children from internalising behaviour problems'. *BMC Psychiatry*, 15, Article 203.

Sunderland, M. 2016. *What every parent needs to know: love, nurture and play with your child.* Penguin, Random House.

Tefferi, H. 2007. 'Reconstructing adolescence after displacement: Experience from Eastern Africa'. *Children and Society, 21*: 297–308. doi:10.111/j.1099-0860.2007.00101.x.

Trickett, E and Jones, C. 2007. 'Adolescent culture brokering and family functioning: A study of families from Vietnam'. *Cultural Diversity and Ethnic Minority Psychology:* 143–150. doi:10.1037/1099-9809.13.2.143.

UNHCR. 2024. *Global trends report: Forced displacement in 2021.* UNHCR.

UNICEF. 2023. *Latest statistics and graphics on refugee and migrant children.* UNICEF. Accessed 10 February 2023. https://data.unicef.org/topic/child-migration-and-displacement/migration/

Volkan, V. 2018. *Immigrants and refugees: Trauma, perennial mourning, prejudice and border psychology.* Routledge.

Yan Lee, T and Lok, D. 2012. 'Bonding as a positive youth development construct: A conceptual review'. *Positive Youth Development: Theory, Research and Application*: 1–11.

Youth and Education Service. 2021. 'Youth and education service for refugees and migrants'. 1 September. Accessed 28 March 2023. https://separatedchildrensservice.wordpress.com/.

Chapter 2

Stress and the Developing Refugee Adolescent Brain

Introduction

Developing an understanding of brain development during adolescence is essential for identifying effective ways to support young people experiencing the 'double burden' of forced displacement and the transition from childhood to adulthood (Tefferi 2007). This chapter examines how biological, genetic, and environmental factors interact with the significant brain remodelling that occurs during adolescence, a critical period that shapes emotional, cognitive, and behavioural characteristics (Aoki et al. 2017) and influences adult brain development (Swanson et al. 2010).

We will explore how recent technological advances in neuroimaging have transformed our understanding of the adolescent brain and trauma. This exploration includes two key areas: first the hierarchical organisation of the brain through Perry's model of brain development (Perry 1999; Perry and Winfrey 2021), which provides a clear framework for explaining the relationships between stress, trauma and brain function to adolescent refugees and second the specific brain structures that undergo significant changes during this developmental stage. Through the experiences of Chima and Natalia, I will investigate how potentially traumatic experiences associated with forced migration affect key brain functions, including the fight-flight-freeze response, learning and memory, sensory processing, and sleep patterns will be investigated. This neurobiological understanding provides the foundation for the trauma-informed approaches detailed in subsequent chapters.

Technological Advances in Studying the Human Brain

Significant technological advances in neuroimaging techniques within the field of developmental neuroscience, which meant that it became possible to gain a deeper knowledge about the way the brain processes information, emerged in the final decades of the twentieth century. This led to a rapid expansion in the number of studies using these techniques to investigate the ways in which the living human brain develops across the lifespan (Crum 2021), also resulting in a transformation of our understanding of trauma. Studies using one of these techniques, Magnetic

DOI: 10.4324/9781003430032-3

Resonance Imaging (MRI), which uses magnets and radio waves to take photos of the brain using a special MRI scanner, shows how the adolescent human brain changes in its anatomy (its structure and morphology) and organisation (the connections between different parts) during this critical period and how this occurs at different rates for different parts of the brain (Blakemore 2011).

The Hierarchical Organisation of the Human Brain

Bruce Perry's conceptualisation of the hierarchical organisation of the human brain provides a highly accessible explanation of its overall structuring, which can also be used to explain the impact of trauma and loss on the brain (Perry, 1999; Perry and Winfrey, 2021) (see Figure 2.1). In addition to informing those who support adolescent refugees, this model can be effectively used as psychoeducation with the adolescents themselves, to help explain and normalise their distressing and frightening responses to traumatic experiences and will be drawn upon throughout the book along with several other models.

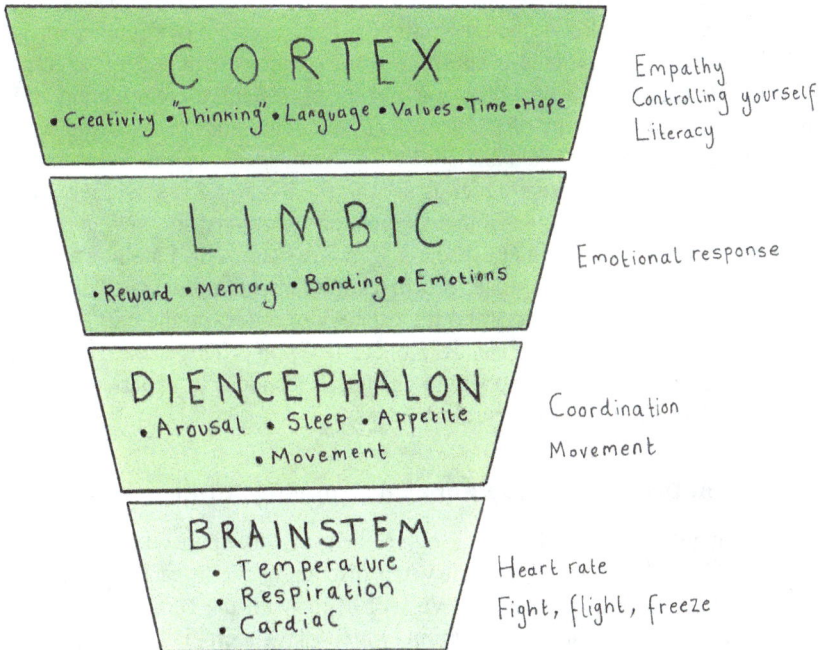

Figure 2.1 The Hierarchical Organisation of the Human Brain.

Perry's Neurosequential Model

Perry's model demonstrates that the structural and functional complexity of these four interconnected areas increases from the lower, more basic areas of the brainstem and the mid-brain up through the limbic brain to the cortex. This sequential 'bottom-up' processing means that the information coming in from our senses is first interpreted by this most primitive, reactive part of the brain, which explains why humans act and feel before they think. This information is then transmitted to higher-order brain regions for further processing (Perry and Winfrey 2021).

The brainstem is the first part of the brain to develop, and it controls less complex, mostly regulatory functions such as breathing, heart rate, body temperature, and emotional regulation. As the brainstem does not register the passing of time, all sensory stimuli (in the form of mainly visual, tactile, sound, and olfactory (smell) input), which enter the brainstem, are immediately matched against stored experiences and transmitted to the amygdala which activates the emotional response. When the brainstem encounters the same or highly similar sensory stimuli, the same emotional response (positive or negative) is activated. In the case of a trauma memory stimulus, this can result in a person feeling as if their mind and body have been taken over again by the trauma memory (van der Kolk 2015).

Moving up the hierarchy to the structures of the midbrain, these serve important functions in visual and auditory reflexes. They regulate eye movement and pupil dilation and are involved in controlling muscle movement and motor control (Ting 2019). Together with the other parts of the brainstem, these midbrain structures control vital functions of the nervous system (the body's command centre which originates from the brain and controls movements, thoughts, and automatic responses). The limbic system which is next in the hierarchy is a useful organising concept for areas of the brain that support our emotional life and are mainly responsible for emotional and unconscious or reflex behaviour. Finally, structures of the cortex are involved in higher processes in the human brain such as speech and language, abstract cognition, and the capacity to reflect on the past and think about the future (Galvan 2017). van der Kolk (2015) points out that each brain area has the capacity to create memory – to change in response to experience and to store those changes in specific neural networks.

Brain Structures with Key Functions during Adolescence

This section will outline the functions of specific brain structures within and across Perry's model, which we will revisit when discussing the impact of trauma on the brain and throughout the book. We will begin with the cerebrum, the largest and most important area of the brain, which plays a crucial role during this developmental stage. The cerebrum consists of grey matter (the cerebral cortex), which is primarily responsible for processing and interpreting information, and white matter, which transmits that information to other parts of the nervous system.

The cerebrum is divided into two halves called the left and right hemispheres (see Figure 2.2).

The two hemispheres process the world differently and are connected by the corpus callosum, allowing communication between them. The left hemisphere contains the verbal centre for speech understanding and formation, and is more linguistic, logical, and linear. The right hemisphere is more connected to bodily sensations and lower brain input. It is emotional, experiential, holistic, and non-verbal, conveying communication through facial expressions, eye contact, tone, posture, and gestures (Siegal 2012, Sunderland 2016).

Although specific areas of the brain are important for certain activities, for most activities both hemispheres are used together in subtly different ways. For example, in relation to speech, the left hemisphere typically plays a specific role

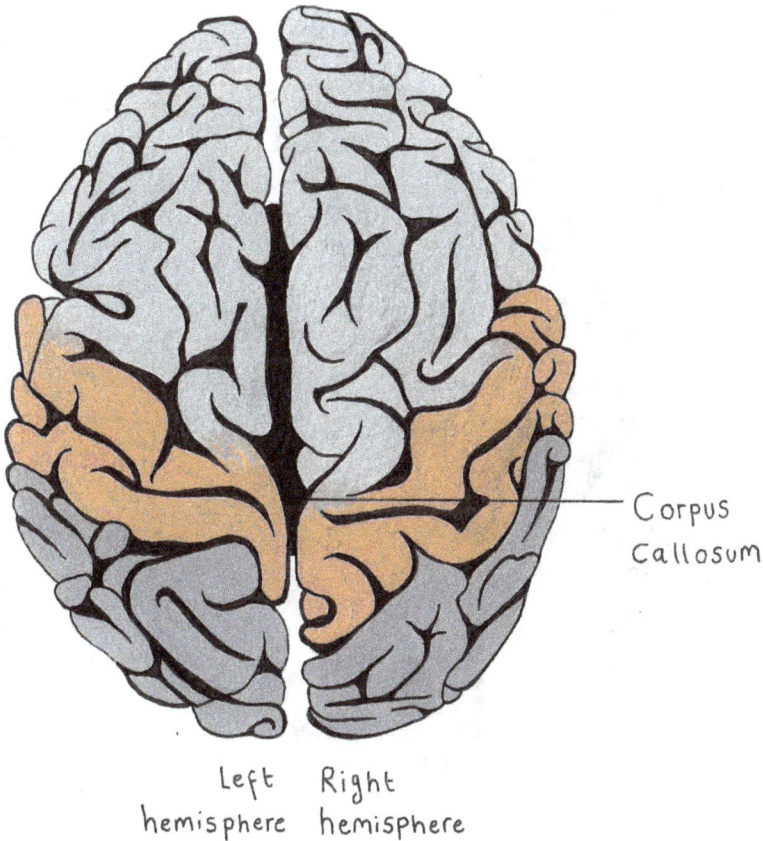

Corpus Callosum

Left hemisphere   Right hemisphere

Figure 2.2 The Hemispheres of the Brain and the Corpus Callosum.

in understanding the syntax, whereas the right hemisphere plays an important role in extracting the implied meaning (Brennan 2022). Listening to or playing music is another important example of integrated hemisphere activity, as the lyrics are interpreted in the left hemisphere while music and sounds are interpreted in the right hemisphere (Albouy et al. 2020).

The two hemispheres are each made up of four lobes which control different functions (see Figure 2.3).

- The temporal lobe is involved in language, hearing, and smell.
- The parietal lobe is involved in processing bodily sensations.

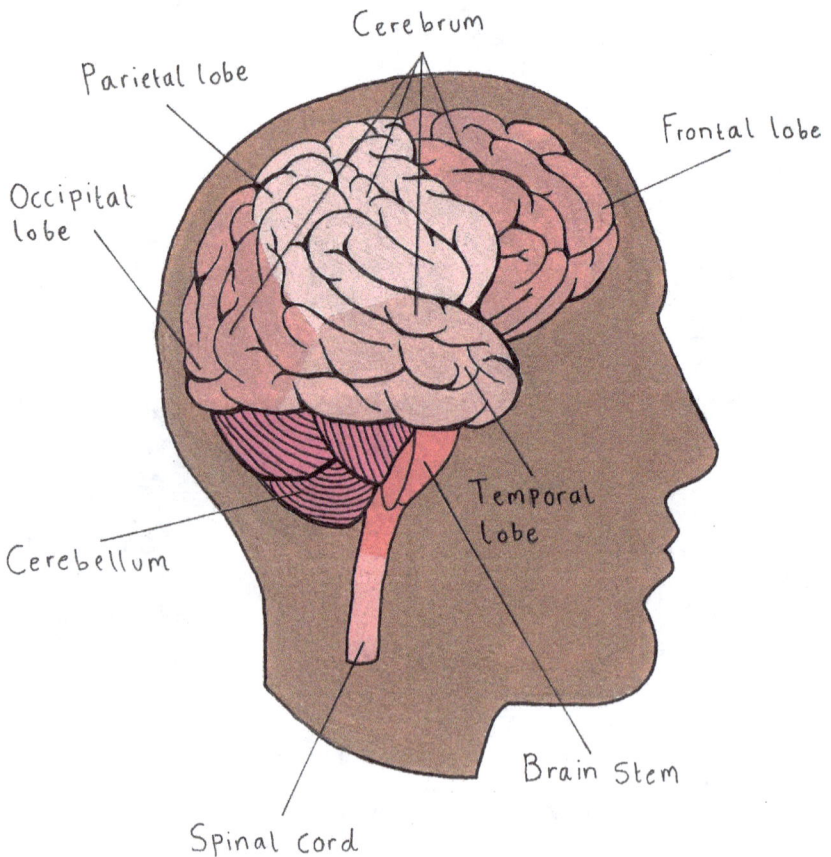

Figure 2.3 The Brain Lobes, the Cerebrum, and the Cerebellum.

- The occipital lobe is involved in visual processing, distance, and depth perception.
- The frontal lobes are considered to be our emotional control centre. They also play a crucial role in our personality and how we act while supporting planning, organisation, and executive function skills. This includes the prefrontal cortex, the part of the frontal lobes lying just behind the forehead, which is responsible for planning complex cognitive behaviour.

The prefrontal cortex (see Figure 2.4) undergoes significant developmental changes during adolescence. This brain region balances emotions, future planning, and empathy, which are easily unsettled by intense emotions and peer influences typical of adolescence (Siegel 2014). The amygdala and hippocampus in the limbic region play important roles during this stage. The amygdala, the brain's 'smoke

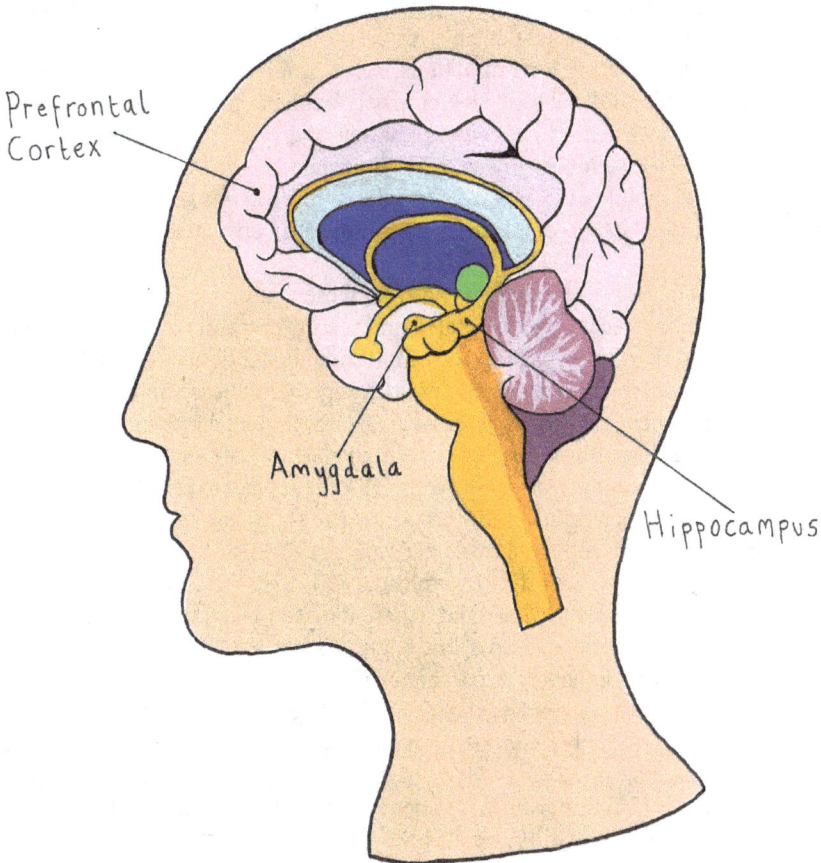

Figure 2.4 The Prefrontal Cortex, Amygdala, and Hippocampus.

detector' (van der Kolk 2015:60), evaluates emotional situations, recognises danger, and prepares the body for fight, flight, or freeze by increasing heart rate and breath frequency. It can take over the brain's thinking part, making us act before we think when sensing danger. The hippocampus and prefrontal cortex are key to learning and autobiographical memory. The maturation of brain areas during adolescence affects these three structures, which contribute significantly to emotional regulation, learning, and memory coding (Siegel 2014).

The Maturation of the Human Brain during Adolescence

Neuroimaging techniques show that the brain matures from the areas at the back (within the brainstem and the mid-brain) which are responsible for older and more basic functions such as vision, movement and processing and progresses to the evolutionary newer and more complex thinking areas of the prefrontal cortex located at the anterior of the frontal lobe (see Figure 2.4). This decision-making part of the brain, which is responsible for the ability of the adolescent to plan and think about the consequences of actions, solve problems, and control impulses, is the last to reach full maturity which partly explains the high vulnerability of adolescents to risk-taking behaviours (Jensen and Nutt 2015). The maturation of the corpus callosum (see Figure 2.2), the connecting bridge between the two hemispheres, is another key change which takes place at this time. This facilitates the multiplication and diversification of connections between different regions of the brain.

The proliferation of research arising from these neuroimaging advances shows more efficient, connected, and integrated information processing to be a key feature of brain maturation during the transition from childhood to adolescence (Blakemore 2012). Brain wiring changes during this critical period increase impulse speed and efficiency, enhancing cognitive processing and developing connections across distant network regions. This period features high plasticity of synapses, the chemical junctions that transmit messages between cells. Genes and experiences shape synaptic connections, determining how brain changes occur through a combination of inherited information and lived experiences (Siegal 2012).

The maturation process during adolescence is also characterised by a combination of expansion and regression where unused connections in the thinking and processing part of a child's brain (the cortex/grey matter) are 'pruned' away while more frequently used connections are strengthened. This process of removing underused wiring to accommodate faster, more efficient, and potentially more effective and interconnected processing of information is the brain's way of maximising efficiency based on the 'use it' or 'lose it' principle (Giedd 2004). This greater brain efficiency typically leads to the development and integration of new skills and abilities, the cultivation of imaginative ideas and creative thinking, and improvements in memory, language, thinking, and reasoning (Galvan 2017).

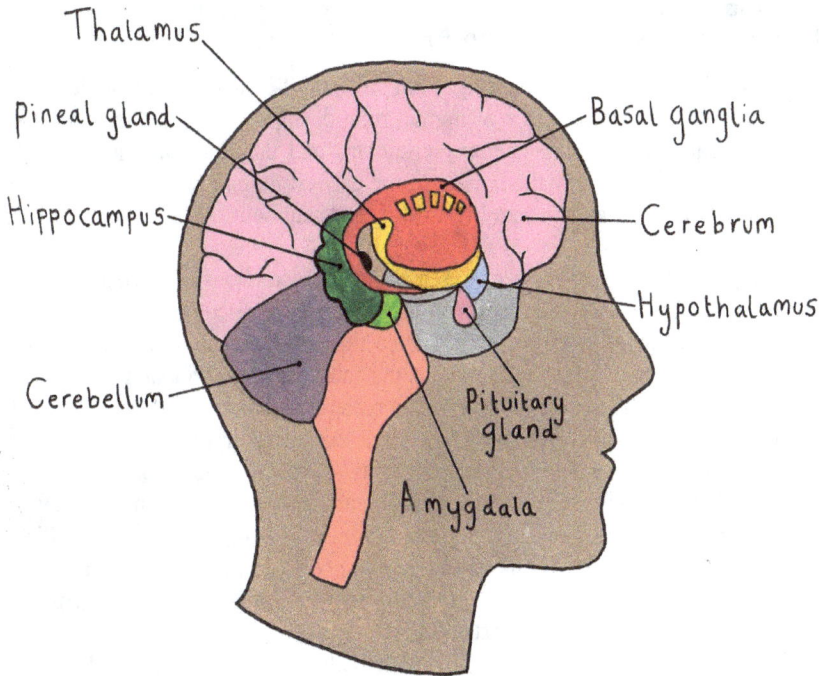

Figure 2.5 The Limbic System.

The limbic system, comprising a collection of structures involved in processing emotion and memory, including the hippocampus, amygdala, and hypothalamus (see Figure 2.5), is also impacted during adolescence. Changes to the balance and activity of neurotransmitters (the body's chemical messengers) within the limbic system, which produce dopamine and serotonin (for positive arousal) and norepinephrine (for stress inoculation), have been documented during this sensitive period (Arain et al. 2013). These neurotransmitters regulate a variety of cognitive and emotional processes, including motivation, reward, mood, and attention, which are believed to contribute to the heightened sensitivity to social cues, as well as mood swings and increased risk-taking behaviour, which characterise the adolescent period (Siegel 2014).

Having focused on the hierarchical and structural features of human brain development in adolescence as well as recognising the importance of genetic influences in the timing of these maturation processes, we will now focus more on the ways in which the nature of adolescent lives and interactions within their social ecologies starting with their earliest relationships, also shape the ways in which the brain circuits are activated and integrated (Bronfenbrenner and Morris 2006; Perry and Szalavitz 2006; Siegel 2014).

The Impact of Early Relationships on the Healthy Development of the Human Brain

Recent scientific evidence resulting from the significant progress made in our knowledge of the brain science of human relationships (interpersonal neurobiology) has confirmed that which many clinicians and theorists have long intuited through their work, namely the impact of the earliest human relationships on psychological wellbeing and the ability to thrive throughout the lifespan (Gerhardt 2004; Sunderland 2016).

Schore (2012) conducted in-depth research on the interactions between primary caregivers and infants during the first three years of life. He discovered that these early caregiving experiences significantly influence the development of the higher social brain, specifically the cortex, and establish the foundation for lifelong relational patterns. Bowlby (1988) refers to the non-verbal patterns acquired unconsciously and the formation of expectations about how others are likely to behave as internal working models. Similarly, Bucci (1997:156) describes these patterns as emotion schemas.

Research shows that women with a healthy attachment to their unborn baby are more likely to protect and nurture their emotional wellbeing during infancy (Pisoni et al. 2014). Sue Gerhardt discusses the 'unfinished' baby, whose systems develop in response to human caregiving, optimising cultural transmission and adaptation to specific socio-ecological contexts (Gerhardt 2004).

The development of a secure attachment with a primary caregiver during the first three years of life helps Gerhardt's 'unfinished' baby to learn to emotionally self-regulate (develop the ability to manage emotions and impulses). When caregiver and infant are sensitively attuned to each other, they are engaging in a mutually regulating process whereby the infant signals hunger, distress, rage, or fear by crying and the sensitively attuned caregiver feeds, soothes, and calms them. Throughout infancy and leading into early childhood and beyond, the child then knows that they have a 'secure base' and that whenever they are hungry, frightened, or unhappy, their caregiver will respond to them in a sensitive, attuned way. Holmes (2014) provides a biographical account of John Bowlby and an exploration of his ground-breaking attachment theory together with a comprehensive introduction to contemporary attachment theory and research.

The importance of this secure attachment in every context, no matter how resource-poor, is supported by Bowen (2021:3), who in a flexible and dynamic re-framing of Maslow's Hierarchy of Needs proposes a *Matrix of Human Needs* where he identifies attachment relationships along with subsistence and communication as core needs. Rather than focusing on stages, this matrix uses the concept of interacting processes to support individual and community development. Attuned attachment leads to the formation of critical connections in the brain which cultivate good coping strategies, form rewarding relationships, effectively regulate emotions, develop kindness and compassion, and foster the development of resilient stress systems (Perry and Szalavitz 2006; Sunderland 2016).

The Impact of Early Mistreatment on the Development of the Human Brain

Early mistreatment from abuse, neglect, or unresponsive parenting can negatively affect brain development (Perry and Szalavitz 2006; van der Kolk 2015). Unconscious brain strategies develop in response to mistreatment to meet unmet needs, leading to adaptations in the brain's chemical systems and reorganisation of its wiring over time (van der Kolk 2015). This makes the brain and body overly sensitive and reactive to environmental threat signals in various ways.

For example, as one of the main functions of the 'smoke detector' amygdala in the limbic system is to warn of impending risk and to activate the stress response of the body, the amygdala of a child who has an alcoholic mother will be in a constant process of detecting threat, resulting in the child being in a state of hypervigilance (increased alertness), where she will repeatedly scan her home environment for potential danger. This response is adaptive for the child here, while the same level of scanning in school may label them as unable to concentrate and disruptive, making it maladaptive for learning.

Besides the impact of clear physical, neglect, and psychological abuse on the developing brain, there is a significant hidden impact when a child lacks consistent, emotionally responsive parenting. Parents may lack awareness of the importance of healthy emotional development and may struggle to provide it due to their own unmet childhood needs, mental health issues, or other limitations (Siegel and Hartzell 2014). For example, research shows that depressed mothers tend to interact less with their infants and are unable to respond and attune consistently to their cues (Field 2010). Within these reduced interactions, these mothers have also been found to be less playful and nurturing and more intrusive and aggressive (Sunderland 2016). These factors have a significant impact on the nature of the bonding and attachment relationship which develops between the infant and the caregiver, thereby establishing the neurological underpinnings of psychological, affective, and relational functioning (Gerhardt 2004).

When the caregiver is unable to provide responsive, attentive, and consistent caregiving, the infant typically stops looking for this connection, and this is often the beginning of a long process of trying to self-regulate without having experienced co-regulation (emotional regulation within a securely attached relationship) (Sunderland 2016). Without co-regulation, a child is likely to experience dysregulation which may take the form of outbursts or aggression and result in the development of maladaptive coping strategies, such as the suppression of emotions. Co-regulation is therefore essential in helping a child to create calming connections in their brain, and its presence or absence ultimately becomes part of the infant's worldview about humans (Jennings 2010). The plethora of research conducted after some of the most shocking images of neglect in Romania's orphanages were exposed in 1989, showed that infants provided with basic physical care but deprived of love, affection, comfort and connection, learned that they would not be responded to so eventually stopped crying and became completely quiet (Fisher et al. 1997).

These examples of mistreatment illustrate that when a child or adolescent experiences repeated toxic stress, their brain develops ways of surviving and remaining alert. Over time, these behaviours can alter the brain's structure with the parts controlling fear and anxiety (the amygdala and the hippocampus) growing to protect them, while the parts controlling logical or more critical thinking (the frontal lobes) become constricted (Schore 2012). They also show that these coping (or survival) strategies do not automatically switch off when the trauma exposure ends and that the child or adolescent remains stuck in 'survival mode' and operates out of the lower brain. This means that very little information can be passed to other parts of the brain where it would usually be rationalised, interpreted, and processed, as illustrated by Bruce Perry's model (Perry 1999).

Like adolescents in so many different communities worldwide, some adolescent refugees are likely to have experienced less than optimal early caregiving experiences due to a variety of factors. These experiences will have impacted the extent to which they have developed resilience and the strategies they are capable of using to cope with the potentially traumatic experiences resulting from forced migration, the outcomes of which will be explored in more detail throughout the case studies.

Chima's early years, marked by daily stressors in conflict-affected settings, were supported by loving adults in his mesosystem, likely helping him develop critical connections and coping strategies. Natalia, however, did not experience emotionally consistent caregiving which, even though partly mitigated by her loving relationship with her grandmother, was likely to have contributed to her struggles with anxiety, fear, and low self-esteem. The impact of these experiences on the adolescent refugee brain will now be explored in more detail, drawing on the experiences of Chima and Natalia.

The Impact of Potentially Traumatic Experiences Associated with Forced Displacement on Adolescent Refugee Brain Functions

The Neurobiology of Stress Responses: Fight, Flight, and Freeze

Many adolescents who arrive in host countries having fled their home countries, with or without an accompanying adult, have experienced armed conflict and situations of violence and persecution, all of which can have a significant impact on the brain and cause considerable psychological distress (Bennouna et al. 2020). The world is experienced differently by the brain after a traumatic experience, with the survivor's energy being diverted into trying to control unbearable physiological responses (Cozoloni 2010).

Van der Kolk (2015) describes how the amygdala triggers stress hormones like cortisol and adrenaline, increasing heart rate, blood pressure, and breathing rate. Pre-programmed physical escape plans, which automatically drive the body to run, hide, fight, or freeze, are instinctively triggered in the brain stem and the mid-brain. When these brain structures take over, the cortex (conscious mind) shuts down, and by the time full awareness returns, the body has likely already responded. If danger is avoided through fight/flight/freeze, internal equilibrium can be reestablished.

Malchiodi (2020) states that the ability to react and protect oneself is crucial in determining a terrifying experience's lasting impact. Chima's family member restrained him to prevent revealing his uncle and cousin's hiding place during an attack by government forces. This prevented him from helping them escape danger or fleeing himself. Immobilisation kept Chima in shock and helplessness, impeding his instinctive fight/flight/freeze response. Chima felt 'very agitated and shaky' because his body was always primed to defend itself. Fragments of sensory stimuli from his trauma evoked memories, emotions, and physiological reactions.

Sensory Processing and Trauma Triggers

Visual Triggers and Trauma Responses

The brainstem acts as a crucial relay centre that receives, filters, and forwards sensory input to higher brain regions for further processing and appropriate responses. This includes input associated with both positive and potentially traumatic experiences. For example, whenever Chima sees a bright yellow colour, the brainstem matches this colour with the clothes of his favourite aunt who always wore yellow and was a warm and nurturing presence in his life. The brainstem then forwards the input to the amygdala which activates the same emotional response of happiness whenever he sees this colour: 'it takes me right back to sitting on her knee when I was small and her telling me lovely stories about herself and my mum when they were kids.'

Chima also experienced an emotional response when the first person he encountered in the host country was wearing a uniform. Sensory visual components of the traumatic experience of being tortured by a government official wearing a uniform entered the brainstem and the matching process in the brainstem connected these experiences. As the brainstem cannot compute the fact that any time has passed, it activated the same emotional fear response which meant that the feelings of overwhelm and powerlessness were re-experienced by Chima. An awareness on the part of the border agency staff of the nature of trauma responses (i.e. being trauma-informed) would have equipped them with knowledge of how to recognise that Chima was experiencing a flashback and how to use simple grounding techniques to help anchor him in the present moment (see Chapters 9 and 12 for explanations and examples of grounding techniques).

Olfactory Processing and Emotional Memory

Smell can be a powerful trigger for emotional responses due to the way the brain processes olfactory (smell) information and its close connection to the amygdala which activates an emotional response and the hippocampus which helps consolidate the memory of that event (Vermetten and Douglas Bremner 2003). This means that encountering the same smell in the future can trigger the recall of the memory and the associated emotions.

Natalia reported a strong emotional response to the smell of Borscht, a traditional soup from her country, at a welcome event. She felt the same safety and trust in her grandmother's house, where Borscht was often cooked during difficult times with her mother.

Auditory Triggers and Flashback Experiences

The sound of a car backfiring triggered a flashback for Natalia, who had witnessed shelling in her home country, reminding her of diving for cover soon after arriving in the host country.

Cognitive Functioning and Learning Challenges

Childhood and adolescent trauma can directly affect learning and cognitive functioning. This can manifest in inability to concentrate, difficulties in processing information, impaired short-term memory recall, and the inability to store long-term memories (Ainamani et al. 2017). In order to process, store, retrieve and respond to new learning, the brain must be in a calm and attentive state whereas when a trauma survivor is in a state of fear, the brainstem is involved in the fight, flight, or freeze response, and information is blocked from entering the brain's areas of higher cognitive memory consolidation and storage (Dyregrov 2010). A refugee adolescent experiencing a trauma trigger cannot, therefore, be fully present in the current moment and cannot absorb any new information.

Information Processing Barriers during Stress States

Chima describes being overwhelmed and confused by the amount of information about the asylum process which was communicated by border agency officials when he first arrived in the host country and says that even with the help of an interpreter, he found it very difficult to understand and retain the information. However, he also describes the much more sensitive way in which his social worker communicates information to him, taking into account the best ways in which he can retain information (see Chapter 4).

Memory Consolidation Difficulties

Natalia recalls her first days attending an access programme which was designed to prepare her for mainstream school. Although she understood the information which was being delivered, she reported finding it very difficult to remember any of it. The different ways in which information can be presented in trauma-informed ways will be demonstrated in the case studies.

Trauma Triggers

Natalia also described an incident where she was triggered by the sound of balloons being burst at a party. This resulted in a flashback where she relived the experience of hearing shots being fired just outside her house. This made her feel helpless, panicked, and unsafe. Luckily, the teacher had undertaken some trauma-informed practice training and knew how to help Natalia by using grounding techniques and by accompanying her to a quiet comfortable space (see Chapters 9 and 12 for illustrations of grounding techniques). This example illustrates how seemingly innocuous stimuli can activate the brain threat detection system in trauma survivors, causing the body to respond as if the danger were present in the moment. The teacher's appropriate response helped Natalia's nervous system return to a regulated state by creating physical safety, engaging her prefrontal cortex through grounding exercises, and avoiding further sensory overload that could have intensified her distress. Without such trauma-informed interventions, these triggering events can reinforce neural pathways associated with the original trauma and potentially contribute to the development of more persistent trauma responses.

Sleep Disruption and its Cognitive Consequences

Trauma-Induced Sleep Architecture

Sleep is crucial for brain health and function, and it plays an important role in memory consolidation, emotional regulation, and overall cognitive performance (Coleman 2021). The brain goes through various stages during sleep, each of which serves different functions. Emotional processing takes place during the rapid eye movement (REM) stage, and memory consolidation takes place in the non-rapid eye movement (NREM) stage (Germain 2013). These processes can be disrupted by traumatic experiences. For example, trauma-induced nightmares can interfere with REM sleep, affecting emotional regulation and memory consolidation (Smit 2016). Sleep disturbances can impact the ability of the brain to manage stress which leads to heightened anxiety and emotional reactivity.

In addition to affecting cognitive functions, emotional regulation, and decision-making, the significant changes in structure and function (especially synaptic pruning, myelination, and the development of the prefrontal cortex) which the brain undergoes during adolescence influence sleep patterns. There is a shift in circadian rhythms during adolescence which leads to a delayed sleep phase preference where adolescents naturally feel more awake later at night and struggle to wake up early (Coleman 2021). The interplay between moving from childhood to adolescence and the trauma associated with forced displacement can lead to more pronounced sleep disturbances. Chima describes experiencing highly disrupted sleep during pre-flight due to the fear of attack, during flight due to the comings and goings at all times of the night and day at the mosque where he was hiding, and during post-flight due to the constant nightmares which he experienced once in a place of safety. He described the reversal of his sleep patterns, and Chapter 10 looks in detail at different ways of supporting refugee adolescents to cope with disrupted sleep and nightmares.

Conclusions

Drawing on research based on technological advances which have made detailed exploration of the brain maturation process possible in recent times, this chapter has demonstrated the impact of traumatic stress on the developing adolescent refugee brain, including that of early relationships and the potentially traumatic experiences associated with forced displacement. Chapter 3 will move on to explore some of the culturally diverse understandings of mental health among adolescent refugees and will look at different ways of addressing the stigma surrounding mental health help-seeking and improving mental health literacy among these young people.

References

Ainamani, H, Elbert, T, Olema, D and Hecker, T. 2017. 'PTSD symptom severity relates to cognitive and psycho-social dysfunctioning – a study with Congolese refugees in Uganda'. *European Journal of Psychotraumatology*, 8(1): 1–10. doi:10.1080/2000819 8.2017.1283086.

Albouy, P, Benjamin, L, Morillon, B and Zatorre, R J. 2020. 'Distinct sensitivity to spectrotemporal modulation supports brain assymetry for speech and melody'. *Science* 367: 1043–1047.

Aoki, C, Romeo, R and Smith, S. 2017. 'Adolescence as a critical period for developmental plasticity'. *Brain Research* 1654 (Part B): 85–86.

Arain, M, Haque, M, Johal, L, Mathur, P, Nel, W, Rais, A, Sandho, R and Sharma, S. 2013. 'Maturation of the adolescent brain'. *Neuropsychiatric Disease and Treatment* 9: 449–461.

Bennouna, C, Stark, L and Wessells, M. 2020. 'Children and adolescents in conflict and displacement'. In A Song and P Ventevogel, *Child, adolescent and family refugee mental health*, 54–95. Springer Nature Switzerland.

Blakemore, S-J. 2011. 'Imaging brain development: The adolescent brain, 61: *Neuroimage*: 1–10.

Blakemore, S-J. 2012. 'Imaging brain development: The adolescent brain'. *Neuroimage*, *61*: 397–406.

Bowen, B. 2021. 'The matrix of needs: Reframing Maslow's hierarchy'. *Health*: 538–563. doi:10.4236/health.2021.135041.

Bowlby, J. 1988. *A secure base: Parent-child attachment and healthy human development*. Basic Books.

Brennan, J. 2022. *Language and the brain: A slim guide to neurolinguistics*. Oxford University Press.

Bronfenbrenner, U and Morris, P A. 2006. 'The bioecological model of human development'. In R M Lerner and W Damon, *Handbook of child psychology: Theoretical models of human development*, 793–828. John Wiley & Sons.

Bucci, W. 1997. *Psychoanalysis and cognitive science*. Guilford Press.

Coleman, J. 2021. *The teacher and the teenage brain*. Routledge.

Cozoloni, L. 2010. *The neuroscience of psychotherapy: Healing the social brain*. Norton.

Crum, J. 2021. 'Future applications of real-world neuroimaging to clinical psychology'. *Psychological Reports*, *124*(6): 2403–2426.

Dyregrov, A. 2010. *Supporting traumatised children and teenagers*. Jessica Kingsley Publishers.

Field, T. 2010. 'Postpartum depression effects on early interactions, parenting and safety practices: A review'. *Infant Behavioural Development*, 33: 1–6.

Fisher, L, Ames, E W, Chisholm, K and Savoie, L. 1997. 'Problems reported by parents of Romanian orphans adopted to British Columbia, 20(1):*International Journal of Behavioural Development*: 67–82.

Galvan, A. 2017. *The neuroscience of adolescence*. Cambridge University Press.

Gerhardt, S. 2004. *Why Love Matters: How affection shapes a baby's brain*. Brunner-Routledge.

Germain, A. 2013. 'Sleep disturbances as the hallmark of PTSD: Where are we now?' *American Journal of Psychiatry*, 170(4): 372–382.

Giedd, J. 2004. 'Structural magnetic resonance imaging of the adolescent brain'. In R Dahl and L Speal, *Adolescent brain development: Vulnerabilities and opportunities*, 77–85. Annals of the New York Academy of Sciences.

Holmes, J. 2014. *John Bowlby and attachment theory (makers of modern psychotherapy)*. Routledge.

Jennings, S. 2010. *Healthy attachments and neuro-dramatic play*. Jessica Kingsley Publishers.

Jensen, F and Nutt A. 2015. *The teenage brain: A neuroscientist's survival guide to raising adolescents and young adults*. Harper Thorsons.

Malchiodi, C. 2020. *Trauma and expressive arts therapy: Brain, body and imagination in the healing process*. The Guilford Press.

Perry, B. 1999. 'The memories of states: How the brain stores and retrieves traumatic experiences'. In J Goodwin and R Attias, *Splintered reflections: Images of the body in trauma*, 9–39. Basic Books.

Perry, B and Szalavitz M. 2006. *The boy who was raised as a dog and other stories from a child psychiatrist's notebook*. Basic Books.

Perry, B and Winfrey, O. 2021. *What happened to you: Conversations on trauma, resilience, and healing*. Bluebird Books for Life.

Philips Swanson, D, Chaka Edwards, M and Beale Spencer, M. 2010. *Adolescence: Development during a global era.* Elsevier.

Pisoni, C, Garofoli, F, Tzialla, C, Orcesi, S, Spinillo, A, Politi, P, Balottin, U, Manzoni, P and Stronati, M. 2014. 'Risk and protective factors in maternal-foetal attachment development'. *Early Human Development*, 90:S45–S46.

Schore, A. 2012. *The science of the art of psychotherapy.* W.W. Norton and Company.

Siegal, D. 2012. *The developing mind: How relationships and the brain interact to shape who we are.* Guilford Press.

Siegel, D. 2014. *Brainstorm the power and purpose of the teenage brain.* Scribe Publications Pty Ltd.

Siegel, D and Hartzell, M. 2014. *Parenting from the inside out.* Scribe.

Smit, S. 2016. 'Trauma-induced insomnia: A novel model for trauma and sleep research'. *Sleep Medicime Reviews*: 74–83. doi:10.1016/j.smrv.2015.01.008.

Sunderland, M. 2016. *What every parent needs to know: love, nurture and play with your child.* Penguin, Random House.

Tefferi, H. 2007. 'Reconstructing adolescence after displacement: Experience from Eastern Africa'. *Children and Society, 21*: 297–308. doi:10.111/j.1099-0860.2007.00101.x.

Ting, D. 2019. *The forgotten midbrain.* Partridge.

van der Kolk, B. 2015. *The body keeps the score: Mind, brain and body in the transformation of trauma.* Penguin.

Vermetten, E and J Douglas Bremner. 2003. 'Olfaction as a traumatic reminder in posttraumatic stress disorder: Case reports and reviews'. *Journal of Clinical Psychiatry, 64*(2): 202–207. doi:10.4088/jcp.v64n0214.

Chapter 3

Reframing Adolescent Refugee Mental Health as Wellbeing

Optimising Help-Seeking Opportunities and Overcoming Stigma

Introduction

Asylum seekers and refugees often face barriers to accessing mental health and psychosocial support services (MHPSS) in destination countries, beyond appointment availability in overstretched systems (Bartolomei et al. 2016). This chapter, grounded in Bronfenbrenner's social ecology model, explores factors affecting access to and perceptions of MHPSS for adolescent refugees. Factors include diverse understandings of mental health, stigma's impact, and varied perceptions of trauma and loss in social and cultural contexts. This exploration concludes with a critique of the Western bio-medical model that pathologises responses which may be better understood as normal reactions to devastating events and loss (Boyles 2017).

Barriers to MHPSS Access for Refugee Adolescents

Culturally Diverse Understandings of Mental Health

Access to mental health supports for refugee adolescents in European host countries can be viewed as a dynamic and interconnected process that involves multiple systems and factors. Bronfenbrenner's socio-ecological model provides a comprehensive conceptual framework for understanding the complexity of pathways to access and provision (Arakelyan and Ager 2020; Siddiq et al. 2023). For example, the macrosystem effectively captures the diversity of culturally embedded refugee perceptions and understandings of mental health, which often differ from prevailing belief systems in European host countries. The mesosystem demonstrates the interaction between different systems such as schools and health systems, which can shape MHPSS referral processes.

Case Example: Chima's Understanding of Mental Health

Chima's foster carer recognised soon after he came to her that he was likely to benefit from therapy. However, she realised that introducing this idea only three weeks after he had arrived in Ireland was likely to be overwhelming given that he

DOI: 10.4324/9781003430032-4

had little English and that there was so much going on for him in relation to the new culture, the new family, and starting in the migrant access programme. Therefore, she spoke to his social worker who, given that she knew there was a waiting list of around three months, decided to make a referral and to talk to Chima about it after a couple of months. Once Chima had settled into his new placement and the education programme, his foster mother first talked to him (through an interpreter) about seeing a therapist, and he recalled that this terrified him as he remembered someone in his village whom he described as 'crazy' being taken away and he was very frightened that this could happen to him.

Chima discussed cultural practices in his community for 'crazy people' aimed at expelling evil spirits from the body. He remembered someone from the village being tied to a tree for several days and various rituals taking place. The social worker, aware of Chima's fears, arranged for the therapist and herself to talk to him at home (with an interpreter). They gently discussed support with him in this familiar setting during this difficult time. Chima met the therapist before entering the therapy room for reassuring pre-engagement. Chima told the therapist he didn't fully understand but would try it once since he sometimes felt crazy and wanted help. He said that he also felt reassured that he wouldn't be taken away.

Shannon et al. (2015) found that the different cultural understandings and practices of refugee populations in European host countries, together with a lack of information about the meaning of 'mental health' and its conceptualisation in these host countries, constituted barriers to seeking MHPSS. Furthermore, scholars have questioned how a single medicalised model of mental health could account for and treat psychosocial distress in every context, including that of forced migration (Mills and Davar 2016).

Cultural idioms of distress are specific expressions and symbols of emotional suffering or culturally acceptable ways for individuals to communicate distress within specific contexts (Rabiau 2019). Riley et al. (2020) identify being the victim of black magic or being possessed by an evil spirit as local idioms of distress used to express mental health concerns among Rohingya refugees in Bangladesh. The cultural idiom of 'thinking too much' has also been identified in cultural settings worldwide as a way of expressing feelings of psychological, somatic, and social distress (Backe et al. 2021).

Mental Health versus Mental Illness

In many cases, different cultural understandings lead to confusion between the term 'mental health' and serious mental illness (Majumder et al. 2015). This perception can be partially attributed to the fact that mental health services may be available only for the most serious cases of mental illness in some of the low- and middle-income countries from which many adolescent refugees and their families have been forced to flee, as the public health focus in these countries often prioritises the control of infectious diseases.

For example, according to the World Health Organisation, Somalia has only three psychiatrists for a country of 15 million (0.02 per 100,000 inhabitants) and Afghanistan has only 300 psychiatrists for a population of over 40 million (0.75 per 100,000 inhabitants) (World Health Organization 2023), whereas Monaco, which has the highest ratio of psychiatrists in Europe per capita, has 41 psychiatrists per 100,000 inhabitants, for a population of 39,000 (Eurostat 2023).

It is important to note that although mental health and mental illness are related concepts that should both be approached in a culturally sensitive and inclusive way, they refer to different aspects of an individual's psychological wellbeing and resilience (Vaillant 2012):

- Mental health is a broader concept that encompasses an individual's overall psychological wellbeing and includes positive aspects of mental functioning (Fusar-Poli et al. 2020).
- Mental illness refers to specific conditions that can negatively impact mental health and functioning (Keyes 2005).

Maintaining good mental health involves promoting wellbeing and resilience, while addressing mental illness often requires diagnosis and treatment (Vaillant 2012).

Confusion between these terms was evident in the Canadian study conducted by Filler et al. (2019), which explored Syrian refugee adolescents' perceptions of mental health. The term mental health triggered fear among many participants, as they often equated it with mental illness, which they typically associated with serious psychiatric conditions like psychosis. This finding prompted researchers to explore alternative ways of discussing mental health with the participants, including:

- Different ways of dealing with stress and pressure;
- Building resilience and coping skills; and
- Promoting wellbeing.

This resulted in participants being more receptive to engaging in such discussions and more open to seeking appropriate support, thereby ultimately reducing stigma.

Reducing Mental Health Stigma

The Multi-Layered Nature of Stigma

In the years following Erving Goffman's seminal essay where he conceptualised stigma as 'the situation of the individual who is disqualified from full social acceptance' (Goffman 1963:3), research on stigma focused on how it manifests at individual and micro levels and its impact on psychological wellbeing (e.g. Cahnman 1968). More recent research by social scientists has considered the stigma's social and institutional origins (Kreitzer et al. 2022).

This research broadly aligns with the nested levels of Bronfenbrenner's socio-ecological framework. Using this framework to examine mental health stigma suggests that its persistence within and across Bronfenbrenner's levels can perpetuate suffering and prevent adolescent refugees from accessing the help they need (Theisen-Womersley 2021).

Types of Stigma Affecting Refugee Adolescents

Social stigma may arise for refugee adolescents fearing negative judgement from family, peers, or teachers regarding mental health difficulties, aligning with Bronfenbrenner's microsystem. Institutional stigma may be experienced throughout the mesosystem when unaccompanied minors worry that their asylum application or educational opportunities will be disadvantaged if mental health difficulties are identified and at the individual level, the internalisation of social or institutional stigma can result in the devaluing of self and the anticipation of social rejection (Bar et al. 2021). It is also important to highlight the importance of the nature of the language used to describe these difficulties which can have a significant impact on help-seeking behaviours.

Case Example: Contrasting Experiences of Natalia and Chima

Natalia's experience was in sharp contrast to Chima's. Having engaged with therapy in her home country, Natalia experienced no stigma related to help-seeking and actively requested therapy upon arrival in Ireland. This illustrates how prior positive exposure to mental health support can mitigate stigma barriers.

Language and Stigma

The stigma associated with using the term 'mental health' was identified by the carers of unaccompanied minors who had fled to the UK (Majumder 2019). Both carers and minors were participants in this research which explored their perceptions and beliefs about mental health. The unaccompanied minors described people with mental health difficulties as 'crazy,' 'mental,' or 'mad,' fearing that engaging with services would result in stigmatisation and rejection by friends and family (Majumder 2019:278). They also described people with these difficulties as being withdrawn, neglectful of their basic hygiene routines, and likely to be in a psychiatric institution. The carers strongly recommended avoiding terms such as 'mental' and replacing them with more neutral terms that did not carry stigma. Many unaccompanied minors expressed their challenges by describing physical or somatic symptoms such as difficulties sleeping, stomach pain, or headaches.

Alternative language frameworks for practitioners are as follows:

- 'Supporting your wellbeing' instead of 'mental health support';
- 'Ways to cope with stress' rather than 'therapy';

- 'Building strength after difficult experiences' instead of 'trauma treatment'; and
- 'Feeling strong in your body and mind' rather than 'psychological health.'

Shifting the Narrative away from Illness

To reduce stigma, Majumder strongly advocates shifting the narrative of service provision away from *illness* towards *wellbeing*. This requires:

(1) Short-term approach: Engaging with the immediate environments, relationships, and connections within the young person's micro- and mesosystems (close family, social workers, educational and religious settings) to gently introduce the idea of seeking support.
(2) Long-term approach: Drawing on research evidence at the exo- and macrosystem levels to inform policy recommendations for structurally embedding less stigmatising and more socially acceptable ways of framing mental health.

I have found that avoiding the use of the potentially stigmatising terms 'therapy' and 'mental health' and framing the engagement as 'providing the opportunity for you to explore different ways of coping and improve your wellbeing given everything you've been through' is very effective in the (pre-) engagement phase of my clinical practice, when I am supporting a parent, foster carer or social care worker to introduce the adolescent refugee to the idea of seeking support, as well as throughout the entire therapeutic process. Creative ways of connecting with adolescent refugees in the pre-engagement phase of psychotherapy will be explored throughout the case studies in Chapters 7–12.

Humanising Post-Traumatic Stress as a Normal Response to Devastating Events and Loss

Moving beyond Diagnostic Categories

Dr Tony Bates suggests in his book *Breaking the Heart Open: The Making of a Psychologist* that one unforeseen consequence of addressing mental health stigma has been the increased use of diagnostic psychiatric categories to label 'disorders' (Bates 2023). While welcoming reduced stigma, he expresses deep discomfort with the process by which the impact of a traumatising experience becomes defined and treated as a medical problem through the language of the medical psychiatric model. Bates proposes that human suffering and emotional distress should be thought about and conceptualised in more meaningful and less pathologising ways in relation to our experiences. This shift in perspective is also captured in the title of Bruce Perry and Oprah Winfrey's book *What happened to you?*, which recognises and honours the power of our past experiences in shaping our current functioning, changing the fundamental question when recognising and responding to the issue of trauma from 'What's wrong with you?' to 'What happened to you?' (Perry and Winfrey 2021).

The Refugee Experience as Loss rather than Disorder

The integration of this perspective shift is especially important in the context of forced displacement. Im et al. (2017) point out that medicalised models of mental healthcare often give limited attention to lived experiences and cultural explanations of distress. Many practitioners, researchers, and policymakers questioned the usefulness of framing the pain, suffering, and challenges associated with forced migration as mental health difficulties (Jalonen and Corte 2018). The specific stressors connected with pre-flight, flight, and post-flight stages can often be more usefully conceptualised using Bronfenbrenner's socio-ecological framework (Bronfenbrenner 1979; Bronfenbrenner and Morris 2006).

Case Example: Trauma Triggers and Supportive Responses

Natalia recounted being triggered by bursting balloons at a party, which caused a flashback of hearing gunshots outside her home. Her teacher's trauma-informed training helped her with grounding techniques and went with her to a quiet space. This example shows how innocuous stimuli can activate trauma responses and how appropriate non-medical support can help regulate them.

Categorising post-trauma experiences of hypervigilance, flashbacks, and hopelessness as symptoms of post-traumatic stress disorder (PTSD) disregards the social context leading to these reactions. Pathologising what could be conceptualised as adaptive reactions to adversity and loss causes further distress and can increase stigma (Theisen-Womersley 2021). It may be more pertinent to conceptualise the refugee experience as a profound loss (of family, friends, home, identity, trust, and life as it was). The loss of home in particular creates a deep sense of disorientation and absence (Cohen and Yadlin 2019; Perry and Winfrey 2021) and sociocultural factors (Levine 2013).

While reconceptualising trauma responses as normal reactions to devastating events offers a theoretical shift, practitioners need practical approaches that can bypass cultural barriers and stigma. Given the linguistic and cultural challenges in traditional talk-based interventions, alternative modalities that do not rely on Western medical frameworks or extensive verbal processing become particularly valuable. Among these alternatives, expressive arts approaches stand out for their ability to transcend cultural and language divides while honouring diverse ways of expressing and processing distress.

Using Expressive Arts to Bridge Cultural Divides

While the previous sections have outlined barriers to traditional mental health approaches, expressive arts offer unique advantages for working with refugee adolescents across cultural boundaries. Artistic expression often transcends language barriers and cultural differences, providing accessible entry points for emotional processing without the stigma of 'mental health' services. The non-verbal nature of many expressive arts approaches allows for:

- communication of complex emotions without requiring specialised vocabulary;
- engagement that does not rely on direct discussion of 'problems' or 'symptoms'; and
- cultural expression that honours diverse traditions and understandings.

Later chapters will explore specific techniques, but practitioners should consider how expressive arts can be framed as cultural celebration, skills development, or community building rather than 'therapy' when introducing these approaches to refugee adolescents.

Conclusions: A Paradigm Shift in Supporting Refugee Adolescent Wellbeing

Supporting refugee adolescents requires a fundamental shift away from diagnosing and treating disorders towards understanding and responding to the complex interplay of cultural, social, and individual factors that shape their experiences. This shift begins with recognising and respecting diverse cultural understandings of distress, which may differ significantly from Western clinical conceptualisations. Equally important is the adoption of non-stigmatising language that emphasises wellbeing over illness, making services more accessible and culturally appropriate.

By framing responses to trauma as normal rather than pathological, practitioners acknowledge the adaptive nature of these reactions to extraordinary circumstances. This approach reduces stigma while honouring the resilience refugees demonstrate. Engaging with young people through accessible, culturally responsive approaches creates space for healing that respects their existing frameworks for understanding suffering and recovery.

Practitioners can create pathways to support that do not require young people to accept Western medicalised models of mental health in order to receive help. This shift not only reduces barriers to accessing support but also honours the resilience, cultural wisdom, and healing traditions that refugee adolescents bring with them. It is essential for all professionals supporting adolescent refugees to have an empathic, creative, and trauma-informed understanding of these young people's experiences during all stages of forced displacement, irrespective of whether they express interest in accessing therapy. Chapter 4 will explore therapeutic (without having to be a therapist), trauma-informed, and culturally sensitive ways in which all professionals can engage with adolescent refugees.

References

Arakelyan, S and Ager, A. 2020. 'Annual research review: A multilevel bioecological analysis of factors influencing the mental health and psychological wellbeing of refugee children'. *Journal of Child Psychology and Psychiatry, 61*(4): 1–26.

Backe, E, Bosire, E, Kim, A W and Mendenhall, E. 2021. '"Thinking too much" A systematic review of the idiom of distress in Sub-Saharan Africa'. *Cultural Medical Psychiatry, 45*: 655–682.

Bar, J, Pabst, A, Rohr, S, Luppa, M, Renner, A, Nagl, M, ... Riedel-Heller, S. 2021. 'Mental health self-stigma of Syrian refugees with post-traumatic stress symptoms: Investigating sociodemographic and psychopathological correlates'. *Frontiers in Psychiatry, 12*: 1–11.

Bartolomei, J, Baeriswyl-Cottin, R, Framorando, D, Kasina, F, Premand, N, Eytan, A and Khazaal, Y. 2016. 'What are the barriers to access to mental healthcare and the primary needs of asylum seekers?' A survey of mental health caregivers and primary care workers. *BMC Psychiatry, 16*: 1–8.

Bates, T. 2023. *Breaking the heart open: The shaping of a psychologist.* Gill Books.

Boyles, J. 2017. 'Assessing survivors of torture for psychological therapy'. In Boyles, J., Psychological therapies for survivors of torture: A human-rights approach with people seeking asylum. 395-912. PCCS Books

Bronfenbrenner, U. 1979. *The Ecology of Human Development.* Massachusetts: Harvard University Press.

Bronfenbrenner, U and Morris, P. 2006. 'The bioecological model of human development'. In R Lerner and W Damon, *Handbook of child psychology: Theoretical models of human development,* 793–828. John Wiley and Sons.

Cahnman, W. 1968. 'The stigma of obesity'. *The Sociological Quarterly*: 283–299. doi:10.1111/j.1533-8525.1968.tb01121.x

Cohen, A and Yadlin, Y. 2019. 'Time and memory in the therapeutic journey with unaccompanied asylum-seeking children'. *Journal of Child Psychotherapy, 44*(3): 348–367. doi:10.1080/0075417X.2018.1556315

Eurostat. 2023. 'Number of psychiatrists: How do countries compare?' Accessed 2 October 2023. https://ec.europa.eu/eurostat/web/products-eurostat-news/-/ddn-20200506-1

Filler, T, Georgiades, K, Khanlou, N and Wahoush, O. 2019. 'Understanding mental health and identity from Syrian refugee adolescents' perspectives'. *International Journal of Mental Health and Addiction*: 764–777.

Fusar-Poli, P, Salazar de Pablo, G, De Micheli, A, Nieman, D. H, Correll, C. U, Vedel Kessing, L, ... van Amelsvoort, T. 2020. *What is good mental health? A Scopng review,* 31. European Neuropsychopharmacology.

Goffman, E. 1963. *Stigma: Notes on the management of spoiled identity.* Touchstone.

Im, H, Ferguson, A and Hunter, M. 2017. 'Cultural translation of refugee trauma: Cultural idioms of distress among Somali Refugees in Displacement'. *Transcultural Psychiatry, 5–6*: 626–652.

Jalonen, A and Corte, P. 2018. *A practical guide to therapeutic work with asylum seekers and refugees.* Jessica Kingsley Publishers.

Keyes, C. 2005. 'Mental illness and/or mental health? Investigating axioms of the complete state model of health'. *Journal of Consulting and Clinical Psychology, 73*(3): 539–48.

Kreitzer, L, McMenemy, C and Yohani, S. 2022. 'Expanding our understanding of the environmental impacts on refugee resettlement through the application of Bronfenbrenner's bioecological theory'. *Local Development and Society, 6(2):*1–23.

Levine, P. (Director). 2013. *Trauma and the unspoken voice of the body* [Motion Picture].

Majumder, P. 2019. 'Exploring stigma and its effect on access to mental health services in unaccompanied refugee childre'. *British Journal of Psychiatry Bulletin*, 43:275–281.

Majumder, P, O'Reilly, M, Karim, K and Vostanis, P. 2015. '"This doctor, I not trust him, I'm not safe": The perceptions of mental health and services by unaccompanied refugee adolescents'. *International Journal of Social Psychiatry, 61*(2): 129–136.

Mills, C and Davar, B. 2016. 'A local critique of global mental health'. *Disability in the Global South*: 437–451.

Perry, B and Winfrey, O. 2021. *What happened to you?* Flatiron Books.

Rabiau, M. 2019. 'Culture, migration and identity formation in adolescent refugees: A family perspective'. In M Denov and M Shevell, *Social work practice with war-affected children: The importance of family, art, culture and context*, 83–100. Routledge.

Riley, A, Akther, Y, Noor, M, Ali, R and Weldon-Mitchell, C. 2020. 'Systematic human rights violations, traumatic events, daily stressors and mental health of Rohingya Refugees in Blangadesh'. *Conflict and Health, 14*(60): 1–14.

Shannon, P, Wieling, E, Simmelink-McCleary, J and Becher, E. 2015. 'Beyond stigma: Barriers to discussing mental health in refugee populations'. *Journal of Loss and Trauma, 20*: 281–296.

Siddiq, H, Elhaija, A and Wells, K. 2023. 'An integrative review of community-based mental health interventions among resettled refugees from Muslim-majority countries'. *Community Mental Health Journal, 59*: 160–174.

Theisen-Womersley, G. 2021. *Trauma and resilience among displaced populations: A sociocultural exploration.* Springer.

Vaillant, G. 2012. 'Positive mental health: Is there a cross-cultural definition?' *World Psychiatry, 11*(2): 93–99.

World Health Organization. 2023. *Urgent need to scale up mental health services in Somalia.* World Health Organization. https://www.emro.who.int/somalia/news/urgent -need-to-scale-up-mental-health-services-in-somalia.html#:~:text=According%20to %20estimates%2C%20one%20in,nurses%20dealing%20with%20mental%20health.

Chapter 4

A Trauma-Informed, Therapeutic Approach for All Professionals Working with Refugee Adolescents

Introduction

Therapeutic skills are extremely valuable for all service providers who engage with refugee adolescents and provide the foundation of trauma-informed practice. While 'therapy' is not being delivered, the use of therapeutic skills fosters the development of supportive relationships. This chapter will first briefly outline those fundamental and intersecting therapeutic skills which the author has found to be essential for the development of caring, compassionate, and responsive relationships with adolescent refugees. It will then explore the key principles of trauma-informed practice with adolescent refugees, starting with ways of establishing physical safety before moving on to explore pathways to building trust within an accepting relationship. This will be followed by suggestions of different ways of restoring control and building in choice, including trauma-informed instruction and engagement in accessible learning and acts of resistance in language brokering. Finally, it will look at ways of supporting coping and the importance of adopting a culturally sensitive approach. These foundational skills create the necessary framework for effective trauma-informed work with refugee adolescents.

Key Therapeutic Skills for Developing Supportive Relationships with Adolescent Refugees

Many of the therapeutic skills outlined in this section and throughout the book are informed by the work of Carl Rogers (1902–1987), the American psychologist who was one of the founders of the humanistic psychology movement in the 1950s and 1960s (Rogers 1951/2012). Rogers developed a person-centred therapeutic approach which emphasises the importance of the therapeutic relationship. Although there are many factors involved in developing effective relationships, the following have been found by the author to be particularly beneficial in developing healing connections in all helping relationships with adolescent refugees.

DOI: 10.4324/9781003430032-5

Patience

The importance of being patient in our interactions with refugee adolescents cannot be overstated. Yohani (2010:870) identified this as a key therapeutic skill in her study of refugee children and adolescents' resettlement experiences. A participant described taking 'tiny baby steps' to help refugee youth catch up academically. In my practice, I recognise the importance of patience in nurturing hope at the refugee adolescent's pace. Lester (2023) suggests true patience involves understanding the causes of behaviours instead of trying to change them. Perry and Winfrey's (2021) shift from 'what's wrong with you' to 'what happened to you' reshapes thoughts, feelings, and actions. Lester (2023) suggests asking 'what's right with you' to help individuals lacking self-worth identify positives, no matter how insignificant, to begin their repair process. When Natalia first attended therapy, she struggled to identify anything right with her. After exploration, we identified that she felt 'less worse' watching a comedy show from her home country, which we then built on. Introducing the idea of 'less worse' was crucial when she couldn't find anything to improve her mood.

Kindness

Research shows that conceptualisations of kindness take on different meanings depending on the context (Cotney and Banerjee 2019). As part of the research process through which they developed a framework and a self-report measure for considering kindness, Canter et al. (2017) conceptualised a core essence which they suggested underpins all states of kindness. They described this core essence as 'a tendency towards active gestures motivated by genuine warm feelings for others' (Canter et al. 2017:18). They stressed that while empathy was an essential aspect of this essence, it also required translation into human actions. This conceptualisation aligns closely with the author's experiences of engaging adolescent refugees with kindness and with the latter's perceptions of their experiences of acts of kindness in different contexts, which were then explored in therapy sessions.

Kindness towards refugee adolescents can include offering a drink, food, a hot water bottle, or a blanket on a cold day, simple actions in the author's everyday practice. Wahlstrom-Smith (2020) describes undocumented refugee children in Sweden, hiding from authorities to avoid deportation, as 'surviving through the kindness of strangers' in music classes, school, church, and voluntary organisations. Acts of kindness benefit both giver and recipient by enhancing mood, reducing stress, strengthening relationships, and cultivating empathy and trust (Hui et al. 2020). Research shows that those who act kindly often underestimate their positive impact, emphasising the need to raise awareness of these actions' benefits (Kumar and Epley 2022).

Paying Attention to Our Biases and Cultivating Acceptance

As already illustrated in Chapter 2, to feel safe and thrive in this world, children need their parents' unconditional love and acceptance (Sunderland 2016). Roger's person-centred approach extends the fundamental need for acceptance beyond the child-parent relationship to all helping relationships, an approach which requires the helping professional to unconditionally accept the person being supported, irrespective of their background and without judgement. However, it is important to point out that all human beings have the natural capacity for judgement and that it is an integral aspect of cognitive processes which allows individuals to evaluate situations, make decisions, and navigate life's complexities (Winslade 2013).

Recognising that judging others is an instinctive human response, Thompson and Pascal (2012) point out that it is more realistic and helpful to start noticing, in a purposeful way, situations in which we make assumptions or form opinions about others, by paying attention to our own thoughts, biases, preconceptions, and judgements. Expanding our reflective practice in this way will help us to challenge and alter our judgements, thereby cultivating our self-awareness (Brown 2021). Byrne and Tanasini (2015) provide an insightful discussion for helping professionals of the different ways in which they can raise their awareness of implicit bias by applying a continuous process of practice, feedback, and reflection, which then leads to the possibility for acceptance.

Empathy

Although the concept of empathy has been variously defined by scholars and practitioners, there is no single agreed definition (Nembhard et al. 2022; Tan et al. 2021). Those who work within the humanistic tradition often favour Carl Rogers' definition of empathy as 'the ability to understand the client's internal frame of reference and to perceive the world as they see it' (Rogers 1949:84). However, although many helping professionals interpret this as the ability to put themselves in somebody else's shoes or to 'feel their pain,' Brené Brown (2021:122), in her bestselling *Atlas of the Heart*, emphasises that we can only respond empathically if we are willing to 'be present to' a person's pain.

Proposing a framework that promotes the development of meaningful connections, Brown writes:

> We need to dispel the myth that empathy is 'walking in someone else's shoes.' Rather than walking in your shoes I need to listen to the story you tell about what it's like in your shoes and believe you even when it doesn't match my experiences.

Therefore, when Chima tells us that he is feeling lonely because he is away from his family, rather than feeling lonely for him, we should reach back into our own experiences of loneliness, so that we can understand and connect with his pain.

Recent developments in neuroscience indicate that the capacity for empathy evolves through the combination of genetic predisposition and social learning (Ratka 2018). Roth-Hanania et al. (2011) found that modest levels of affective empathy (the ability to *share and feel* the emotional experiences) and cognitive empathy (the ability to 'understand' another person's perspective or emotions), for a person in distress, were evident during the first year of life, thereby suggesting innate biological factors. However, contextual influences and social learning have also been identified as key elements. Stern and Cassidy (2018) show that individuals learn more complex empathic responses through the modelling and reinforcement of empathetic behaviours by significant figures within their social ecologies. This demonstrates the potential for interventions which develop and enhance empathy. Weisz and Zaki (2017) document the effectiveness of the experiential interventions of role-play, perspective-taking, and information sharing, which have been shown to increase internal feelings of empathy. Given the unique challenges and experiences brought by refugee adolescents to the therapeutic setting, empathy can be considered fundamental to the provision of effective, culturally sensitive support.

Consistency

Consistency can be defined as the stability and predictability of actions, attitudes, and behaviours over time (O'Neill 2001). Consistent empathy, openness, and a non-judgemental attitude foster a reliable therapeutic environment for refugee adolescents, enhancing trust and safety (Geroski 2017; Jalonen and Corte 2018). In her trauma awareness training, developed for helping professionals working with people in humanitarian crisis contexts, Nicola Lester emphasises the importance of the consistent provision of support and kindness, as well as being caring and empathic, irrespective of the presentation, behaviour, or background of the person (Lester 2023). Chima recounted how his social worker treated him the same after a fight following a racially motivated attack. Despite looking bloodied and agitated, she treated him with her usual respect, and a year later he noted the calming effect of this predictable response.

Honesty, Openness, and Transparency

There is a mutual need for honesty, openness, and transparency when working with adolescent refugees, who need clear, truthful, consistent explanations appropriate to this developmental stage (Lester 2023). A genuine, honest, and open relationship is one in which the supporting professional validates the beliefs and attitudes of the adolescent refugee, even if these beliefs do not correspond with their own, showing them that they are valued as a person. It is also important for the supporting professional to be honest with refugee adolescents about any gaps in their own knowledge and for them to be open and transparent about their role and its limits, including the limits of confidentiality. Furthermore, Geldard et al. (2019) point out that all professionals should ensure transparency around who controls the direction of the conversation, while empowering the young person to control their direction as appropriate. Managing expectations and establishing boundaries from the outset is critical.

Willingness to Bear Witness to Another's Distress

Bearing witness to the distress of refugee adolescents requires the management of feelings of impotency and anguish when faced with unimaginable and overwhelming accounts of persecution, cruelty, and loss. To accompany the young person on this difficult journey, the service provider needs to develop a good understanding of the impact of all the factors associated with the double burden of moving to a new country and moving from childhood to adulthood (Volkan 2018). The different factors that contribute to this double burden for Chima and Natalia before, during, and after forced migration are outlined in Chapter 1 where the challenges of forced displacement are conceptualised in relation to Bronfenbrenner's bioecological model and in Chapter 2 which explores the impact of these experiences on the adolescent brain. Lester (2023) also highlights the significant value of paying attention to the strength and resilience of the young person, or 'what is right with them.' Most importantly, we should not underestimate the power of our presence and our willingness to listen if the young person wants to tell their story (Lester 2023). When integrated into a comprehensive approach, these skills become powerful tools within a structured trauma-informed framework specifically tailored to the unique needs of adolescent refugees.

Trauma-Informed Practice with Adolescent Refugees

Trauma-informed practice with adolescent refugees integrates the understanding of trauma's impact on them into care and support interactions (Miller et al. 2019). It involves understanding trauma's impact on wellbeing and responding sensitively to avoid re-traumatisation. Practitioners using a trauma-informed approach with refugee adolescents acknowledge how displacement, violence, and loss affect their psychological and emotional development. Guidance will be provided for integrating core principles of trauma-informed practice into support for refugee adolescents by all service providers.

1. Establishing physical and emotional safety
2. Establishing trust within an accepting relationship
3. Building in choice and restoring control
4. Supporting coping
5. Ensuring a culturally sensitive approach

Of these five core principles, establishing safety forms the essential foundation. Without addressing basic safety needs first, all other trauma-informed efforts have limited effectiveness.

Establishing Physical and Emotional Safety

From the first meeting, the adolescent refugee must feel welcome and safe. A confidential and secure physical environment is especially important for these young people, given that many of them will have experienced physical and emotional abuse and put their trust in different people before and during displacement, only to have had that trust broken, often with serious consequences in relation to their safety and migratory route possibilities (Ni Raghallaigh 2013). Chima recounted experiences of having money taken by disappearing people smugglers. Creating a safe environment is crucial for therapy, yet often neglected in settings with refugee adolescents. Chima and Natalia shared positive experiences of feeling safe in therapy, noting that practical measures for comfort could apply in various settings.

Natalia felt a strong sense of relief upon entering the therapy room, knowing she could talk confidentially to the therapist. He contrasted this experience with his first meeting with his social worker after claiming asylum in Ireland as an unaccompanied minor, recalling how this meeting had been conducted in a very busy open-plan office, which he had found especially difficult as he did not feel physically safe in Ireland, fearing that the people smugglers to whom he still owed money could track him down. When asked to tell his story in this communal space, even in hushed tones with verbal reassurances of confidentiality, he did not feel safe and therefore said very little. This lack of safety had understandably made him feel very anxious and stressed. Ravi Kohli describes the ways in which restricting talk and being silent are used as powerful protective tools by child and adolescent refugees when they feel that their security is being threatened (Kohli 2009). While safety creates necessary conditions for engagement, trust built through consistent, warm interactions enables refugee adolescents to move beyond protective silence towards authentic engagement.

Establishing Trust within an Accepting Relationship

A warm, friendly connection between the service provider and the refugee adolescent during their first meeting is absolutely critical to the development of a trusting, collaborative, and authentic relationship irrespective of its expected duration. It is also important to note here that the pronoun 'we' should be used by all service providers as the language of collaboration when engaging with these young people. This will help them to feel that they are not alone and that they are being accompanied by a supportive adult regardless of their reasons for engaging with the specific service. In situations where the adolescent is accompanied by a parent, other carer, or social worker (e.g. to therapy, a medical appointment, or another specialist service), it is important that the service provider talks to the adolescent first, introducing themselves and checking how the adolescent would like to be addressed.

If the refugee adolescent's name is unfamiliar to the service provider, it is important for them to check the pronunciation before the first meeting, either with someone from the community or with their carer, and it is always a good idea to check again with the young person. Chima was relieved when meeting his social worker for the first time, she asked him if she was pronouncing his name correctly. His name had an important meaning in his own language which had been lost when other service providers had either mis-pronounced it or asked for the 'English equivalent,' after which Chima had reported feeling a strong rejection of his identity. He described having multiple names which did not always fit with European understandings of naming conventions, but in his home culture were believed to protect him from his identity being mis-used, from discovery by the authorities and even from witchcraft.

Close attention should also be paid to refugee adolescent perceptions of the confidentiality of interpreters (see Chapter 14 for a full exploration of the challenges and opportunities associated with working with interpreters). Adolescent refugees may be anxious about being identified by the interpreter or worried about the interpreter sharing information with members of their community. It is therefore good practice, before engaging in the first session, to remind the interpreter of the importance of confidentiality and to explain its significance in relation to this specific group. It is also important to explain the concept of confidentiality to the refugee adolescent as well as discuss with them whether they would like to be matched with the interpreter for gender and ethnicity or whether there are other considerations to be made around the choice of interpreter, if indeed it is possible to make such requests.

This should also help to avoid distressing situations such as that experienced by Chima when meeting his interpreter for the first time; he realised very quickly that the interpreter was from an opposing tribe in his own country. This triggered some traumatic memories, which meant that he was unable to continue with the session. Although Natalia also experienced discomfort when she was allocated a male interpreter with whom she did not feel comfortable sharing some intimate personal issues, she also reported a very positive experience with another interpreter whom she found to be very empathic and non-intrusive. Furthermore, she communicated to the therapist that through this process she had learned how to clearly express her needs which started the longer journey towards empowerment and self-advocacy. In addition to setting aside time for a conversation with the interpreter in advance of the first session, it is important for the service provider to allocate individual debriefing time after the session for the interpreter and the adolescent refugee (Tribe and Thompson 2017). As trust develops, attention must shift to restoring the sense of control and agency that displacement and trauma often diminish through meaningful choices and opportunities for self-determination.

Building in Choice and Restoring Control

Trauma-Informed Instruction and Engagement in Accessible Learning

The profound impact of traumatic experiences on adolescent refugees' cognitive, emotional, and social functioning, and therefore their ability to learn and retain information, as discussed in Chapter 2, manifests in numerous ways (Sellars 2020). Moreover, the time constraints under which service providers are typically operating can lead to the tendency to repeat the same instructions in the same way to many different people without really giving much thought to how it comes across or whether it is understood.

The use of trauma-informed instruction partnered with the Universal Design for Learning (UDL) framework provides an effective way of facilitating engagement in accessible learning for adolescent refugees who have experienced trauma. The UDL framework emerged from architectural universal design principles that sought to create accessible environments for all users, regardless of ability. Developed in the 1990s by CAST (Centre for Applied Special Technology), UDL was initially conceived as an educational approach to support learners with disabilities by designing flexible learning environments that accommodate individual learning differences (CAST 2025). Since then, it has evolved into a widely adopted framework across educational contexts that recognises the natural variability in how all people learn. For refugee adolescents whose learning may be affected by trauma, language barriers, and cultural differences, UDL offers particularly valuable strategies that can be adapted beyond classroom settings to all services they encounter.

The overall goal of UDL is to remove barriers to learning and make education more accessible for all learners, promoting intentional design for learner variability while offering the choice of different learning pathways. By embracing UDL principles, educators aim to create a more inclusive and effective learning experience that meets the diverse needs of learners through the following three principles:

> **Multiple means of engagement**: Fostering an inclusive and supportive learning environment by offering varied ways for learners to engage with the information.
> **Multiple means of representation**: Presenting information in multiple ways to cater for diverse learning styles and preferences (e.g. using multimedia, visual aids, audio resources, and other varied forms of content delivery).
> **Multiple means of action and expression**: Providing learners with a variety of ways to demonstrate their understanding and skills.

For refugee adolescents, in addition to instruction in the educational context, these principles can be usefully applied to information provision from all of the services with which they engage, not just educational settings. Although the third principle is probably more applicable in the school or college setting, given the absence of a formal requirement for refugee adolescents to demonstrate their understanding of information in other settings, it is always useful for these young people to be able to show their understanding in ways that feel most comfortable for them. This information may range from different aspects of their rights and the asylum-seeking process to information on health and wellbeing, employment, and educational opportunities (Banes et al. 2019).

When an adolescent refugee starts a new service, substantial information needs to be communicated and absorbed. Presenting information in various formats in a supportive environment allows young people to access content through different cognitive pathways. This enhances individual learning, promotes choice, and improves understanding and retention. This flexible provision of information accommodates diverse sensory needs, reducing trauma re-triggering, and maintaining adolescent refugees' interest and motivation.

Chima found his first meeting with the social worker overwhelming due to the detailed information provided. He valued her methods to ensure he understood and retained the information. After explaining his rights and the asylum process using a bilingual leaflet and interpreter, she provided links to informative subtitled videos and advised him to watch them with his keyworker to interpret the information and ask questions. She texted him the main points of their conversation with visual cues and said she would check back in a few days for questions.

Chima felt that reviewing the material with his social worker and keyworker fostered a collaborative, equal, and supportive relationship. He also found it useful that his social worker had checked in with him at the start to talk about his preferred way of receiving information. He told her that although he preferred images and short videos because of his difficulties with English, he also liked receiving written bullet points as he copied them into his phone's notes section for ease of access and cross-checked them with Google Translate.[1]

Chima's experiences illustrate the importance of reinforcing linguistic and cultural information that refugee adolescents may find difficult to understand at first, using different channels of communication (including written, auditory, and visual pathways). This approach is particularly important for unaccompanied refugee adolescents who, in addition to contending with traumatic experiences and arriving in a new country without their families, must deal with complicated asylum claims and family reunification processes (Dashab and Mokhtarzade 2021). Chima also pointed out that the different ways in which his social worker had presented the information over a longer period of time had helped him to develop a deeper understanding of it.

Natalia also experienced the feeling of overwhelm associated with being provided with a large volume of information during the registration process upon her arrival in Ireland, estimating that she had retained less than 50% of the content even with the help of an interpreter. Although, unlike Chima, Natalia was accompanied by her mother, she described how exhausting it was trying to interpret the information for them both due to her more advanced knowledge of English. This activity has been described as 'language brokering' (Rumbaut and Portes 2001) and refers to the practice of individuals, usually children and adolescents, serving as informal interpreters or translators for their families and communities.

Language Brokering: Acts of Resistance, Restoration of Control, and Feelings of Validation

Language brokering refers to the practice where individuals, usually children and adolescents, serve as informal interpreters or translators for their families and communities. (Rumbaut and Portes 2001). This practice represents a complex intersection of responsibility, identity, and power for refugee adolescents, directly connecting to our discussion of control and agency.

Language brokering can empower and burden many refugee adolescents. They become essential cultural and linguistic mediators, gaining unique status and responsibility in family dynamics. This role reversal can restore control and competence where they may feel powerless. It pressures young people managing their own trauma and adaptation challenges.

In their study of adolescent language brokering in the healthcare context, Iqbal and Crafter (2023) found that some brokers experienced this role negatively. To regain control within these unequal language brokering relationships, some participants intentionally disrupted the process by using delay tactics or selectively modifying the message, demonstrating acts of resistance that helped maintain their sense of agency. Conversely, Melander and Schmulyar Green (2023) reported that some young people experienced validation and empowerment through language brokering, as this role was perceived as valuable within their family, community, and host society.

This dual nature of language brokering – as both a potential burden and opportunity for agency – highlights the importance of recognising refugee adolescents' complex roles within their families and providing appropriate support that acknowledges their contributions while not overwhelming them with adult responsibilities.

In addition, research suggests that as transnational family communication increasingly relies on an understanding of the 'language' of smartphones, social media, and video-calling apps, adolescents also feel obligated to engage in the digital equivalent of this task by helping their parents use this communication technology to sustain post-migratory transnational relationships (Worrell 2021).

Fostering a Sense of Belonging

The experiences of Natalia and Chima illustrate the importance of ensuring that information has been fully understood by presenting it through different modalities and revisiting it several times in a collaborative way. It is especially important for this group that we treat each young person as an individual with different ways of understanding and interpreting the information that we communicate to them, thereby fostering a sense that they matter, that they are included, and that they can experience a sense of belonging in the host country.

Having explored how to restore agency through informed choice and opportunities for self-determination, we now turn to strategies for supporting refugee adolescents' natural coping abilities. Building on the foundation of safety, trust, and empowerment enables more effective development of resilience in coping resources.

Supporting Coping

Although research into coping dates back to the beginnings of the psychoanalytic movement at the turn of the 18th century (Frydenberg 2014), coping only started to be viewed as a process in the 1980s, through the work of theorists such as Billings and Moos (1981) and Lazarus and Folkman (1984), for whom this process was conceptualised as the range of active responses developed by an individual to manage stressful experiences. In the decades which followed, there has been an increased focus on individual differences in coping styles and understanding coping in different contexts such as health, work, and relationships, all underpinned by this original conceptualisation. Greater attention has also been paid to the recognition and acknowledgement of positive coping strategies as advocated by Folkman and Moskowitz (2003) and concretised by Lahad et al. (2013).

Identifying Existing Coping Strategies

Lester (2023) asserts that the first thing which needs to be considered when supporting the coping of those who have experienced trauma is to recognise how they are already coping rather than how they are not coping. Lester argues that we need to recognise 'wise' adaptations and uncover that which is right with someone. She demonstrates the power of reframing ways of coping from negative to positive, a practice frequently utilised by the author in her clinical work. For example, Chima was worried that he was relying too much on his friends when he wasn't feeling good in himself: 'When I feel down, I contact my friends because I'm too scared to be alone and this makes me feel ashamed and weak.' We worked together to reframe this as 'when I'm feeling down, I contact my friends because I enjoy their company and this makes me feel valued, accepted and included.' Lester argues that when an individual lacks self-worth, a shift to recognise what is right with them can start the process of healing.

This is especially challenging when coping strategies cause physical harm and carry a level of risk; for example, when adolescent refugees cope with strong emotions by hurting themselves. However, in such cases, it is important to acknowledge that what appears to us to be harmful is helping to keep them alive, offering them a form of release from the intensity of their distress.

The BASIC Ph Model

The BASIC Ph integrative model of coping and resiliency, created by Lahad et al. (2013), and used by the authors to identify and harness the natural coping strategies of refugee adolescents, is underpinned by the belief that all humans have unique healthy and instinctual internal coping resources which can be mobilised in stressful situations. Lahad et al. identified the following six natural styles or 'channels' of coping, the categorisation of which gives the model its name and exemplifies human attempts to survive and thrive:

1. **Belief**

The adolescent refugees we work with often turn to their core belief system as a means of coping. For example, Chima reaches out to his faith community and consults religious texts to help him to cope. Beliefs can also include political positions and moral values or strong feelings of purpose. Ayalon (2013) includes traditional belief systems and rituals of mourning and leave-taking in this coping channel and the authors find this very helpful for refugee adolescents who have experienced loss. Chapter 12 presents Ovie's story which considers the different ways in which expressive arts can be integrated into the therapeutic process of grieving, loss and the ritual of mourning.

2. **Affect**

Adolescent refugees who utlise their affect as a coping strategy typically seek opportunities to share anxieties, fears, anger, sorrow and loss and to have these emotions validated by the adults in their lives. Carers and support workers can nurture and cultivate this by modelling open and genuine expressions of feeling. If adolescent refugees see their carers expressing affect then they will be more likely to feel comfortable doing the same.

3. **Social**

Adolescent refugees who cope with adversity through social channels typically seek support and control through their friendships. This is a much used channel for the adolescent refugees we work with (cf. Hoare 2022) and Chima and Natalia both make extensive use of this way of coping through their many family and friendship networks.

4. **Imagination**

Adolescent refugees frequently turn to their imagination and creativity as a means of coping with trauma through daydreaming or engaging in pleasant thoughts. Supportive adults can help them to divert their attention using guided visualisation or imagery which at its simplest is using the imagination to put the body into a calmer state. The authors use this with adolescent refugees to create the sense of a 'safe space' and practise it with them to support them in its use. See Chapter 9 for an explanation and description of the 'create a safe space' activity with Nabeel.

5. Cognition

Cognitive strategies of coping include information gathering, problem solving, self-navigation, internal positive self-talk, making lists of activities and preferences as well as the cognitive reframing technique already mentioned. Psychoeducation, which offers evidence-based, age-appropriate information to the young person to explain the possible underlying causes of any difficulties, can also offer an effective source of coping within this channel (Im et al. 2018).

6. Physical

Many adolescent refugees also frequently use the physical channel through playing sport and going to the gym. Others might cope with stress through relaxation (see Chapter 8 for relaxation techniques engaged in with Daahir). This was an important coping channel for Natalia who liked to dance and move her body to alleviate stress, while Chima enjoyed playing football.

Lahad et al. (2013) suggest that people respond in more than one of these modes and that everyone is capable of coping in all six modes but that over time and depending on life experiences and innate tendencies, each person develops his or her own preferred mode. This model has been used for the identification and development of coping skills and the building of resilience during and in the wake of natural and man-made disasters in many different contexts, including the Second Lebanon War (Shacham et al. 2013), the Yugoslav War (Krkeljic et al. 2013), and post-hurricane Katrina (Rogel 2013). As these contexts are all characterised by forced displacement, using it as a flexible framework has been helpful in identifying and developing the internal coping and resilience resources of the adolescent refugees with whom we work.

Supporting Adaptive Coping Development

Once you have identified a refugee adolescent's natural coping channels using the BASIC Ph model, the next step is to help them expand and strengthen these adaptive strategies. This process involves three key approaches:

1. Affirm and validate their existing coping strategies. Acknowledge the creativity and resilience demonstrated in their current approaches, rather than immediately trying to replace them with 'better' strategies. For example,

when Natalia shared that dancing helped her release tension, her support team encouraged this activity by helping her find dance classes.

2. Help broaden their coping repertoire by gently introducing complementary channels. For example, if an adolescent refugee primarily uses social coping, you might introduce cognitive techniques that can be employed when friends are not available. This expansion provides more options when their primary coping strategy is not accessible or appropriate. With Chima, whose primary coping channel was social connection, his foster carer gradually introduced physical activities (running and football) that he could use when feeling overwhelmed but unable to reach friends.

3. Support the adolescent refugee in recognising when certain coping strategies are most effective. Different situations may call for different approaches. A strategy that works well for everyday stress might be insufficient during acute distress or triggering situations. Developing awareness of emotional states and which coping techniques match different intensity levels builds this metacognitive skill. This awareness enhances autonomy and strengthens the ability to self-regulate across various contexts.

By working collaboratively to build upon natural coping tendencies rather than imposing unfamiliar strategies, professionals can honour the young person's agency while expanding their capacity for resilience. This approach recognises that effective coping is highly individualised and influenced by cultural background, personal history, and developmental stage. Effective application of coping frameworks requires cultural humility, and understanding how culture shapes expressions of distress, preferred coping mechanisms, and healing practices is essential for meaningful support.

A Culturally Sensitive Approach

Although the word 'culture' is neither a static nor tangible concept with an agreed-upon definition, of the many discussions of culture across the social sciences literature, I have found that the following definition from the context of treating psychological trauma across cultures fits best with my work:

> The concept of culture is about the process of being and becoming a social creature, about the rules of a society and about the ways in which these are enacted, experienced, and transmitted. ... Culture regulates the impact and expression of emotions and shapes individual expressions and perceptions of how to suffer under stress and these modes are taught sometimes openly, sometimes indirectly.
>
> Droždek and Wilson (2007:6)

Rather than requiring knowledge of the different cultural backgrounds of all the refugee adolescents with whom we work, adopting a culturally sensitive approach encourages us to remain curious, pay attention to our judgements, and seek to understand how an individual is experiencing their world (Lester 2023). Crucially, Spencer (2014) highlights the danger associated with adopting a narrow definition of culture which reduces the concept to ethnic characteristics while ignoring critical interactions between history and power.

Lester (2023) highlights the importance of recognising power differentials and manifestations of inequality between practitioner and refugee. Every encounter can lead to different assumptions, judgements, and considerable distress. Exploring these ideas in a trauma-informed way can enhance engagement and relationships, increasing awareness and protecting a person's story. Chima recalls a newly qualified youth worker's gentle curiosity about Islamic death rituals, which allowed him to share his norms after his cousin's death, helping him feel validated in his religion rather than 'othered' (Juergensmeyer et al. 2023).

Conclusions

Drawing on the experiences of Chima and Natalia, this chapter has explored the different ways in which *all professionals* can work in a trauma-informed and therapeutic way with adolescent refugees. The integration of key therapeutic skills of patience, kindness, awareness of bias, empathy, consistency, honesty, and the willingness to bear witness creates the relational foundation necessary for effective support. These skills, when combined with the principles of trauma-informed practice, create environments where refugee adolescents can feel safe, heard, understood, supported, validated, and empowered.

The chapter highlights several crucial considerations for practice. First, establishing physical and emotional safety forms the cornerstone of all interventions, recognising that many refugee adolescents have experienced profound betrayals of trust. Second, information must be provided in accessible, culturally appropriate ways that accommodate trauma-related cognitive challenges. Third, supporting coping involves identifying and building upon existing strengths rather than focusing solely on deficits. Finally, cultural sensitivity requires ongoing curiosity, humility, and awareness of power differentials.

This trauma-informed approach complements the neurobiological insights from Chapter 2 and builds on Chapter 3's focus on reframing mental health as wellbeing, recognising trauma's impact on adolescent development while avoiding pathologising language. Professionals can foster healing and growth. The following chapters will explore creative approaches that apply these principles in various contexts, showing how expressive arts can address challenges faced by refugee adolescents, such as sleep disturbances, self-harm, and grief. The skills and principles in this chapter are essential for practice.

Note

1   Google Translate is a free online language translation service provided by Google, which allows users to translate text, speech, or even images from one language to another.

References

Ayalon, O. 2013. Caring – 'Children at risk intervention groups BASIC Ph guide for coping and healing'. In M Lahad, M Shacham and O Ayalon, *The 'BASIC PH' model of coping and resiliency*, 71–103. Jessica Kingsley Publishers.

Banes, D, Allaf, C and Salem, M. 2019. 'Refugees, education and disability: Addressing the educational needs of arabic-speaking refugees with learning challenges'. In E Sengupta, and P Blessinger, *Language, teaching and pedagogy for refugee education innovations in higher education teaching and learning*, 109–124. Emerald Publishing Limited.

Billings, A.G, and Moos, R.H. 1981. 'The role of coping resources and social resources in attenuating the stress of live events.' *Journal of Behavioural Medicine*, *4*, 139–157. doi: 10.1007/BF00844267.

Brown, B. 2021. *Atlas of the heart: Mapping meaningful connection and the language of human experience*. Vermilion.

Byrne, A and Tanesini, A. 2015. Instilling new habits: addressing implicit bias in healthcare professionals. *Advances in Health Sciences Education*, *20*(5): 1255–1262. DOI: 10.1007/210459-015-9600-6.

Canter, D, Youngs, D and Yaneva, M. 2017. 'Towards a measure of kindness: An exploration of a neglected interpersonal trait'. *Personality and Individual Differences*, *106*, 15–20.

CAST 2025. UDL Guidelines. Accessed 29/7/25.https://udlguidelines.cast.org/.

Cotney, J and Banerjee, R. 2019. 'Adolescents' conceptualisations of kindness and its links with wellbeing: A focus group study'. *Journal of Social and Personal Relationships*: 599–617. doi:10.1177/0265407517738584

Dashab, M and Mokhtarzade, S. 2021. 'The necessity to protect unaccompanied refugee children focusing on the right to family reunification'. *Public Law Studies Quarterly*, *513*. doi:10.22059/jplsq.2019.284163.2059

Drożđek, B and Wilson, J. 2007. *Voices of trauma: Treating psychological trauma across cultures*. Springer.

Folkman, S and Moskowitz, J. 2003. 'Replacing stressful challenges with positive coping strategies: A resilience programme for clinical placement'. *Psychological Inquiry*, *14*(2): 121–125.

Frydenberg, E. 2014. 'Coping research: Historical background, links with emotion, and new research directions on adaptive processes'. *Australian Journal of Psychology*, *66*: 82–92.

Geldard, K, Geldard, D and Yin Foo, R. 2019. *Counselling adolescents: The proactive approach.* Sage Publications Ltd.

Geroski, A. 2017. *Skills for helping professionals.* Sage Publications.

Hoare, R. 2022. 'Friends as family: Using composite psychotherapy case material to explore the importance of friendships for unaccompanied adolescent refugees coping with the challenges of resettlement in Ireland'. *Journal of Refugee Studies, 35*(3): 1160–1185.

Hui, B, Ng, J, E, Cunningham-Amos, L and Kogan, A. 2020. 'Rewards of kindness? A meta-analysis of the link between prosociality and wellbeing'. *Psychological Bulletin, 146*(12): 1084–1116.

Im, H, Jettner, J. A, Warsame, A, Isse, M, Khoury, D and Ross, A. 2018. 'Trauma-informed psychoeducation for Somali refugee youth in urban Kenya: Effects on PTSD and psychosocial outcomes'. *Journal of Child and Adolescent Trauma, 11*: 431–441. doi:10.1007/s40653-017-0200-x

Iqbal, H and Crafter, S. 2023. 'Child language brokering in healthcare: Exploring the intersection of power and age in mediation practices'. *Journal of Child and Family Studies*: 586–597. doi:10.1007/s10826-022-02376-0

Jalonen, A and Corte, P. 2018. *A practical guide to therapeutic work with asylum seekers and refugees*. Jessica Kingsley Publishers.

Juergensmeyer, M, Moore, K and Sachsenmaier, D. 2023. 'Thank God we're not like them'. In M Juergensmeyer, K Moore and D Sachsenmaier, *Religious othering global dimensions*, 111–473. Routledge.

Kohli, R. 2009. 'Understanding silences and secrets when working with unaccompanied asylum-seeking children'. In Thomas, N *Children, Politics and Communication*, 107-123, Cambridge University Press, doi: 10.51952/9781847421852.ch006.

Krkeljic, L, Pavlicic, P and Pavlicic, N. 2013. 'During and after the Yugoslav War: Stress and trauma among adolescent schoolchildren'. In *The 'Basic PH' model of coping and resiliency: Theory, research and cross-cultural application*, 264–277. Jessica kingsley Publishers.

Kumar, A and Epley, N. 2022. 'A little good goes an unexpectedly long way: Underestimating the positive impact of kindness on recipients'. *Journal of Experimental Psychology*: 1–17. doi:10.1037/xge0001271

Lahad, M, Shacham, M and Ayalon, O. 2013. *The 'Basic PH' model of coping and resiliency*. Jessica Kingsley.

Lazarus, R and Folkman, S. 1984. *Stress, appraisal and coping*. Springer.

Lester, N. 2023. *The gift of reconnection: Trauma-informed practice training*. Psychological Trauma Consultancy.

Melander, C and Shmulyar Green, O. 2023. 'Language brokering as acts of care: experiences of young migrants born in Poland and Romania living in Sweden'. *Nordic Social Work Research*: 1–12. doi:10.1080/2156857X.2023.2199417

Miller, K, Brown, C, Shramko, M and Svetaz, M. 2019. 'Applying trauma-informed practices to the care of refugee and immigrant youth: 10 clinical pearls'. *Children*, 694. doi:10.3390/children6080094

Nembhard, I, David, G and Ezzeddine, I. 2022. 'A systematic review of research on empathy in health care'. *Health Services Research, 58*: 250–263.

Ni Raghallaigh, M. 2013. 'The causes of mistrust amongst asylum-seekers and refugees: Insights from research with unaccompanied asylum-seeking minors living in the Republic of Ireland'. *Journal of Refugee Studies, 271*: 82–100. doi:10.1093/jrs/fet006

O'Neill, O 2001. 'Consistency in action'. In E. Millgram, *Varieties of Practical Reasoning*, 316–329. Bradford Books.

Perry, B and Winfrey, O. 2021. *What happened to you: Conversations on trauma, resilience, and healing*. Bluebird Books for Life.

Ratka, A. 2018. 'Empathy and the development of affective skills'. *American Journal of Pharmaceutical Education, 82*(10): 1140–1143.

Rogel, R 2013. 'Implementing the BASIC Ph Model in post "Katrina" Mississippi Gulf Coast'. In *The 'Basic PH' model of coping and resiliency: Theory, research and cross-cultural application*, 277–295. Jessica Kingsley Publishers.

Rogers, C. 1949. 'The attitude and orientation of the counselor in client-centred therapy'. *Journal of Consulting Psychology, 13*(2): 82–94.

Rogers, C. 1951/2012. *Client-centred therapy: Its current practice, implications and theory*. Constable.

Roth-Hanania, R, Davidov, M and Zahn-Waxler, C. 2011. 'Empathy development from 8 to 16 months: Early signs of concern for others'. *Infant Behavior and Development, 34*: 447–458.

Rumbaut, R and Portes, A. 2001. *Ethnicities: Children of immigrants in America.* Russell Sage Foundation.

Sellars, M. 2020. *Educating students with refugee and asylum seeker experiences.* Verlag Barbara Budrich.

Shacham, M, Lahad, M and Shacham, Y. 2013. 'How Jewish and Arab parents perceived their children's resiliency during the Second Lebanon War'. In *The 'Basic PH' model of coping and resiliency: Theory, research and cross-cultural application,* 177–197. Jessica Kingsley Publishers.

Spencer, S. 2014. *Race and ethnicity: Culture, identity and representation.* Routledge.

Stern, J A and Cassidy, J. 2018. Empathy from infancy to adolescence: An attachment perspective on the development of individual differences. Developmental Review, 47, 1022. doi:org/10.1016/j.dr.2017.09.002.

Sunderland, M. 2016. *What every parent needs to know: Love, nurture and play with your child.* Penguin, Random House.

Tan, L, Le, M, Yu, C C, Liaw, S, Tierney, T, Ho, Y, ... Low, J. 2021. 'Defining clinical empathy: A grounded theory approach from the perspective of healthcare workers and patients in a multicultural setting'. *BMJ Open, 11*: 1–9.

Thompson, N and Pascal, J. 2012. 'Developing critically reflective practice'. *Reflective Practice, 132*: 311–325. doi:10.1080/14623943.2012.657795

Tribe, R and Thompson, K. 2017. *Working with interpreters: Guidelines for psychologists.* The British Psychological Society.

Volkan, V. 2018. *Immigrants and refugees: Trauma, perennial mourning, prejudice and border psychology.* Routledge.

Wahlstrom Smith, A. 2020. 'Surviving through the kindness of strangers: can there be 'wellbeing' among undocumented refugee children?' *International Journal of Qualitative Studies on Health and Well-Being, 152*: 1–11. doi:10.1080/17482631.2020.1724757.

Weisz, E and Zaki, J. 2017. 'Empathy-building interventions: A review of existing work and suggestions for future directions'. In E Seppela, S Simon-Thomas, M Brown, C Worline, C Cameron and R Doty, *The Oxford handbook of compassion science,* 205–217. Oxford University Press.

Winslade, J. 2013. 'From being non-judgemental to deconstructing normalising judgement'. *British Journal of Guidance and Counselling*: 518–529. doi:10.1080/03069885.2013.7 7177:

Worrell, S. 2021. 'From language brokering to digital brokering: Refugee settlement in a smartphone age'. *Social Media and Society*: 1–11. doi:10.1177/20563051211-12365

Yohani, S. 2010. 'Nurturing hope in refugee children during early years of post-war adjustment'. *Children and Youth Services Review, 32*(6): 865–873.

Chapter 5

Expressive Arts in Psychotherapy with Traumatised Refugee Adolescents

Introduction

This chapter explores the role of expressive arts in psychotherapy with refugee adolescents who have experienced potentially traumatic events. Expressive arts offer unique healing pathways beyond traditional talk therapy. Drawing on neuroscience research, cross-cultural healing traditions and contemporary clinical practice, the chapter explores how various creative modalities can help refugee adolescents process trauma, overcome language barriers, express emotions, enhance self-regulation, and build resilience. The chapter establishes why non-verbal, body-centred approaches are essential in trauma recovery. It then examines the core principles of expressive arts psychotherapy and provides an overview of key modalities including art, music, drama, dance/movement therapies, and therapeutic writing. The chapter reviews applications of these approaches with refugee adolescents, highlighting practices that address their unique needs. The chapter emphasises the importance of culturally responsive, trauma-informed care that recognises and builds on the strengths and resilience of refugee adolescents.

Theoretical Foundations

The Neuroscience and Mind-Body Connection in Trauma Recovery

Neuroscience research since the 1990s shows that conventional talk therapy is unlikely to be optimal for trauma survivors (van der Kolk 2015; Levine 2013, 2015; Mate 2019). This research shows that trauma primarily impacts the body, with secondary psychological effects. Chapter 2 discusses the effects of traumatic experiences from forced displacement on refugee adolescents' brain functions.

Research conducted by van der Kolk in the early 1990s (cited in van der Kolk 2015) found a significant reduction in the capacity of Broca's area, one of the speech centres of the brain, to put thoughts and feelings into words after a traumatic experience. Scans also showed that Broca's area was deactivated whenever a flashback was triggered. For these reasons, healing approaches should seek to

DOI: 10.4324/9781003430032-6

re-establish a connection with the body and the senses through the combination of expressive arts, mindfulness, and body awareness approaches (Rappaport 2014).

Expressive arts approaches have been found to be particularly effective for those who have experienced potentially traumatic events, given that even years after the event, most still find it extremely difficult to talk about what happened to them and to articulate the accompanying feelings and impulses (Levine 2008). van der Kolk states that: 'Trauma by its very nature drives us to the edge of comprehension, cutting us off from language based on common experience or an imaginable past' (van der Kolk, 2015:43). Although some individuals can still talk about a traumatic event, the story which they tell is highly unlikely to capture their internal emotional reality. Many survivors create a safer surface-level story for friends and family which may help to explain their responses and conduct.

Given this mind-body trauma connection, the organisation of traumatic experiences into a coherent account with a beginning, middle, and an end is extremely difficult to achieve through talking alone (van der Kolk 2015). The brain systems responsible for creating autobiographical memories cease to function effectively following trauma. In contrast to ordinary memories, which are stored as stories that change and fade over time, the imprints of trauma are stored as physical sensations and movements, intense negative emotions (fear, shame, rage, collapse), and immediate threats to life (Levine 2015).

The neurobiological underpinnings may also result in more subtle physical responses such as breath holding and muscle tensing, which can be brought into conscious awareness through the sensory aspects of the expressive arts (van der Kolk 2015). Incorporating mindfulness and body awareness techniques into expressive arts-focused individual or group therapy can be transformative through its promotion of the learning of new ways of being in the world, allowing those who engage to express all aspects of their experiences in the most intuitive ways (Malchiodi 2020; Rappaport 2014).

Historical and Cross-Cultural Healing Practices through the Expressive Arts

The healing powers of the visual arts, storytelling, drama, comedy, dance, music, play, poetry, and communal rituals, collectively known as the expressive arts, have long been recognised as integral to ancient civilisations and the cultures of indigenous peoples (Jennings 2018; Malchiodi 2020). As well as being instinctive responses to grief, loss, and trauma, these ancient practices continue to be used to celebrate and honour new life and life's transitions (Linklater 2014).

Throughout human history, creative expression has been central to healing practices across diverse cultures (Womack 2010). Indigenous healing traditions consistently incorporate rhythmic movement, symbolic representation, and communal participation as essential elements in restoration and recovery. Degges-White (2017) points out that Navajo healers still include sandpainting and music in their healing rituals. Similarly, Aboriginal healing circles, African drumming ceremonies, and

East Asian meditative arts all represent culturally diverse approaches that recognise the profound connection between creative expression and psychological well-being (Elendu 2024).

These traditional practices demonstrate a sophisticated understanding of the mind-body connection that modern neuroscience is now beginning to validate (van der Kolk 2015). Coming of age initiations, marriages, and traditions of burial and mourning are all examples of these rites of passage (Archibald and Dewar 2010). These rituals harness the power of symbolic action, community witness, and embodied expression to facilitate transitions through difficult life experiences.

In his foreword to Cathy Malchiodi's (2015) book on creative interventions with traumatised children, Bruce Perry, child psychiatrist, researcher, and educator, sees the enduring nature of these ancient traditions and time-honoured principles as clear evidence of their fundamental roles in healing from trauma and loss:

> Amid the current pressure for 'evidence-based practice' parameters, we should remind ourselves that the most powerful evidence is that which comes from hundreds of separate cultures across the thousands of generations independently converging on rhythm, touch, storytelling and reconnection to community.

The western world's more recent recognition of the therapeutic benefits of the arts is reflected in the World Health Organization (WHO) Arts and Health Programme which organises events, supports research, and raises awareness of the potential value of the arts in the promotion of good health (Fancourt and Finn 2019). This institutional validation represents a significant shift towards acknowledging what many cultures have understood for millennia – that creative expression is not merely an adjunct to healing but often central to it.

These historical healing practices and their contemporary validation through neuroscience research provide the foundation for modern expressive arts psychotherapy. Building on this rich heritage, the ways in which expressive arts psychotherapy has evolved as a structured therapeutic approach that integrates these timeless healing elements within contemporary clinical frameworks will now be examined.

Expressive Arts Psychotherapy: Definitions and Core Concepts

Expressive arts psychotherapy, founded in the early 1970s, is a specialised action-oriented psychotherapy modality grounded in sensory practices that harness the healing power of creative expression. Unlike specialised expressive approaches which focus on a single modality such as visual arts, music, drama, or dance/movement, expressive arts psychotherapy embraces an innovative intermodal approach which supports the inclusion of multiple forms of creative arts in clinical practice (Levine and Levine 1999).

Expressive arts psychotherapists typically incorporate art, music, dance/movement, dramatic enactment, creative writing, and imaginative play as tools for communicating, transforming, and healing traumatic experiences (Malchiodi 2020). Richardson (2016:6) offers a comprehensive interpretation, describing expressive arts therapy as including every form of creativity that an individual or group can conceive of, stating that: 'it is the body, mind and soul in harmony or chaos finding a way to be witnessed, heard, healed, changed, challenged, deepened, discovered or surrendered through a relationship between self, the arts, and the therapist.' This is the interpretation embraced by the author in her engagement with adolescent refugees.

This specialist modality – also referred to as the expressive therapies, creative therapies, integrative therapies, and intermodal expressive arts, or action therapies (Richardson 2016) focuses on the process of creative endeavour to foster therapeutic growth rather than on formal analysis by the therapist. The approach recognises that individuals possess diverse preferences for communicating and coping styles, which might include visual expression, tactile engagement, music, drama, or dance/movement as a means of self-expression. This aligns with the Universal Design for Learning and BASIC Ph models described in Chapter 4.

The expressive arts approach enables refugee adolescents to go beyond everyday experiences and connect with aspects of themselves that might not be as accessible through conventional talk therapy (Degges-White 2017). Examples include utilising symbols to articulate internal conflicts and feelings and communicating inner struggles in a physical way. This exploration can lead to more profound self-discovery and expression compared to traditional talk therapy alone.

In addition to being a specialist modality, expressive arts approaches and techniques can enhance the existing skill set of all clinicians. Integrating expressive arts into existing psychotherapy practices provides both therapist and young person with the possibility of moving beyond the constraints of talk, thereby deepening and advancing the process of healing from trauma (Malchiodi 2011). This integration harnesses touch, synchrony, rhythm, and other forms of intuitive expressive processes to promote the integration of sensory-oriented and brain-focused aspects of arts-based expression into the therapeutic process (Malchiodi 2023; Rappaport 2014).

Therapeutic Process

As well as acknowledging these preferences, it is important to recognise the powerful role of the expressive arts as a means of accessing inner emotions and the unconscious mind. Degges-White (2017) demonstrate how the expressive arts approach enables us to go beyond everyday experiences and connect with aspects of ourselves which might not be as accessible through conventional talk therapy. Examples include utilising symbols to articulate internal conflicts and feelings and communicating our inner struggles in a physical way. This exploration can lead to more profound self-discovery and expression compared to traditional talk therapy alone. Fundamentally, the focus is on the process of the creative endeavour to foster therapeutic growth rather than on its formal analysis by the therapist.

The Integration of the Expressive Arts with Other Psychotherapy Modalities

In addition to being a specialist modality, expressive arts approaches and techniques can enhance the existing skill sets of all clinicians. Integrating expressive arts into existing psychotherapy practices provides both therapist and young person with the possibility of moving beyond the constraints of talk, thereby deepening and advancing the process of healing from trauma (Degges-White 2017). This can be achieved by harnessing and integrating touch, synchrony, rhythm, and other forms of intuitive expressive processes which promote the integration of sensory-oriented and brain-focused aspects of arts-based expression into the therapeutic process (Malchiodi 2023; Rappaport 2014). Using these different pathways to activate the creative process opens up different possibilities for individual self-expression which has the potential to expand and progress the opportunities afforded by the therapy process.

Degges-White (2017) demonstrates that the expressive arts are suitable for psychotherapists who work with clients of all ages in diverse clinical settings from private practice to educational establishments to residential treatment centres. The following sections provide brief overviews of the principal expressive arts modalities, highlighting their unique characteristics and therapeutic applications. This exploration establishes a foundation for understanding how these approaches can be effectively adapted for work with refugee adolescents, with each modality offering distinct pathways for expression and healing while sharing the common element of embodied non-verbal therapeutic engagement. These modalities are further illustrated through detailed case studies.

With this understanding of expressive arts psychotherapy as both a specialist modality and an enhancement to existing therapeutic approaches, we can now explore the specific modalities that comprise the expressive arts repertoire. Each of these modalities offers unique pathways for expression and healing while sharing the common element of embodied non-verbal therapeutic engagement.

Key Expressive Arts Modalities

Art Therapy

Art therapy uses different art media ranging from the more traditional crayons, oil pastels, chalks, pencils, and paints to collage supplies which include pictures from magazines, ribbons, and coloured card, to more natural materials such as clay, twigs, and leaves (Malchiodi 2015). Furthermore, the more recent development of digital tools has introduced possibilities for digital drawing and collaging technologies, photography, virtual reality, and digital storytelling platforms (Zubala et al.

2021). The art-making process elicits verbal and non-verbal communication within the safe space of an attuned therapeutic relationship where the therapist and client work together to understand the meaning of the artwork produced. This artwork provides a focus for discussion, increased awareness, and reflection, and as it is typically a physical object, it embodies a memory of the making of the object and the interaction between therapist and client (Case et al. 2023). Furthermore, there is growing evidence from the field of neuroscience that the creative process of art therapy enhances neuroplasticity and that the materials and methods employed facilitate self-expression and assist in self-regulation (King 2022).

Music Therapy

As a universal and ubiquitous form of language, music provides a powerful means of communication, regardless of age, background, location, or capacity (Thaut 2013). Elliott et al. (2011) point out that music can instantly evoke specific memories and that it has calming, connecting, energising, and inspiring properties. Music has been a source of healing for centuries, and in recent times sophisticated scanning techniques have shown that, unlike spoken language, it can activate virtually all brain regions and networks (Thaut 2013). The observation that the playing of music to wounded and traumatised soldiers during the First and Second World Wars alleviated pain, boosted morale, and improved mood led to the more formal identification of its therapeutic qualities and the eventual professionalisation of music therapy. Music therapy interventions are used to address physical, emotional, cognitive, and social needs within a therapeutic relationship across a variety of populations (Browne 2008; de Witte et al. 2022; Bunt and Stige 2014). These interventions can be active (making music) and/or receptive (receiving or listening to music).

Drama Therapy

Summarising the many definitions of dramatherapy in his seminal book on the subject, Phil Jones (2007:795) conceives of dramatherapy as 'involvement with drama with a healing intention' and talks about its potential to reflect and transform life experiences by enabling clients to express and process difficulties in their lives within a trusting therapeutic relationship. In parallel with the ways in which many expressive arts modalities evolve in practice, drama therapy uses a therapeutic framework to facilitate participants to make use of the content of drama activities, the process of creating enactments, and the relationships formed between those taking part. A connection is therefore created between the client's internal world, their challenging life experiences, and the dramatherapy session activities (Feniger-Schaal and Orkibi 2020). The participant seeks to achieve a new perspective on the challenges they bring to dramatherapy, and this modality helps them to think in different ways about situations, offering new understandings, reframing, and support.

Dance/Movement Therapy

Throughout history, dance and movement, like all other forms of expressive arts, have been deeply integrated into the heart of healing ceremonies across diverse cultures (Gray and Fargnoli 2022). Across the ages, dance has been used to stimulate bountiful harvests, offer reverence to deities, safeguard against malevolent forces and ailments, enhance fertility, commemorate significant life stages, and collectively process shared traumas within communities (Purser 2019). Dance/ movement therapy (DMT), also known as dance therapy, movement therapy, dance movement psychotherapy, movement psychotherapy, dance/movement therapy, and dance-movement therapy, is a form of psychotherapy which uses the creative movement process as its foundation, drawing from this rich multicultural history of dance as healing. The Association for Dance Movement Psychotherapy UK defines DMP as 'a relational process in which client(s and therapist use body movement and dance as an instrument of communication during the therapy process' (ADMP UK 2025). Expanding this definition in her work on harnessing soul and spirit in DMP, Hayes (2013) explores the different ways in which DMP reveals and captures the ways in which we sense, feel, and imagine, and how we connect to and engage with the world.

Therapeutic Writing

Storytelling and narratives have played a powerful and enduring role in human psychology, from therapeutic reading in the asylums of Europe in the 1700s, to the prescribing of books to help hospital patients in the early 19th century and the bibliotherapy and therapeutic writing interventions of the 20th and 21st centuries (Baraitser 2014). Pardeck and Pardeck (2021:1), describe oral and written texts as having been 'silent therapists' for centuries. The unique capacity, motivation, and skill of humans for telling stories and using the written word creatively, combined with the power of writing to facilitate connections among individuals, groups, and the wider cultural context, make it a highly effective vehicle for healing (Malchiodi 2023).

Therapeutic writing uses language, symbol, and story within the safety of a supportive therapeutic relationship (Bolton et al. 2011). Producing a written record of our truths empowers and foregrounds our voice, enabling us to put some form to chaotic thoughts and emotions. Metaphor, imagery, and memory can stimulate the imagination (Geldard et al. 2019), and experiences, thoughts, and ideas can be mapped creatively (Pennebaker 2014; Bolton et al., 2011). Repressed memories can be brought into conscious awareness (Malchiodi 2020), and emotions and experiences which cannot be spoken out loud can be safely contained (Baraitser 2014). Bolton et al. (2011) highlight the increased self-confidence associated with expressive writing compared with talking, as well as the greater likelihood of being able to access traumatic material.

While each of these modalities has developed as a distinctive therapeutic approach, their application to work with adolescent refugees requires consideration of the specific needs, challenges, and strengths of this population. Before exploring specific modality-based applications, it is important to first understand several foundational therapeutic principles that are particularly relevant for refugee adolescents.

Providing Ways to Understand, Explore, and Express Emotional Experiences

Margot Sunderland, a British child and adolescent psychologist, psychotherapist, and author, highlights the lack of support provided for children and adolescents to help them understand and sensitively explore and express their emotions in their families, communities, and schools (Sunderland 2018). This perceived disregard for emotional experiences is likely to be particularly acute for unaccompanied refugee adolescents, given the additional challenges which they typically face, as outlined in Chapter 1. In addition, for those who arrive with their family, the emotional availability of parents who have been forcibly displaced is likely to be seriously compromised due to emotional exhaustion, although in one study some parents reported experiencing post-traumatic growth through increased compassion for their children during the resettlement phase (Eltanamly et al. 2019).

Sunderland (2012) asserts that when young people have no safe person with whom to explore, feel, and think about their key emotional experiences, this can have a significant and enduring impact on their ability to effectively:

- understand and manage their emotions;
- build and maintain healthy relationships;
- develop self-awareness;
- navigate obstacles; and
- develop resilience and healthy coping mechanisms.

The advantages of the expressive arts for exploring key emotional experiences have been conceptualised in various ways. Fonagy (2006) frames expressive arts methods as alternative ways of promoting mentalisation, which he defines as the ability to reflect on the thoughts, feelings, and intentions of self and others. Prendiville (2017) describes feelings being identified through the unconscious projection of life experiences and relationships onto all elements of the expressive arts, including play and symbols. Malchiodi (2021:23) describes the use of the expressive arts for exploring feelings as 'a way for us to understand things with our hearts when we cannot with our minds.' Malchiodi's conceptualisation is embodied in Feen-Calligan et al's (2020) art therapy programme for Syrian refugee youth, which focuses on exploring feelings through non-verbalised kinaesthetic sensory experiences with a variety of art media. Malchiodi's simple and warm description is often used by the author to explain the expressive arts approach to their adolescent refugee participants.

Sunderland has produced a series of therapeutic stories and accompanying guidebooks for professionals and parents entitled 'Helping Children with Feelings' to help children to connect with unresolved feelings including loss, anger, rage, anxiety, low self-esteem and fear, all of which are commonly experienced by child and adolescent refugees (Sunderland 2022a). The guidebooks provide imaginative ideas rooted in relational neuroscience of how to help children to safely and creatively explore and express their feelings using visual arts, movement, and music, which also provide optimal conditions for working with adolescent refugees (e.g. Sunderland 2022a, 2022b).

Although Margot Sunderland also writes specifically for teenagers (Sunderland 2012), her focus in this work is on different ways of having thoughtful, reflective and empowering *conversations* with them, and I have found the creative guidebooks for children to be more useful when working with adolescent refugees given their cultural and trauma-impacted linguistic challenges. Finally, Sunderland emphasises the importance of adults actively participating in all activities with children and adolescents, thereby creating a supportive and empathic atmosphere which promotes emotional exploration, understanding, and expression (Sunderland 2019).

Enhancing Self-Regulation and Building Resilience

Self-regulation and resilience are closely interrelated capacities that are often compromised in adolescent refugees who have experienced trauma. This section explores how expressive arts approaches can help develop these essential life skills through embodied creative interventions.

Self-Regulation through the Expressive Arts

Self-regulation refers to an individual's capacity to manage impulses, calm the body's stress responses, and regulate affective, sensory, and physical responses that are likely to have an impact on emotions, physiology, and cognitions (Forgas et al. 2015). Self-regulated individuals can exercise patience and self-control, are aware of the possible consequences of their actions, and are able to respond appropriately. Expressive arts approaches are particularly effective for enhancing self-regulation because they can mediate the kinaesthetic sensory qualities of rhythm, movement, touch, and sound that influence autonomic nervous system functions (Porges 2011).

Although the expressive arts offer many possibilities when supporting adolescent refugees to improve self-regulation, Malchiodi (2020) suggests that integrating these techniques into the following two broad processes is particularly helpful:

(i) Grounding and anchoring,

(ii) Relaxation and stress reduction.

Developing an understanding of the positive effect of these self-regulatory skills and the ways in which they can be enhanced by the expressive arts within the safe space of a therapeutic relationship ensures that practitioners can help adolescent refugees to reduce the impact of being emotionally hijacked and experiencing distressing sensations of alarm, fear, and terror (van der Kolk 2015).

Grounding and Anchoring

Grounding techniques can assist refugee adolescents in diminishing stress responses by shifting their focus away from internal feelings of anxiety, panic, and fear, and redirecting it instead towards their immediate external environment and present reality (Jalonen and Corte 2018). These techniques frequently employ the senses to strengthen a sense of presence in the here and now. Grounding techniques can be as straightforward as identifying things that one can see, hear, or smell in the present (Levine 2008). However, this may pose a challenge during highly stressful periods, and the expressive arts can help increase focus on something which is not distressing or can serve as an immediate distraction.

Bilateral Drawing

Malchiodi (2011) identifies bilateral drawing, which involves drawing or doodling simultaneously with both hands, as an effective grounding tool. She asserts that making marks or scribbles on paper with both hands simultaneously can be experienced as a non-threatening and embodied experience that shifts attention away from the distressing sensations in the body to an action-oriented and self-empowered focus. Malchiodi points out that as bilateral drawing engages both hemispheres of the brain concurrently, it connects 'thinking' to 'feeling' and therefore has a positive impact on an individual's internal rhythms and the regulation and grounding of the body and the mind.

Creating Anchors and Safe Spaces

The term 'anchoring' describes the process of using specific prompts or experiences to direct attention to the current moment or transform anxiety into peace of mind (Siegel 2010). Anchoring lends itself well to the use of expressive arts approaches often employing sensory cues such as sounds, music, or objects created by the individual, which can be accessed at any time to support self-regulation. For practitioners who work with adolescent refugees, this often involves creating a therapeutic safe space as an anchor to be evoked during periods of distress. The notion of a safe space, sometimes called a safe haven, recalls or imagines the safety of secure childhood attachment which is cultivated through attuned dyadic regulation with a trusted caregiver (Jennings 2010). This safe space can then be anchored and given a form through the expressive arts such as a painting, a clay model, a song, a dance, or a movement, and returned to when needed (Dieterich-Hartwell and Koch 2017).

Relaxation and Stress Reduction

Complementing grounding techniques, the following relaxation techniques help reduce hyperarousal symptoms, which are common after traumatic experiences. They have been found to be particularly effective with refugee adolescents (Fondacaro et al. 2021).

Progressive Muscle Relaxation (PMR)

PMR is based on the simple practice of tensing one muscle group at a time followed by a relaxation–tension–release phase (Wilczynska et al. 2019), which can be enhanced through music or guided imagery (see Chapter 10).

Body-Based Techniques

The body-based stress reduction techniques developed by psychologist and trauma-specialist, Peter Levine (2008), comprise a series of easily learned postures to help the body to simply 'slow down' when an individual is feeling anxious or scared. These positions involve placement of the hands on the head, heart, and stomach, accompanied by rhythmic breathing (see Chapters 8, 10, 11).

Movement-Based Practices

Movement-based practices help release tension and restore a sense of physical safety by engaging the body in expressive, rhythmic motion. These practices can include gently stretching, dance, or simple repetitive movements that help regulate the autonomic nervous system and release trapped energy from the body (Levine 2013). For refugee adolescents who have experienced significant trauma, movement offers a way to reconnect with their bodies in a safe, controlled manner, allowing them to experience agency and embodied presence in the present moment. These practices can be particularly effective when adapted to incorporate culturally familiar movements that resonate with the adolescent's background and experience (Harris, 2007) (see Chapters 11, 12, 14).

These self-regulation techniques provide essential tools for adolescent refugees to manage trauma symptoms. Equally important is the creation of psychological safety, which is particularly significant for those who have experienced the profound loss of their physical home.

Creating a Safe Space: Expressive Arts as Temporary Home

Papadopoulos (2002), in his exploration of refugees, home and trauma, conceptualises 'home' as a complex concept rooted in its etymological origins and modern interpretations, which extends beyond personal spaces to include family, other relationships, feelings, and cultural practices. Described as 'the seat of domestic life' by the *Oxford English Dictionary*, 'home' symbolises refuge and emotional fulfilment. In her multidisciplinary exploration of this multi-dimensional notion, Mallett (2004) points out that the elusive ideal of feeling 'at home' often surfaces in absence, revealing its significance at the heart of human experience. Taylor (2013) suggests that refugees are primarily defined by their displacement from home, experiencing a profound longing to restore that which has been lost.

However, refugees facing the impossibility of returning to their homeland due to conflict or adversity encounter an additional layer of complexity: home becomes intertwined not only with longing but also with fear and other negative emotions. The expressive arts offer adolescent refugees who are living in this liminal space between the danger they have fled and the safety which they seek, a temporary home characterised by a sense of belonging and refuge, serving as a sanctuary where they can find solace and express themselves during the turmoil and uncertainty of forced displacement (Callaghan 1998; DeMott, 2014). The expressive arts can provide a temporary sanctuary which supports restoration and integration.

Having established these key therapeutic concepts of emotional expression, self-regulation, and the creation of safe spaces, we can now examine how specific expressive arts modalities can be adapted and applied to address the unique circumstances of refugee adolescents.

Applications with Adolescent Refugees: Modality-Based Approaches

Using the expressive arts as the main therapy modality or integrating them into a different modality are both approaches which have been found to be highly effective in situations where identities have been lost or are in conflict with the host culture (Marshall 2007), making them an ideal medium through which to work with adolescent refugees (Kalaf and Plante 2019). These therapeutic approaches can be delivered individually or in groups, with each modality offering unique benefits while addressing common therapeutic goals:

- Overcoming language and cultural barriers using creative and symbolic strategies;
- Creating a safe space, a temporary home, and a bridge to the host culture;
- De-stigmatising mental health difficulties and help-seeking;
- Providing ways to express feelings;
- Enhancing self-regulation; and
- Developing coping strategies and resilience.

Visual Arts Applications with Refugee Adolescents

Therapy using the visual arts offers refugee adolescents concrete, tactile means of expression that transcend language barriers and access emotions that may be difficult to visualise.

Overcoming Language and Cultural Barriers

One of the most significant benefits of the visual arts lies in their capacity to bypass the constraints of language by offering additional pathways for communication (Richardson 2016). Adnams Jones (2018) describes the expressive arts as an innate form of 'literacy,' accessible to anyone of any age in any culture, which offers the possibility of externalising implicit experiences without the spoken word.

Symbolic strategies using visual objects are particularly appealing to adolescents because they involve actively choosing visual objects as symbols, which helps to keep them engaged in the therapeutic process (Geldard et al. 2019; Jung 1968) believed that symbols could help uncover unconscious material, enabling adolescents to bring unconscious content into conscious awareness. Objects that can effectively serve as symbols include:

- stones, shells, pieces of wood, feathers
- small containers with lids
- beads
- marbles
- keys, padlocks
- miniature dwellings
- toy boats, cars and other means of transport
- small diverse human figures
- fantasy figures
- animals
- trees, fences, bridges, walls

CASE VIGNETTE: CHIMA'S SILENT EXPRESSION

When Chima first began therapy, his limited English and the impact of trauma on his verbal expression would have made traditional talk therapy challenging. During his third session, his therapist introduced a collection of miniature objects, including small human figures, animals, and transport. Without prompting, Chima selected a small boat, placed it between two larger objects, and positioned several figures both inside and outside the boat. Through this symbolic arrangement, he was able to communicate his family's separation during flight in a way that words could not capture. The therapist observed how this non-verbal expression allowed Chima to externalise his experience without the pressure of language, creating a foundation for later therapeutic integration when he felt ready. This symbolic work provided a bridge that transcended both language barriers and trauma-induced emotional disconnection, allowing therapeutic connection despite these challenges.

CREATING VISUAL SAFE SPACES

Fitzpatrick (2002), in her study of the role of art therapy in understanding the experiences of Bosnian refugees in Western Australia, documents the ways in which they can illustrate their homes, loved ones, aspects of themselves, and their stories using visual lifelines and other arts media. She describes engaging in a collaging activity where they depicted current strengths and supports on one side and 'hoped for' things on the other side. As a symbolic means of connecting the two sides, groupmembers were asked to draw a bridge between them, showing how this could provide a powerful way of remembering, mourning, and reconstructing their experiences and strengthening their identities.

Visual Expression of Feelings and Building Resilience

CASE VIGNETTE: CHIMA'S INSIDE-OUTSIDE MASK

Chima's therapist noticed his tendency to present a composed exterior while holding significant internal distress. When introduced to the inside-outside mask activity described by Feen-Calligan et al. (2020), Chima engaged deeply with the process. On the outside of his mask, he depicted a smiling face with bright colours and strong features that conveyed confidence and resilience as the self he showed to others at school and in his foster home. Inside the mask, however, he created a chaotic pattern of dark colours interspersed with small red dots and jagged lines, representing his internal experience of fear, uncertainty, and hyper-vigilance.

This creative expression allowed Chima to acknowledge his inner emotional reality without having to verbally articulate feelings that were difficult to name. The concrete external representation of his internal experience created a shared understanding between Chima and his therapist that became a reference point in subsequent sessions. When Chima was struggling to express himself, the therapist could ask, 'is this an inside mask feeling or an outside mask feeling,' providing a shorthand that bypassed language barriers while honouring the complexity of his emotional experience.

Enhancing Self-Regulation through Visual Arts

CASE VIGNETTE: BILATERAL DRAWING WITH NATALIA

Natalia often experienced intrusive memories related to the sounds of shelling in her home country. During one session when she appeared particularly distressed after hearing a loud motorbike outside, her therapist introduced bilateral drawing. Starting with simple mirrored movements using coloured markers on a large sheet of paper, Natalia began making symmetrical patterns with both hands simultaneously. As she engaged in this process, her breathing visibly slowed, and her body tension decreased. When asked about her experience afterwards, Natalia said that drawing with both hands helped her to feel more grounded and present when she was starting to drift away into frightening memories. She explained that concentrating on making the balanced pattern took up so much of her attention that the scary images in her head became fainter and less powerful. Together, Natalia and her therapist practised and refined this technique as a portable self-regulation tool that she could use anywhere at school or in other settings when she felt her anxiety building.

Music Applications with Refugee Adolescents

Music provides a universal language that can help refugee adolescents connect with their cultural heritage while building bridges to the new environment. Music offers pathways for emotional expression, regulation, and social connection.

Creating a Psychological Home and Cultural Bridge

CASE VIGNETTE: HOW MUSIC CREATED A PSYCHOLOGICAL HOME FOR NATALIA

Natalia, who had experienced therapy in her home country, was initially hesitant to engage in expressive arts, preferring to rely on verbal communication in spite of her emerging English (developing language proficiency). During her fourth session, her therapist played background music from her home country while they worked. Natalia immediately recognised the melody and appeared visibly moved. In subsequent sessions, they collaboratively created a 'musical home' playlist that integrated songs from both her homeland and her host country. This playlist became a transitional object that Natalia could access between sessions, providing both a connection to her cultural identity and a bridge to her new environment. The music created that which Papadopoulos (2002) describes as a 'temporary home,' a safe psychological space that acknowledged both her past and present. This musical bridge allowed Natalia to begin exploring more challenging aspects of her displacement experience through other expressive modalities.

Working in refugee camp settings with small groups, Mallon and Hoog Antink (2021) encouraged participants to share songs from their home countries, helping them to maintain their connections with home, develop a sense of belonging, experience validation of their music and culture, and construct a cultural bridge during music-making activities. Heynen et al. (2022) found that when therapists and refugees collaboratively explored music from the refugee's homeland, this shared discovery process fostered greater safety, trust, and social bonds while strengthening connections to cultural roots.

Building Social Connections through Music

CASE VIGNETTE: GROUP CONNECTION THROUGH MUSIC

Natalia participated in a six-week music therapy group with other refugee adolescents from diverse backgrounds. Despite significant language differences in the group, collaborative drumming created an immediate sense of connection. During the third session, the music therapist introduced a rhythmic activity where each participant could contribute a personal rhythm that represented something from their home country, and Natalia offered a rhythm that evoked a dance from her homeland. As the group members learned and incorporated each other's rhythmic patterns, a complex collaborative composition emerged. The therapist noticed increased eye contact, spontaneous smiling, and synchronisation of body movements among participants who had previously appeared isolated or withdrawn. After the session, Chima commented that it was 'the first time I felt understood without words' since arriving in the host country. This experience illustrates how shared creative expression can transcend language barriers and cultural differences, creating meaningful social connections through non-verbal collaboration.

Hunt (2005) found that being in a music therapy group enhanced peer support and encouraged group participation for adolescent refugees, while the act of playing music together provided a solid basis for participation and group cohesion. Participants reported experiencing a sense of togetherness and empowerment which contributed to their psychological wellbeing and capacity to navigate challenges in their new environment.

De-Stigmatising Mental Health Support through Music

The non-clinical associations of music can help reduce stigma around accessing support services. Therapy sessions focused on sharing and creating music often feel less clinical and more culturally familiar, making them more accessible to refugee adolescents who might otherwise avoid traditional mental health services. The communal aspects of music-making connect with cultural traditions of healing through community engagement rather than individualised treatment models that may feel stigmatising.

Drama and Movement Applications with Refugee Adolescents

Drama therapy and dance/movement therapy offer embodied approaches to healing that engage the whole person, addressing the semantic aspects of trauma that may be inaccessible through verbal approaches alone.

Embodied Expression and Narrative Reconstruction

Rousseau et al. (2005) identified empowerment through collective effort in drama therapy workshops with adolescent refugees, where stories were shared through 'playback theatre.' Small groups were provided with lengths of fabric and cubes as props to convey their stories, opening up multiple levels of awareness for their own group members as well as other participants. This was a high-school-based intervention and teachers reported a clear strengthening of ties between the students after the workshops, reporting how it mobilised them to support one another.

Movement, Visualisation, and Trauma Recovery

Abu Sway et al. (2005) combined guided visualisation with movement in their work with a group of families whose homes had been demolished in the West Bank and Gaza. The prolonged stress experienced by the group members resulted in elevated cortisol levels, negatively impacting both their physical and mental wellbeing. Stimulating the group members both physically and mentally helped them to remain attuned to their sensations. They were first asked to stand in a circle and exercise all their muscles, starting with the head and moving down their bodies until every muscle was used. They were then prompted to mimic the movements of their hands and feet as they typically performed their daily tasks, including kneading dough, grinding grain, or harvesting fruits. Visualisation guided the participants back to their previous homes, prompting them to replicate their real-life movements. This process aimed to revive a mental image of their home, allowing them to reconstruct it within themselves after its physical demolition.

Physical Integration and Resilience Building

Engaging in movement-based expressive arts activities helps refugees who have experienced trauma to reconnect with their bodies, release tension, and restore a sense of physical autonomy and safety (Levine 2013). When people are active rather than passive, they are experiencing, perceiving, and expressing themselves with their own bodies in motion which leads to positive results after traumatic experiences (Wang et al. 2023). Harris (2007) documents a Dance/Movement Therapy Programme for South Sudanese refugee youth in the USA which combines Sudanese Dinka movement, dance, and ritual, reporting improved solidarity, increased group cohesion, and healing through mind-body integration.

Connecting the mind, body, and spirit through expressive activities was one of the main goals of a therapeutic Capoeira programme for adolescent refugees in Australia (Momartin et al. 2019), which simulated non-contact combat between two players using a blend of music, singing, dance, acrobatics, and martial arts movements. Pre- and post-intervention assessment using the Teacher's Strengths and Difficulties Questionnaire (SDQ) demonstrated a significant improvement in the participants' daily lives after a weekly programme which ran for the academic year. Positive outcomes included improved relationships with teachers, caregivers, and peers, refined social skills, and enhanced mind-body connection through moving the body in unfamiliar ways and developing physical awareness, confidence, and control.

Football has also been identified as a useful tool for coping. Horn et al. (2019) document the benefits of a joint programme delivered by *London-based Arsenal Football Club and Freedom from Torture clinicians*. Participation outcomes included improved relationships, a sense of belonging, hope for the future, emotional regulation, and improved physical health.

Therapeutic Writing Applications with Refugee Adolescents

Therapeutic writing uses language, symbol, and story within the safety of a supportive therapeutic relationship to help refugee adolescents process traumatic experiences and construct new narratives of identity and belonging (Baraitser 2014).

Reframing Narratives and Making Meaning

Expressive arts activities grounded in storytelling and writing empower individuals to cognitively reframe and re-interpret their experiences and to construct narratives of resilience and growth. James Pennebaker's pioneering research into expressive writing and trauma highlights the ways in which it can support trauma survivors who favour cognitive coping strategies, to reframe and make sense of their traumatic experiences (Pennebaker 2014).

Applying Pennebaker's work to the refugee context, Baraitser (2014) illustrates how therapists can utilise carefully chosen literature with refugee youth to help them verbalise and reshape their experiences of conflict and displacement-related trauma, bridging their past with the present through narrative transformation. Although the positive impact of reframing through the expressive arts is also highlighted by Rowe et al. (2017) in their evaluation of a school-based art therapy programme for refugee adolescents in the USA, they also point out that the deficit-focused quantitative assessment tools typically used to evaluate such programmes are unable to capture the positive impact òf reframing.

Reducing Stigma through Poetry

Mohammadian et al. (2011) describe how poetry therapy with small collaborative groups of emerging adults was found to be non-stigmatising and yielded promising reductions in signs of depression, anxiety, and stress for these young people. The creative distance provided by poetry allows for the expression of difficult emotions without direct disclosure, which can feel safer for adolescents concerned about stigma.

The modality-based approaches described above demonstrate the versatility of expressive arts with refugee adolescents. To further understand how these creative interventions support resilience, we can view them through the lens of the BASIC Ph model, which offers a comprehensive framework for identifying and enhancing natural coping mechanisms.

Expressive Arts Applications within the BASIC Ph Framework: Enhancing Resilience ~~Through~~ Creative Expression

Building on the BASIC Ph model introduced in Chapter 4, this section explores how expressive arts can specifically enhance each coping channel for adolescent refugees. The focus here is on the unique ways in which creative expression amplifies and extends these natural coping mechanisms. The expressive arts offer particularly powerful tools for activating multiple resilience channels simultaneously. Each creative modality can engage different combinations of the BASIC Ph channels, providing flexible pathways that respect individual preferences while expanding coping repertoires:

Visual arts may simultaneously engage imagination, affect, and physical channels through tactile experiences.

Music often activates social, physical (through rhythm), and belief channels (through cultural connections).

Drama typically engages social, imaginative, and cognitive channels through role-play and perspective-taking.

Movement/dance naturally combines physical and affective channels while often incorporating social dimensions.

Writing frequently integrates cognitive and affective channels while providing imaginative exploration.

The following sections, which include case vignettes, outline how the expressive arts can be integrated into each component of the BASIC Ph model to support resilience building in refugee adolescents.

Belief through Ritual and Symbolism

For those adolescent refugees who draw on beliefs and values to guide them through times of stress, personally and culturally significant rituals and symbols enhanced by the expressive arts can be incorporated into the therapeutic process. This may include creating and participating in ceremonies, using symbolic objects, or engaging in spiritual practices (Land 2014).

Zwart and Nieuwenhuis (1998) document a powerful mourning ceremony planned and conducted with therapists in the host country with a young adult refugee who had witnessed his family being slaughtered in his home village and was forced to flee. His preparation for the one-year anniversary ceremony in his expressive arts therapy sessions included working on an 'ugly stone' that represented his pain. He buried this stone at the beach after the ceremony, knowing that eventually the sea would carry it away and connect him with his home country. Music representing his mixed faith background also played a significant role in the ceremony. Through the expressive arts, this mourning ritual gave form and structure to his beliefs and individual grief over his tragic loss, which slowly advanced his therapeutic process.

Affect through Creative Expression

All of the expressive arts offer powerful ways to express and process emotions non-verbally. By engaging in creative activities, individuals can explore and release repressed emotions, leading to emotional catharsis. Feen-Calligan et al. (2020) document creative activities for refugee youth which encourage self-expression using different media. These activities include the 'inside-outside-mask' where the 'self you show to others' is portrayed on the outside of the mask and 'what you keep on the inside' is depicted inside the mask. Collaging with coloured paper and magazines has also been found to be a highly effective non-intrusive and embodied way for refugee youth to express feelings non-verbally (Palit and Levin 2016; Vacchelli 2018) (see Chapters 5 and 9).

Social Connection through Collaborative Arts

Expressive arts therapy groups promote social connection and support and can foster a sense of belonging and shared experience among refugee youth, reducing feelings of isolation and alienation. The collaborative nature of many expressive arts activities creates natural opportunities for building relationships, developing trust, and experiencing positive social interactions.

Imagination through Visualisations and Guided Imagery

Blending expressive arts with guided imagery and visualisation techniques can greatly enhance imaginative stimulation and inner exploration for adolescent refugees who use their imagination to cope. Daniel-Becks et al. (2018) integrated music into trauma-focused guided imagery with young adult refugees and found that the embodied sensory experience of listening to music helped to anchor and integrate the therapeutic experience. Clinicians can also support refugee adolescents to create visual artworks, dramatic enactments, music, movement and expressive writing based on their guided journeys, allowing them to externalise and reflect upon their inner landscapes (see Chapters 8–12 and Chapter 15)

Cognition through Reframing Narratives and Storytelling

Cognitive coping strategies include information gathering, problem solving, reframing, self-navigation, internal conversations, and lists of activities and preferences, all of which can be enhanced by the expressive arts. Feen-Calligan et al. (2020) describe the different ways in which adolescent refugees coped through problem solving in their expressive arts therapy groups: hot glue was applied to leaky meditation jars, missing puppets were recreated, and new techniques were attempted. Reframing is also a critical aspect of this coping channel as it empowers individuals to shift their perspective and view challenging situations in a more positive light, ultimately reducing stress and enhancing adaptive responses (Beck 1979).

Physical Integration through Expressive Movement and Sport

Expressive somatic practices such as yoga, Tai chi, or DMT combine physical movement with emotional processing and creative techniques. Grasser et al. (2019) use expressive tactile objects such as parachutes and art creations in DMT to help anchor participants while they are given the opportunity to lead and follow movement, observe the movement of others, and be seen themselves. These structured movement experiences provide refugee adolescents with embodied ways to process trauma and build resilience through physical expression.

Integrative Cross-Modality Approaches

The strength of expressive arts therapy with refugee adolescents is the flexibility to integrate multiple modalities based on individual preferences, cultural backgrounds, and therapeutic needs. This integrative approach recognises that healing occurs through multiple pathways and that different expressive forms may resonate more strongly at different points in the therapeutic journey.

De-stigmatising mental health support-seeking together with its confusion with mental illness has been found to pose a significant barrier to those refugee adolescents who would likely benefit from psychological support. De Anstiss and Ziaian (2010) assert that expressive arts therapies can effectively address this stigma by offering a more inclusive and less intrusive approach to mental healthcare than that afforded by more conventional forms of talk therapy, while also respecting individual preferences for self-expression. Moreover, Knettel et al. (2023) documented clinician and academic perspectives that highlighted how trauma-informed and culturally responsive approaches to understanding stress and building resilience significantly contribute to reducing stigma.

The stigma associated with seeking psychological support has also led to expressive arts therapists seeking to engage with adolescent and adult refugees in diverse ways and in contexts that are often different from those found in regular practice. For the author, therapy sessions would often be preceded by engagement with the refugee adolescent accompanied by their carers (and an interpreter where needed – see Chapter 13) in a venue of their choice such as a park or a community space, to talk about how they could be supported given the difficulties associated with being uprooted and transplanted into a completely different culture. The word 'therapy' would never be used. Knettel et al. (2023) found that providing services in community settings and schools was likely to further reduce stigma.

Mapping out the Dutch context, Wertheim-Cahen (1998) describes the setting up of a 'drama course' with young male unaccompanied minors in a dilapidated community centre for the unemployed. He also details how sessions held in a Dutch reception centre for asylum seekers, which started as a simple drop-in session with an invitation to draw and paint, gradually evolved into a regular art therapy group where the asylum seekers used the art sessions to visualise, represent and process their past experiences together with their hopes and dreams for the future with an art therapist who could hold space while providing valuable insights into their thoughts and feelings.

Conclusions

By enhancing their own therapeutic modality with the expressive arts, clinicians can develop a more comprehensive and inclusive approach to trauma recovery where adolescent refugees have the opportunity to explore different avenues of expression based on their preferences, strengths, and therapeutic goals. This approach allows for a more personalised, holistic, and empowering healing journey which recognises and develops the resilience and creativity of adolescent refugees.

References

Abu Sway, R, Nashashibi, R, Salah, R and Schweiki, R. 2005. 'Expressive arts therapy – healing the traumatised: The Palestinian experience'. In D. Kalmanowitz, and B. Lloyd, *Art therapy and political violence: With art, without illusion,* 154–171. Routledge.

Adnams Jones, S. 2018. *Art-making with refugees and survivors.* Jessica Kingsley Publishers.

Archibald, L, Dewar, J. 2010. *Creative arts, culture and healing*: Building an evidence base. Aboriginal Healing Foundation.

Association for Dance Movement Psychotherapy UK. 2025. Association for Dance Movement Psychotherapy UK, 31 March. admp.org.uk

Baraitser, M. 2014. *Reading and expressive writing with traumatised children, young refugees and asylum seekers: Unpack my Heart with words.* Jessica Kingsley.

Beck, A.1979. *Cognitive therapy and the emotional disorders.* Meridian, Penguin Books.

Bolton, G, Field, V and Thompson, K. 2011. *Writing routes: A resource handbook of therapeutic writing.* Jessica Kingsley Publishers.

Browne, I 2008. *Music and madness.* Cork University Press.

Bunt, L and Stige, B. 2014. *Music therapy.* Routledge.

Callaghan, K. 1998. 'In limbo: Movement psychotherapy with refugees and asylum-seekers'. In D. Dokter, *Arts therapists, refugees and migrants: Reaching across Borders,* 25–41. Jessica Kingsley Publishers.

Case, C and Dalley, T R. 2023. *The* handbook *of* art *therapy,* 4th edn. Routledge.

Daniels Beck, B, Messel, C, Meyer , S, Cordtz, T, Sogaard, U, Simonsen, E, 2018 'Feasibility of trauma-focused guided imagery and music with adult refugees diagnosed with PTSD: A pilot study'. *Nordic Journal of Music Therapy,* 27(1), 67-86. doi: 10.1080/08098131.2017.1286368.

De Anstiss, H and Ziaian, Z. 2010. 'Mental health help-seeking and refugee adolescents: Qualitative findings from a mixed-methods investigation'. *Australian Psychologist*: 45(1), 29–37.

Degges-White, S. 2017. 'Introduction to the use of expressive arts in counselling'. In S. Degges-White and N. Davis, *Integrating the expressive arts into counseling practice; Theory-based interventions,* 1–7, 2nd edn. Springer Publishing Company.

DeMott, M. 2014. 'Breaking the silence: Expressive arts as testimony'. In G Overland, E Guribye and B Lie, *Nordic work with traumatised refugees: Do we really care?,* 192–201. Cambridge Scholars Publishing.

de Witt, M, da Silva Pinho, A, Stams, G, Moonen, X, Bros, A, Stams, G, Moonen, X, Bos, A, van Hooren, S. 2022. 'Music therapy for stress reduction: A systematic review and meta-analysis'. *Health Psychology Review,* 16(1), 134-159.

Dieterich-Hartwell, R and Koch, S. 2017. 'Creative arts therapies as temporary home for refugees: Insights from literature and practice'. *Behavioural Sciences, 69*: 1–11.

Elendu, C. 2024. 'The evolution of ancient healing practices: From Shamanism to Hippocratic medicine: A review'. *Medicine, 103*(28): 1–17. doi:10.1097/MD.0000000000039005

Elliott, D, Polman, R and McGregor, R. 2011. 'Relaxing music for anxiety control'. *Journal of Music Therapy, 48*(3): 264–288. doi:10.1093/jmt/48.3.264

Eltanamly, H, Leijten, P, van Rooij, F and Overbeek, G. 2019. 'Parenting in times of refuge: A qualitative investigation'. *Family Process, 61*: 1248–1263.

Fancourt, D and Finn, S. 2019. *What is the evidence on the role of the arts in improving health and well-being? A scoping review.* World Health Organisation. https://iris.who.int/handle/10665/329834.

Feen-Calligan, H, Grasser, L, Debryn, J, Nasser, S, Jackson, C, Seguin, D and Javanbakht, A. 2020. 'Art therapy with Syrian refugee youth in the United States: An intervention study'. *The Arts in Psychotherapy, 69*: 1–16.

Feniger-Schaal, R, & Orkibi, H. 2020. 'Integrative systematic review of drama therapy intervention research'. Psychology of Aesthetics, Creativity, and the Arts, 14(1), 68-80. doi.org/10.1037/aca0000257

Fitzpatrick, F. 2002. 'A search for home: The role of art therapy in understanding the experiences of Bosnian refugees in Western Australia'. *Art Therapy: Journal of the American Art Therapy Association, 19*(4): 151–158.

Fonagy, P. 2006. 'The mentalization-focused approach to social development'. In J Allen and P Fonagy, *Handbook of mentalization-based treatment,* 51–99. John Wiley and Sons Ltd.

Fondacaro, K, Mazzulla, E and Weldon, H. 2021. 'The chronic traumatic stress Treatment (CTS-T): A resilience-focused, culturally responsive intervention for refugees and survivors of torture – including a mobile and mental health application'. *Torture Journal, 31*(2): 110–125.

Forgas, J, Baumeister, R and Tice, D. 2015. 'The psychology of self-regulation: An introductory review'. In J Forgas, R Baumeister and D Tice, *Psychology of self-regulation,* 1–17. Routledge.

Geldard, K, Geldard, D and Yin Foo, R. 2019. *Counselling adolescents: The proactive approach.* Sage Publications Ltd.

Grasser, L, Al-Saghir, H, Wanna, C, Spinei, J and Javanbakht, A. 2019. 'Moving through the trauma: Dance/movement therapy as a somatic-based intervention for addressing trauma and stress among Syrian refugee children'. *Journal of the American Academy of Child and Adolescent Psychiatry, 58*(11): 1124–1126.

Gray, A and Fargnoli, A. 2022. 'Theoretical underpinnings of dance/movement therapy in the treatment of psychological trauma'. In R Dieterich-Hartwell and A Melsom, *Dance/ Movement therapy for trauma survivors,* 1–17. Routledge.

Harris, D. 2007. 'Dance/movement therapy approaches to fostering resilience and recovery among African adolescent torture survivors'. *Torture, 17*(2, 134–155.

Hayes, J. 2013. *Soul and spirit in dance movement psychotherapy: A transpersonal approach.* Jessica Kingsley Publishers.

Heynen, E, Bruls, V, van Goor, S, Pat-El, R. T, Schoot, T and van Hooren, S. 2022. 'A music therapy intervention for refugee children and adolescents in schools: A process evaluation using a mixed method design'. *Children, 9*(14): 1–21.

Horn, R, Ewart-Biggs, R, Hudson, F, Berilgen, S, Ironside, J and Prodromou, A. 2019. 'The role of a trauma-sensitive football group in the recovery of survivors of torture'. *Torture Journal, 29*(1): 97–109.

Hunt, M. 2005. 'Action research and music therapy: Group music therapy with young refugees in a school community'. *Voices: A World Forum for Music Therapy, 5*(2). doi:10.15845/voices.v5i2.223

Jalonen, A and Corte, P. 2018. *A practical guide to therapeutic work with asylum seekers and refugees.* Jessica Kingsley Publishers.

Jennings, S. 2010. *Healthy attachments and neuro-dramatic play.* Jessica Kingsley Publishers.

Jennings, S. 2018. *Theatre, ritual and transformation: The Senoi Temiars.* Routledge.

Jones, P. 2007. *Drama as therapy volume 1: Theory, practice and research.* 2nd edn. Routledge.

Jung, C. 1968. *Man and his symbols.* Dell Publishing.

Kalaf, L and Plante, P. 2019. 'The lived experience of young Syrian refugees with an expressive arts workshop about resilience'. *Canadian Art Therapy Association Journal,* *32*(1): 18–30. doi:10.1080/08322473.2019.1600895

King, J and Strang, C. 2022. *Art therapy and the neuroscience of trauma: Theoretical and practical perspectives.* Taylor & Francis.

Knettel, B, Oliver-Steinberg, A, Lee, M, Rusesin, H, Duke, N, Esmaili, E and Puffer, E. 2023. 'Clinician and academic perspectives on expressive arts therapy for refugee children and families: a qualitative study'. *International Journal of Migration, Health and Social Care, 19*(3/4): 260–272.

Lahad, M, Shachan, M and Ayalon, O. 2013. *The 'Basic Ph' model of coping and resiliency.* Jessica Kingsley.

Land, H. 2014. *Spirituality, religion and faith in psychotherapy: Evidence-based expressive methods for mind, brain and body.* Lyceum Books.

Linklater, R. 2014. *Decolonizing trauma work: Indigenous stories and strategies.* Fernwood Publishing.

Levine, P, Levine, E, 1999. Foundations of expressive arts therapy: Theoretical and clinical perspectives. Jessica Kingsley Publishers.

Levine, P. 2008. *Healing trauma. A pioneering programme for restoring the wisdom of your body.* Sounds True, Inc.

Levine, P. (Director). 2013. *Trauma and the unspoken voice of the body* [Motion Picture].

Levine, P. 2015. *Trauma and memory: Brain and body in a search for the living past: A practical guide for understanding and working with traumatic memory.*North Atlantic Books.

Malchiodi, C. 2011. 'Art therapy and the brain'. In C Malchodi, *Handbook of art therapy,* 17–26. Guilford Press.

Malchiodi, C. 2015.*Creative interventions with traumatized children,* 4th edn. The Guilford Press.

Malchiodi, C. 2020. 'Expressive arts therapy as self-regulatory and relational interventions with children and caregivers'. In J Mitchell, J Tucci and E Tronick, *The handbook of therapeutic care for children: Evidence-informed approaches to working with traumatised children and adolescents in foster, kinship and adoptive care,* 289–313. Jessica Kingsley Publishers.

Malchiodi, C. 2021. *Creative interventions with traumatised children,* 2nd edn. The Guilford Press.

Malchiodi, C. 2023. 'What is expressive arts therapy?' In C. Malchiodo, *Handbook of expressive arts therapy,* 153–569.s The Guilford Press.

Mallett, S. 2004. 'Understanding home: A critical review of the literature'. *Sociological Review, 52*: 62–89.

Mallon, T and Hoog Antink, M. 2021. 'The sound of lost homes – Introducing the COVER model – Theoretical framework and practical insight into music therapy with refugees and asylum-seekers'. *Voices: A World Forum for Music Therapy, 21*(2): 1–10.

Marshall, C. 2007. 'Cultural identity, creative processes and imagination: Creating cultural connections through art-making'. *Journal of Cultural Research in Art Education, 25*(1): 1–12.

Maté, G. 2019. *In the realm of hungry ghosts: Close encounters with addiction* (10th anniversary ed.). Scribe Publications.

Mohammadian, Y, Shahidi, S, Mahaki, B, Mohammadi, A, Baghban, A and Zayeri, F. 2011. 'Evaluating the use of poetry to reduce signs of depression, anxiety and stress in Iranian female students'. *The Arts in Psychotherapy, 38*(1): 59–63.

Momartin, S, Coello, M, Pittaway, E R D and Aroche, J. 2019. 'Caspoeira Angola: An alternative intervention programme for traumatised refugees from war-torn countries'. *Torture, 29*(1), 85–96.

Palit, M and Levin, S. 2016. 'Collaborative therapy with women and children refugees in houston: Moving toward rehabilitation in the United States after enduring the atrocities of war'. In L Charles and G Samarasinghe, *Family therapy in global humanitarian contexts*, 38–50. Springer.

Papadopoulos, R. 2002. 'Refugees, home and trauma'. In R Papadopoulos, *Therapeutic care for refugees. No place like home*, 9–40. Karnac.

Pardeck, J and Pardeck, J. 2021. *Bibliotherapy: A clinical approach for helping children.* Routledge.

Pennebaker, J. 2014. *Expressive writing: Words that heal.* Idyll Arbor Inc.

Porges, S. 2011. *The polyvagel theory: Neurophysiological foundations of emotions, attachment, communication and self-regulation.* W W Norton and Company.

Prendiville, E. 2017. 'Neurobiology for psychotherapists'. In E Prendiville and J Howard, *Creative psychotherapy: Applying the principles of neurobiology to play and expressive-arts-based practice*, 7–21. Routledge.

Richardson, C 2016. *Expressive arts therapy for traumatised children and adolescents.* Routledge.

Purser, A. 2019. 'Dancing intercorporeality: A health humanities perspective on dance as a healing art'. *Journal of Medical Humanities, 40*, 253–263. doi:10.1007/s10912-017-9502-0

Rappaport, L. 2014. 'Mindfulness and the arts therapies: Overview and roots'. In L. Rappaport, *Mindfulness and the arts therapies: Theory and practice*, 24–38. Jessica Kingsley Publishers.

Rousseau, C, Gauthier, M.-F, Lacroix, L, Alain, N, Benoit, M, Moran, A, ... Bourassa, D. 2005. 'Playing with identities and transforming shared realities'. *The Arts in Psychotherapy, 32*: 13–27.

Rowe, C, Watson-Ormond, R, English, L, Rubesin, M. H, Marshall, A, Linton, K, ... Eng, E. 2017. Evaluating art therapy to heal the effects of trauma among refugee youth: The Burma art therapy program sEvaluation. *Health Promotion through Arts and Gardening, 18*(1): 26–33. doi:10.1177/1524839915626413

Schore, A. 2012. *The science of the art of psychotherapy.* W W Norton and Company.

Siegel, D. 2010. Mindsight: *Transform your brain with the new science of kindness.* Oneworld.

Sunderland, M. 2012. *Bothered: Helping teenagers talk about their feelings.* Taylor and Francis.

Sunderland, M. 2018. *Draw on your Emotions.* Routledge.

Sunderland, M. 2019. *Draw on your relationships: Creative ways to understand and work through important relationship issues*, 2nd edn. Routledge.

Sunderland, M. 2022a. *Helping children with Loss a guidebook.* Routledge.

Sunderland, M. 2022b. *The day the sea went out and never came back.* Routledge.

Taylor, H. 2013. 'Refugees, the state and the concept of home'. *Refugee , 32*(2), *Survey Quarterly* 130–152.

Thaut, M. 2013. *Rhythm music and the brain.* Taylor & Francis Ltd.

Vacchelli, E. 2018. 'Embodiment in qualitative research: Collage making with migrant, refugee and asylum seeking women'. *Qualitative Research, 18*(2): 171–190.

van der Kolk, B. 2015. *The body keeps the score: Mind, brain and body in the transformation of trauma.* Penguin.

Wang, Z, Jiang, B, Wang, X, Li, Z, Wang, D, Xue, H and Wang, D. 2023. 'Relationship between physical activity and individual mental health after traumatic events: A systematic review'. *European Journal of Psychotraumatology*:1–15. doi:10.1080/2000 8066.7023.2205667

Wertheim-Cahen, T. 1998. 'Art Therapy with asylum seekers: Humanitarian relief'. In D Dokter, *Arts therapists, refugees and migrants: Reaching across borders*, 41–62. Jessica Kingsley Publishers.

Wilczynska, D, Lysak-Radomska, A, Podczarska-Glowacka, M, Zajt, J, Dornowski, M and Skonieczny, Py. 2019. 'Evaluation of the effectiveness of relaxation in lowering the level of anxiety in young adults —a pilot study'. *International Journal of Occupational Medicine and Environmental Health, 32*(6): 17–824.

Womack, M. 2010. *The anthropology of health and healing.* AltaMira Press.

Zubala, A, Kennell, N and Hackett, S. 2021. 'Art therapy in the digital world: An integrative review of current practice and future directions'. *Frontiers in Psychology*: 1–20. doi:10.3389/fpsyg.2021.600070

Zwart, M and Nieuwenhuis, L. 1998. 'Mourning rituals in non-verbal therapy with traumatised refugees'. In D Dokter, *Arts therapists, refugees and migrants: Reaching across borders,* 1189. Jessica Kingsley Publishers.

Chapter 6

Integrating the Expressive Arts into Non-Clinical Psychosocial Support for Adolescent Refugees

Introduction

The power of expressive arts extends across numerous contexts, offering valuable tools for a wide range of professionals working with adolescent refugees. Social workers, educators, healthcare providers, and community workers – as well as psychotherapists – can harness these creative approaches to address fundamental psychosocial needs that transcend age, gender, and cultural boundaries. The universal language of creativity enables all professionals who support refugee adolescents to contribute meaningfully to their wellbeing. While I refer to approaches developed by others as 'interventions' throughout this chapter to maintain consistency with their original terminology, I personally conceptualise my own work with refugee adolescents as a collaborative, relational process rather than an intervention. This perspective recognises the agency and active participation of young people in their own healing journeys.

This chapter synthesises research on how professionals, as part of adolescent refugee mesosystems, can integrate expressive arts into their practice to address key psychosocial needs, including:

- being empathetic and validating emotions;
- modelling and practising self-regulating techniques;
- developing coping skills and resilience-building strategies;
- encouraging and facilitating opportunities for social connection;
- recognising and respecting adolescent refugee identities, cultures, and backgrounds;
- creating environments that prioritise psychological and physical safety and security;
- empowering adolescent refugees to make choices and participate in decision-making processes; and
- encouraging activities that provide a sense of meaning, purpose, and fulfilment.

Using these needs as an organising framework, we will explore both manualised and non-manualised expressive arts approaches that have been developed for

DOI: 10.4324/9781003430032-7

group settings, followed by applications for individual practice. While profession-als in non-clinical roles cannot provide therapy, they can effectively support refu-gee adolescents through creative approaches that develop nurturing connections, model self-regulation strategies, and bear witness to their stories. Such focused approaches align closely with the key therapeutic skills and principles of trauma-informed practice detailed in Chapter 4.

Additionally, these professionals play a crucial role in facilitating referrals to clinical services and directing adolescent refugees to available mental health resources and community supports when needed. The following sections will examine specific evidence-based programmes, practical implementation strate-gies, and illustrative examples that demonstrate the versatility and accessibility of expressive arts approaches across diverse settings.

Understanding the current research landscape on psychological support for adolescent refugees is essential before exploring specific frameworks. Examining the evidence base contextualises the chapter's approaches and highlights knowl-edge gaps. This assessment aids practitioners in making informed decisions about the most effective approaches for their contexts while acknowledging our current understanding's limitations. Acknowledging the strengths and weak-nesses of existing literature allows us to approach the following frameworks with context, recognising where evidence exists and where practice exceeds research.

Research Context and Gaps

A significant scoping review by Moutsou et al. (2023) on interventions for unac-companied minor refugees highlighted the efficacy of psychotherapy for address-ing trauma and mental health issues, while noting a substantial research gap in psychosocial interventions. This gap is particularly concerning because psychoso-cial support, which focuses broadly on wellbeing, empowerment, social integra-tion, and practical needs, aligns more closely with refugee adolescents' expressed priorities and can be delivered by a wider range of professionals across various settings.

My own comprehensive review of major academic databases (PsychINFO, ERIC, MEDLINE) confirms this research deficit, particularly regarding the use of expressive arts in one-to-one psychosocial interventions with individual adoles-cent refugees. This significant limitation affects our understanding of how these approaches can be effectively applied in individual support contexts, even as group-based interventions show promising results.

Given these limitations in the evidence base, this chapter primarily examines group-based expressive arts interventions implemented across various settings, while also exploring potential individual applications through the experiences of Chima and Natalia. These composite narratives, introduced in Chapter 1 and developed through Chapters 2–5, offer valuable contextual insights for profession-als working in individual settings. While not directly addressing the research gap, these examples serve as a bridge to the more detailed case studies presented in Chapters 8–12.

This dearth of empirical evidence underscores both the significance of this book's contributions and the urgent need for rigorous studies on non-clinical, individualised expressive arts interventions with refugee adolescents. Future research in this area would not only fill a crucial literature gap, but also better inform evidence-based practices, potentially enhancing the efficacy of psychosocial support for this population.

Frameworks for Delivering Expressive Arts-Based Psychosocial Support

We now examine the main frameworks for delivering expressive arts-based psychosocial support to refugee adolescents. These frameworks offer guidance for implementation while allowing adaptation to various contexts and needs.

Psychosocial support frameworks for refugee adolescents range from highly structured to flexible approaches. Standardised interventions with prescribed content, activities, and guidelines are called manualised approaches. Some adaptable frameworks offer general principles and activities while encouraging practitioners to customise content for participants' specific needs and cultural contexts.

Several key considerations influence the selection of an appropriate framework:

(1) **Cultural appropriateness:** Frameworks must be culturally responsive to the diverse backgrounds of refugee adolescents. This may require adaptation of activities, metaphors, and examples to ensure that they resonate with participants' cultural experiences.
(2) **Setting and resources:** Implementation settings vary widely from schools and reception centres to community spaces and healthcare facilities. Each setting presents unique opportunities and constraints that influence which framework can be used effectively.
(3) **Provider expertise:** The training, skills and professional background of facilitators determine which frameworks they can effectively implement. Some approaches require specialised training, while others can be delivered by professionals with basic psychosocial support skills.
(4) **Phase of displacement:** frameworks may be more appropriate depending on whether adolescents are in acute crisis, early resettlement, or longer-term integration phases.
(5) **Scalability needs:** In contexts with large numbers of refugee adolescents, frameworks that can be efficiently scaled while maintaining effectiveness become particularly valuable.

These key considerations directly influence which intervention approach might be most suitable in a particular context. With these factors in mind, we can now examine specific interventions along the continuum from highly structured to more flexible frameworks. We begin with manualised interventions, which offer stand-ardised protocols and detailed implementation guidance, making them particularly valuable in contexts requiring consistency across multiple providers or settings. Following this, we will explore non-manualised approaches that provide greater flexibility for adaptation to specific cultural contexts and individual needs. By understanding both approaches, practitioners can make informed decisions about which interventions might best address the unique circumstances of the adolescent refugees they support, while working within their own professional capacity and setting constraints.

Common Theoretical Foundations

Several key theoretical frameworks appear consistently across many of the approaches discussed in this chapter. Understanding these foundational models provides important context for the specific approaches that follow:

1. **Herman's Triphasic Model of Trauma Recovery:** Developed by Judith Herman (1992), this model outlines three stages in trauma recovery: safety and stabilisation, remembrance and mourning, and reconnection. Many approaches, particularly EXIT and aspects of TRT, explicitly focus on the initial safety stage, recognising that establishing psychological safety and building emotional regulation skills must precede any deeper trauma processing.
2. **Ecological Systems Perspectives:** Bronfenbrenner's bioecological theory (Bronfenbrenner and Morris 2006) informs several interventions, including the Tree of Life and Yohani's hope-focused visual arts project. This perspective recognises that adolescent development and healing occur within inter-connected social systems and relationships.
3. **Narrative Approaches:** Interventions like Tree of Life and Writing for Recovery draw on narrative practices that help refugee adolescents external-ise, reframe, and integrate difficult experiences. These approaches emphasise the power of storytelling in making meaning of experiences and reclaiming personal agency.
4. **Perry's Stress Attunement Model:** Bruce Perry's approach (Perry and Szalavitz 2006) emphasises creating safe emotional spaces, managing stress-ors, and establishing healthy relationships as foundations for healing from trauma. This model informs the Advancing Adolescents programme, which focuses on activities that promote emotional regulation, social connection, and safety within community settings.

Each intervention draws on one or more of these theoretical frameworks, adapt-ing and applying them in ways appropriate to different contexts, cultures, and delivery methods. The frameworks discussed in this chapter have been selected for their appropriateness for non-clinical professionals working with refugee ado-lescents. They incorporate expressive arts elements while remaining accessible to professionals from diverse disciplines, including education, social work, and community development. While some clinical elements may be present, these frameworks can be implemented without clinical expertise when appropriate training and supervision are provided.

Manualised Interventions

Manualised psychosocial interventions, central to evidence-based practice, provide standardised frameworks that ensure reliability, validity, and measurable outcomes, making them central to evidence-based practice with refugee adolescents (Truijens et al. 2017). These interventions typically include materials guiding practitioners through therapeutic content and implementation processes (Urnes-Johnson et al. 2016). While some critiques have raised concerns about flexibility and responsiveness to individual differences (Hamilton et al. 2008; Hauke et al. 2014), research increasingly demonstrates that individual needs can be effectively addressed within group settings through what Kendall and Beidas (2007) term the 'flexibility within fidelity principle,' where personalisation occurs within a consistent framework.

Such approaches can be implemented in two ways: through a structured protocol that follows prescribed activities in a specific sequence or in a more flexible way that allows practitioners to select from a menu of activities while maintaining core principles. The choice of implementation approach ultimately depends on the goals, available resources, and preferences of both practitioners and participants.

Table 6.1 presents key manualised interventions suitable for non-clinical professionals working with refugee adolescent groups, and Table 6.2 maps each of these interventions to their primary theoretical frameworks, illustrating how different approaches draw on common theoretical foundations while implementing them in distinct ways. These interventions were identified through a comprehensive review of electronic databases, including PsycARTICLES, PsycINFO, ERIC, Social Science Database, Medline, PubMed, and Proquest. Following the tables, detailed descriptions of each approach are provided, including their theoretical foundations, implementation requirements, and evidence of effectiveness. These interventions have been organised into three categories based on their primary therapeutic approach: trauma-focused interventions, creative-expression interventions, and community-building interventions.

To further understand the theoretical underpinnings of these approaches, Table 6.2 maps each approach to its primary theoretical frameworks. This mapping illustrates how different approaches draw on common theoretical foundations while implementing them in distinct ways.

Teaching Recovery Techniques (TRT)

The TRT community intervention deliverable by non-specialists was developed by The Children and War Foundation, based in the UK and Norway, as a response to the Bosnian War in the 1990s (Yule et al. 2013). TRT is a group-based, psychosocial

Table 6.1 Manualised interventions for practitioners working with groups of refugee adolescents

Intervention	Developer	Primary approach	Target population	Access information
Teaching Recovery Techniques (TRT)	Children and War Foundation	Trauma-focused	Children and adolescents (8+)	Available after training https://childrenandwar-uk.org/
Writing for Recovery	Children and War Foundation	Trauma-focused	Adolescents and young adults	Available through Children and War Foundation https://childrenandwar-uk.org/
Expressive Arts in Transition (EXIT)	Meyer-Demott et al. (2017)	Creative expression	Adolescents and young adults	Available through the Norwegian Institute for Expressive Arts https://eng.nordicsah.com/courses
Tree of Life	Ncube and Denborough (2007)	Community-building	Children adolescents and adults	Available through Dulwich Centre Foundation https://dulwichcentre.com.au/the-tree-of-life/
Plurality Theatre	Canadian team of school, community and health professionals	Creative expression	Secondary School students	Available through the Refugees Well School… .https://refugeeswellschool.org/
Advancing Adolescents	Mercy Corps	Community-building	Adolescents in crises	Available through Mercy Humanitarian Corps https://www.mercycorps.org/
Capacitar	Cane (2016)	Mind-body healing	Children adolescents and adults	Available through Capacitar International https://capacitar.org/

Source: Author's own elaboration.

Table 6.2 Theoretical frameworks informing manualised interventions

Intervention	Herman's Triphasic Model	Ecological systems	Narrative approaches	Perry's Stress Attunement
TRT Writing for Recovery	✓		✓	
EXIT	✓			
Tree of Life		✓	✓	
Advancing Adolescents				✓
Plurality Theatre		✓	✓	
Capacitar		✓	✓	✓

Source: Author's own elaboration.

approach rooted in trauma-focused Cognitive Behaviour Therapy (CBT) principles which is designed to be delivered as five two-hour group sessions.

The primary aim of TRT is to help children and adolescents understand trauma, cope with loss, and learn strategies to manage post-traumatic stress symptoms such as intrusive memories, hyperarousal, and avoidance. A variety of techniques are employed, including the normalisation of stress reactions, psychoeducation, symbolic and dream work, relaxation techniques, and exposure exercises.

Following preliminary training (see Children and War UK 2024), the TRT intervention is intended for use by 'non-specialist' teachers, youth workers, community leaders, and other professionals supporting these young people, as well as psychologists and psychotherapists (Smith et al. 2023). It has been implemented in a variety of low-, middle-, and high-income countries (as classified by The World Bank 2024). As of March 2025, TRT has been implemented in the following countries: UK, Norway, Sweden, Australia, Canada, Finland, Ireland, Jordan, Kenya, Lebanon, Nepal, Palestine, South Africa, Thailand, and Uganda. The manual is subject to constant revision in response to feedback from its users.

Evaluation data published in peer-reviewed journals show positive results in a variety of settings (Smith et al. 2023). Reductions in post-intervention post-traumatic stress scores were found after the TRT programme was delivered to Palestinian children living in Gaza and the West Bank (Barron et al. 2013, 2016), and to Syrian children living in Jordan and Lebanon (El-Khani et al. 2021). Interestingly, Alzaghoul et al. (2022) found that adding a parenting component to TRT interventions led to the most enduring mental health improvements for children and adolescents displaced to low- and middle-income countries and territories in the Middle East (El-Khani et al. 2021).

Adolescents displaced by war who flee to countries classified as higher income such as Norway (Solhaug et al. 2023) and Sweden (Sarkadi et al. 2018) have also benefited from the intervention. An important finding from the study of Solhaug et al. (2023) was that life satisfaction only significantly increased from pre- to post-intervention, for youth with successful asylum applications. There was no increase for those whose application had been rejected or who were still awaiting a decision. The authors concluded that TRT initiatives should consider the asylum process stage reached by individuals because harsh immigration policies could overburden their coping capacity. The manual was therefore revised to include asylum-seeking-related stressors.

The effectiveness of TRT input *during* the chaos of war has also been documented, as the Russian invasion of Ukraine in February 2022 prompted the provision of mental health input in the form of trauma management, to Ukrainian children and young people aged 7–23 years (Yavna et al. 2024). TRT had already been introduced and formally approved in Ukraine in 2014 after the first Russian invasion. Rapid facilitator cascade training, where a small group of trained facilitators trained others in the same role, ensured the delivery of TRT either in person in Ukraine or online to Ukrainian children and adolescents who had been displaced to 26 different countries. This was the largest documented delivery of TRT during an ongoing war which demonstrated that it could be rapidly upscaled in response to such a crisis (Yavna et al. 2024). Similar to the EXIT programme that will be discussed later, TRT prioritises establishing safety and building emotional regulation skills before addressing deeper trauma processing, reflecting the influence of Herman's Triphasic Model on both interventions.

Writing for Recovery

The 'Writing for Recovery' intervention supports children and adolescents who have experienced trauma and loss from wars or disasters. Its framework is based on James Pennebaker's research showing that writing about thoughts and feelings related to trauma positively affects biological, psychological, and behavioural processes (Pennebaker and Ferrell 2013). This activity helps construct a narrative and encourages participants to shift focus from their trauma (Ruini and Mortara 2022). This has been found to lead to subtle improvements in working memory (Yogo and Fujihara 2008) and academic performance (Pennebaker and Chung 2006). Additionally, Slatcher and Pennebaker (2006) discovered that expressive writing could result in small but measurable improvements in social interactions, such as increased talking, laughter, and social engagement in the months after the intervention (Slatcher and Pennebaker 2006).

This intervention can be administered individually or in groups of up to 50 participants. It typically takes place over three consecutive days, often in school settings. Each day includes two 15-minute sessions which progress from unstructured writing about personal feelings and thoughts related to the traumatic experience to structured writing where participants are asked to imagine offering advice to a person in a similar situation. The final task involves reflecting from a future perspective where participants are asked to imagine looking back after 10 years and to reflect on what they think they are likely to have learned from the experience.

Participants are assured that their responses will be anonymous, confidential, and free from judgement. They are told they will not receive feedback on their writing and, at the end of each day, they can submit their work in a box for researchers to analyse, though this is not copulsory.

Kalantari et al. (2012) found that this brief intervention alleviated symptoms of traumatic grief at the post-test stage among 12- to 18-year-old Afghan war-bereaved refugees forcibly displaced to Iran. Unfortunately, the planned six-month follow-up in this study was not feasible due to the unpredictable and inconsistent circumstances of the participants.

Expressive Arts in Transition (EXIT)

The manualised EXIT early intervention mental health and wellbeing programme was developed by Melinda Meyer-DeMott, Director and Co-founder of the Norwegian Institute for Expressive Arts (Nikut 2024). Meyer-DeMott first used this programme with new arrivals to a refugee reception centre in Norway in 1991 (Norwegian Centre for Violence and Traumatic Stress Studies 2020). Like the TRT programme discussed earlier, EXIT draws on Herman's Triphasic Model of Trauma Recovery, with both interventions emphasising the crucial first stage of establishing psychological safety before deeper trauma work can begin.

EXIT focuses specifically on the first stage of establishing safety. The programme prioritises building psychological safety, emotional regulation skills and providing trauma psychoeducation for new arrivals. The inclusion of specific training for non-clinician facilitators such as teachers, humanitarian workers, and community leaders involves learning how to conduct activities that support trauma recovery and promote resilience without embarking upon in-depth trauma processing, which is the domain of clinically trained professionals.

Meyer-Demott et al. (2017) evaluated EXIT by assigning 145 unaccompanied refugee boys, aged 15 to 18, in Norway to 10 sessions of expressive arts (EXIT) or a life as usual (LAU) control group over five weeks. The LAU group was offered activities to ensure they benefitted from the process. Both groups were assessed initially and four times over 25 months using instruments for post-traumatic stress symptoms. The EXIT group reported improved stress management and fewer trauma-related symptoms. Without psychoeducation for the EXIT group, the LAU group likely lacked the knowledge to manage post-traumatic stress symptoms.

Advancing Adolescents

Founded in 1979, Mercy Corps is a global humanitarian and development organisation that seeks to alleviate suffering, poverty, and oppression by empowering individuals and communities in some of the world's most challenging regions (Mercy Corps 2024a).

Their 'Advancing Adolescents' programme, which can be delivered by non-clinicians, consists of 16 sessions over 8 weeks. This programme is a community-based, psychosocial intervention designed for refugee and host community adolescents in humanitarian crises. It implements Perry's stress attunement approach (see Common Theoretical Foundations, Chapter 6) through practical activities that create safe emotional spaces, manage stressors, and establish healthy relationships. The emphasis on creating safe emotional spaces and building healthy relationships found in Advancing Adolescents reflects similar priorities seen in EXIT and TRT, though approached through Perry's stress attunement framework rather than Herman's Triphasic Model. Male and female volunteers from the local area are trained to serve as instructors, facilitators, mentors, and animators on the programme.

The Advancing Adolescents programme features the following three crucial elements to support adolescent adjustment in complex emergency contexts:

(1) the establishment of a 'safe space' within the community as a base for activities and protection;
(2) the facilitation of social support and self-expression; and;
(3) the implementation of group-based activities.

Sessions are open to groups of 8–15 adolescents, matched by age and gender. Participants can choose from various modalities, including fitness activities (nature walks, football), arts and crafts (sewing, graphic design, photography, singing, folklore, drama, theatre), vocational skills (hairdressing, beautician training), and technical skills (computer repairs, English language, first aid).

Panter-Brick et al. (2020) developed a toolkit for the interdisciplinary evaluation of the 'Advancing Adolescents' programme and identified sustained benefits on self-reported insecurity, stress, and mental health. They created a reliable, culturally relevant measure of resilience, tested cognitive skills, and found that cortisol levels, as a biomarker of chronic stress, decreased by one-third after the intervention. The use of these stress biomarkers provided compelling evidence that mental health and psychosocial interventions could regulate physiological stress as well as improve self-reported mental health and wellbeing. Mercy Corps (2024b) provides detailed evaluations of this programme conducted in Lebanon, Jordan, and Syria.

Tree of Life Psychosocial Support Tool

As noted in Table 6.1, the Tree of Life represents a widely implemented, community-building approach for diverse populations. This intervention has rich historical roots, tracing back to a training handbook for community workers developed by Anne Hope and Sally Timmel in 1984. The approach was further refined through collaboration between the Regional Psychosocial Support Initiatives (REPSSI 2022) and the Dulwich Centre Foundation in Australia, adapting it specifically for work with vulnerable populations. This approach has been found to be particularly beneficial for refugee adolescent populations (Stark et al. 2019).

Theoretically anchored in narrative practices, the Tree of Life employs metaphor to externalise personal stories, allowing participants to view their experiences from a reflective distance. This approach aligns with storytelling traditions common in many refugee adolescent cultures, while providing a framework that helps participants avoid feeling overwhelmed or defined by potentially traumatic narratives (Stiles et al. 2021). By using visual metaphor, the intervention creates space for diverse cultural viewpoints and interpretations (see Chapter 3).

The tree metaphor serves as a powerful organising concept, with each part representing different aspects of participants' lives. This metaphorical structure mirrors Bronfenbrenner's ecological systems theory explored in Chapter 1, reflecting the complex interrelationships between individuals and their environments. Just as trees function symbiotically within broader ecosystems, the metaphor helps participants visualise their connections to family, community, and culture.

Implementation Process

The Tree of Life unfolds through a structured four-part process. In the first part, participants create their personal trees with specific elements representing different aspects of their lives. As White (2006) explains, this creates a different 'territory of identity' or a 'safe place to stand' where the child or adolescent can look out at their life and reflect upon what they have been through.

Roots: Cultural and social backgrounds, including place of origin, ancestry, mentors, religious affiliations, and treasured songs (Hughes 2014).
Ground: Present circumstances such as residence and current activities (Stiles et al. 2021).
Trunk: Strengths and abilities, often identified through others' observations and stories about skill development (Azarova et al. 2018).
Branches: Hopes and dreams for the future.
Leaves: Names of significant individuals from the past and present (Stark et al. 2019).
Fruits: Gifts received, including expressions of kindness, care, or love.

The second part 'thickens individual stories by connecting all trees into a forest, allowing participants to reflect on each other's representations and serve as "outsider witnesses"' (Walther and Fox 2012). This process transforms narratives from stories of loss and trauma into accounts of strength, resilience, and cultural connection. The third part, 'when the storms come,' addresses current challenges collectively, while the final part culminates in a celebration ceremony where participants receive certificates acknowledging their qualities, attributes, and hopes.

The certificate presented to each participant records the specific qualities appreciated by each individual, the attributes which made them proud or valued by others, and their hopes and dreams for the future. The process should con-clude with a discussion about the future of the trees – for example, whether they should be part of an exhibition or if each participant would prefer to take them home. Similar to the Plurality Theatre intervention discussed next, the Tree of Life shares a foundation in narrative approaches and ecological systems theory, with both interventions creating safe spaces for storytelling and meaning making within a group context.

Evidence and Adaptability

Johnson (2022) highlights the Tree of Life's effectiveness in enhancing feelings of belonging among refugee children and adolescents in host countries. Originally developed for clinical settings, the approach was quickly recognised as valuable for non-clinical applications, leading to training programmes for faith leaders, teachers, NGO staff, youth workers, and others offering psychosocial support in group settings (Dulwich Centre Foundation 2024).

The case study of Daahir presented in Chapter 8 provides a practical illustration of this intervention's implementation and impact, demonstrating how the meta-phorical framework supports identity development and community integration. REPSSI (2016) offers a comprehensive workshop methodology guide for profes-sionals working with adolescent refugees as part of their Psychosocial Wellbeing Series.

Plurality Theatre

Classroom-based drama workshops are emerging as an effective non-clinical inter-vention for the promotion of positive mental health among refugees in educational settings (Spaas et al. 2023). Whereas drama therapy is intentional and focuses on a specific issue within a trusting relationship with the therapist (see Chapter 5), the playful nature of drama in a group workshop format lends itself well to the provi-sion of non-clinical psychosocial support to adolescents by expanding experiences, transforming realities and stimulating the imagination (Jennings 2010).

The Plurality Theatre programme developed by a Canadian team of school, community, and health professionals is intended for secondary school teachers and other professionals interested in engaging in creative expression with refu-gee and immigrant adolescents (Equipe Théâtre Pluralité d'Erit 2010). It aims to help develop relationships, refine negotiation skills, and normalise emotional expression.

The workshop consists of 90-minute sessions delivered once weekly for 9 weeks and covers future, family, prejudices, bullying, and racism. This intervention has been widely implemented but evaluated in only a few studies (e.g. Dahne et al. 2024; Spaas et al. 2023). Plurality Theatre, like the Tree of Life intervention, uses creative expression to foster social connections and belonging through collective narrative building.

In their qualitative evaluation of the ways in which Plurality Theatre workshops can build social capital for newly arrived refugee adolescents in Denmark, Dahne et al. (2024) draw on Schaefer-McDaniel's (2024) framework for conceptualising youth social capital through social networks, sociability, trust, reciprocity, and a sense of belonging. Focus groups with adolescent participants, interviews with educators, and reflections from the workshop team revealed that for most participants the workshops fostered trust and improved social relations – key facets of bonding social capital, although caution was needed to ensure participants' emotional wellbeing.

Participants valued the workshops' emancipatory and safe environment, which created social spaces for storytelling, bearing witness, agency building, and enjoyment. Similar positive outcomes were observed in the group-based randomised study carried out by Spaas et al. (2023). The study compared classroom drama and 'Welcome to School' interventions, with the former being found to significantly enhance peer relations and social support.

Non-Manualised Expressive Art Interventions

In addition to the manualised interventions, several single case studies have evaluated impactful non-clinical psychosocial expressive arts interventions with refugee adolescents that have been implemented in educational and community settings. Yohani (2008) documents an inclusive and accessible community-based visual arts project framed by Bronfenbrenner's bioecological theory (Bronfenbrenner and Morris 2006) and delivered by non-clinicians. This project created social ecologies of hope for refugee children and adolescents in Canada through a ten-session after-school programme led by trained staff providing psychoeducational support via visual arts activities. The goal was to create a safe and nurturing environment to support hopeful healing, growth, and acculturation in the host society.

Children and adolescents explored, enhanced, and shared their sense of hope through collage, drawing, painting, photography, and the creation of a story quilt. Participants used disposable cameras to capture images of hope, and the project was evaluated through group and individual photo-assisted interviews. This camera activity served as a therapeutic tool, helping participants articulate their stories of hope. The evaluation emphasised the value of creative non-clinical approaches to share experiences of hope in the participants' social ecologies.

Also developed in Canada, the Open Studio Project is a community-based arts initiative which is aimed at supporting refugee youth to navigate social and cultural integration (Lewis et al. 2018). The Open Studio is structured around seven simple parameters: a focus on intentional art-making, non-judgemental commentary, non-evaluative feedback, voluntary participation, witnessing, sharing, and facilitator participation. The project ran weekly for 2.5 hours over a 16-week period in an after-school community setting. The content emphasised refugee experiences and ideas of belonging through art-making and reflective journaling. Sessions were loosely structured, featuring a weekly core project while also providing materials for personal creativity. Projects included group and individual mosaics, lantern making, still-life drawing, printmaking, papier maché bowls, knitting, and crochet circles.

The project's impact on participants was evaluated using semi-structured interviews, a focus group, and visual arts created by them, ensuring their experiences were expressed verbally, interactively, and visually. Themes of belonging, welcome, connection, and anxiety-free learning emerged from evaluating participants' Open Studio experiences. These themes align with the four Crucial 'C's framework by Bettner and Lew (1990): *Counting* (inclusion), *Competencies* (art-making and leadership skills from refugee youth hosting workshops), *Courage* (risk-taking in school art exhibitions), and *Connections* (new friendships), which supports the psychological and emotional development of children and adolescents.

While these non-manualised group interventions demonstrate the potential of expressive arts in community and educational settings, it is equally important to consider how these approaches can be adapted for individual interactions. The following examples, drawn from the experiences of our composite characters Chima and Natalia, illustrate how simple expressive arts and sensory tools can be effectively integrated into one-on-one interactions with adolescent refugees, such as initial meetings or intake processes.

Individual Practice Possibilities: Chima and Natalia's Experiences as Foundational Narratives for the Case Studies

Chima and Natalia's stories, drawn from clinical case notes, serve as a foundation for both actual and aspirational practice scenarios across multiple service providers. These narratives illustrate the potential for integrating expressive arts into diverse organisational settings. By presenting practices which are easy to engage with, I aim to inspire and guide professionals across different settings to consider adopting and adapting expressive arts approaches for individual work with adolescent refugees.

Chima's arrival as an unaccompanied minor at the port in his destination country was marked by intense anxiety, heightened by the sight of uniformed immigration officers which triggered memories of abuse by security forces in his home country. Contrary to his expectations, Chima found himself in a comfortable and welcoming interview room with soft furnishings and warm lighting. The trauma-informed immigration officer, recognising Chima's distress, reassured him of his safety and quickly recognised the need for grounding techniques. With the help of the interpreter and a simple visual shared via an iPad (also provided to Chima in printed form), the officer guided Chima through the 7/11 breathing exercise (detailed and illustrated in Chapter 8). This straightforward yet effective intervention demonstrates how supportive practices can be implemented in formal settings to alleviate distress and foster a trauma-informed environment.

During Chima's first meeting with his social care worker, Ellen, he was pre-sented with a basket of fidget toys and sensory objects, including playdough. Chima recalls being particularly drawn to the playdough, finding comfort in its softness, pliability, and distinctive smell. The yellow playdough held special significance for him, as it was his aunt's favourite colour and evoked positive memories of her warm presence in his life.

Similarly, when Natalia and her mother arrived at the support hub in the host country, their intake interview room was equipped with an array of expressive arts materials. These included marker pens, paper, crayons, and colouring pencils, as well as baskets of sensory items resembling those offered to Chima by Ellen. Natalia, who had always found doodling to be calming during anxious moments, was offered a Mandala colouring sheet by the support worker. She recalled feeling relieved to have something to occupy her hands and soothe her anxiety during the questioning process.

In both Natalia's and Chima's cases, the professionals engaged with the materials themselves at the start, implicitly giving permission and encouraging the young refugees to do the same. This strategy helped create a more relaxed atmosphere in what were potentially very stressful situations. These instances illustrate how simple, yet thoughtful, collaborative activities can significantly impact the comfort and emotional wellbeing of adolescent refugees in various institutional settings. By incorporating expressive arts and sensory elements into their practice, profes-sionals can create more supportive and trauma-informed environments, facilitating better communication and trust-building.

While these examples focus on initial encounters, it is important to note that such expressive arts and sensory activities can be effectively integrated into mul-tiple one-to-one scenarios throughout the support process for adolescent refugees. These tools offer transformative potential across all settings, proving especially beneficial in formal or potentially intimidating environments where their calming influence can be notably impactful. Chapter 7 presents a six-stage framework for healing and supporting adolescent refugees, with expressive arts at its core. This comprehensive framework details how different professionals can contribute to the healing process. Chapters 8–12 will expand significantly on the introductory exam-ples included here, providing in-depth case studies and offering practical examples of how to implement these expressive arts activities across diverse strategies and settings of refugee support.

Conclusions

The integration of expressive arts into psychosocial support for adolescent refugees offers powerful and accessible approaches for practitioners across diverse profes-sional contexts. This chapter has explored both manualised and non-manualised interventions that could be effectively implemented by non-clinical professionals to address the fundamental psychosocial needs of refugee adolescents in group and individual settings.

Key Takeaways for Practice

Accessibility and Adaptability

Expressive arts approaches can be adapted to various settings – from formal immigration interviews to educational environments and community spaces – making them accessible tools for diverse professionals.

Cultural Responsiveness

The metaphorical and symbolic nature of creative expression allows for culturally sensitive approaches that honour and incorporate the diverse backgrounds and experiences of refugee adolescents.

Safety First

All effective interventions prioritise establishing psychological safety before any deep exploration of trauma, following Herman's Triphasic Model of Recovery.

Non-Verbal Processing

Creative expression provides valuable alternatives to verbal communication, especially when it is hard to articulate experiences of trauma.

Collective Healing

Group-based interventions demonstrate the power of shared experience and collective meaning-making, fostering connection and belonging among refugee adolescents.

Simplicity in Application

Even simple expressive arts tools – such as drawing materials, fidget toys, or breathing exercises – can significantly impact an adolescent's comfort and capacity to engage in potentially stressful situations.

Actionable Insights for Different Settings

For Education Professionals

Classroom-based interventions such as Plurality Theatre and Tree of Life can be integrated into existing curricula, strengthening peer relations while addressing psychosocial needs without stigmatisation.

For Social Care Workers

Simple sensory tools and creative materials can transform initial assessments and ongoing support sessions, as demonstrated in Chima's experience with playdough during meetings with his social worker.

For Immigration and Legal Professionals

Brief grounding techniques and accessible visual supports, such as those used by immigration officers with Chima, can transform potentially triggering interactions into more supportive encounters.

For Community Workers

Programmes such as Advancing Adolescents and the Open Studio Project offer frameworks for creating safe spaces where refugee adolescents can process experiences, build resilience, and foster connections through creative expression.

For All Practitioners

The research highlights that even professionals without clinician training can effectively implement many of these approaches with appropriate guidance, supervision, and respect for boundaries between psychosocial support and specialised therapeutic intervention.

Looking Forward: Connections to Case Studies

The examples of Chima and Natalia serve as bridges to the comprehensive case studies that follow. Chapter 7 will present a six-stage framework for healing that places expressive arts at its core, detailing how different professionals can contribute to the healing process. Chapters 8–12 will then provide in-depth case studies, including Daahir's experience with the Tree of Life activity mentioned in this chapter, offering concrete examples of implementing these expressive arts activities across diverse support settings.

The case study chapters will build upon the theoretical foundations and psychosocial support approaches outlined in this chapter, demonstrating their practical application through authentic, nuanced narratives of adolescent refugee healing journeys. By connecting theory to practice in this way, these chapters will further illuminate how expressive arts can create pathways to healing, resilience, and integration for adolescent refugees navigating complex transitions.

References

Alzaghoul, A, McKinlay, A and Archer, M. 2022. 'Post-traumatic stress disorder interventions for children and adolescents affected by war in low and middle-income countries in the Middle East: Systematic review'. *BJPsych Open*: 1–16. doi:10.1192/bjo.2022.552.

Azarova, V, Law, H, Hughes, G and Basil, N. 2018. 'Celebrating heritage: A mixed-method approach to explore the experiences of refugee children and young people (CYP) in the evaluation of Tree of Life Groups'. *Psychotherapy Section Review*, *61*: 50–67.

Barron, I, Abdallah, G and Heltne, U. 2016. 'Randomised control trial of teaching recovery techniques in rural occupied Palestine: Effect on adolescent dissociation'. *Journal of Aggression, Maltreatment and Trauma*, *25*(9): 955–973.

Barron, I, Abdullah, G and Smith, P. 2013. 'Randomised control trial of a CBT trauma recovery'. *Journal of Loss and Trauma*, *18*(4), 306–321. doi:10.1080/15325024.2012.688712.

Bettner, B and A Lew. 1990. *Raising kids who can.* Connexions Press.

Bronfenbrenner, U and Morris, P A. 2006. 'The bioecological model of human development'. In R M Lerner and W Damon, *Handbook of child psychology: Theoretical models of human development*, 793–828. John Wiley & Sons.

Cane, P.M. 2016 Refugee accompaniment: Capacitar practices of self-care and trauma healng for refugees and those who walk with them. Capacitar International.

Children and War UK. 2024. *Children and war training.* Accessed 16 May 2024. https://childrenandwar-uk.org/training-2/.

Dahne, F, Smith Jervelund, S, Langer Primdahl, N, Siemsen, N, Derlyn, I, Verelst, A, Spaas, C, de Haene, L and Skovdal, M. 2024. 'Understanding how classroom drama workshops can facilitate social capital for newly arrived migration and refugee adolescents: Insights from Denmark'. *Transcultural Psychiatry 61*(2): 260–270. doi:10.1177/13634615231225099.

Dulwich Centre Foundation. 2024. Accessed 9 May 2024. https://dulwichcentre.com.au/.

El-Khani, A, Cartwright, K, Maalouf, W, Haar, K, Zehra, N and Cokamay-Yilmaz, G. 2021. 'Enhancing teaching recovery techniques (TRT) with parenting skills: RCT of TRT + parenting with trauma-affected Syrian refugees in Lebanon utilising remote training with implications for insecure contexts and Covid-19'. *International Journal of Environmental Research in Public Health*, *18*(6): 1–20.

Equipe Théâtre Pluralité d'Erit. 2010. *Théâtre Pluralité.* Montreal. https://refugeeswellschool.org/activeapp/wp-content/uploads/2019/02/Classroom-Drama-Therapy-manual-ENG.pdf.

Hamilton, J D, Kendall, P, Gosch, E, Furr, J and Sood, E. 2008. 'Flexibility within fidelity'. *Journal of the American Academy of Child and Adolescent Psychiatry*: 47(9): 987–993.

Hauke, C, Gloster, A, Gerlach, A and Richter, J. 2014. 'Standardised treatment manuals: Does adherence matter?' *Sensoria: A Journal of Mind, Brain and Culture*, 10: 1–13.

Herman, J. 1992. *Trauma and recovery: The aftermath of violence – from domestic abuse to political terror.* 3rd edn. Basic Books.

Hughes, G. 2014. 'Finding a voice through "The Tree of Life": A strength-based approach to mental health for refugee children and families in schools'. *Clinical Child Psychology and Psychiatry*, *19*(1): 139–153. doi:10.1177/1359104513476719.

Jennings, S. 2010. *Creative drama in groupwork.* Routledge.

Johnson, S. 2022. 'War and conflict: A resource bank'. *Conflict and Mental Health*, *27*(4): 931–937. doi:10.1177/13591045221109277.

Kalantari, M, Yule, W, Dyregrov, A, Neshatdoost, H and Ahmadi, S. 2012. 'Efficacy of writing for recovery on traumatic grief symptoms of Afghani refugee bereaved adolescents: A randomised control trial'. *Omega*, *65*(2): 139–150.

Kendall, O and Beidas, R. 2007. 'Smoothing the trail for dissemination of evidence-based practices for youth: Flexibility within fidelity'. *Professional Psychology: Research and Practice*, *38*: 13–20. doi:10.1037/0735–7028.38.1.13.

Lewis, L, McLeod, H and Li, X. 2018. 'The open studio: Exploring immigrant and refugee youth experiences of belonging through community-arts practice'. *Cultural and Pedagogical Inquiry* 10(1): 5–21.

Mercy Corps. 2024. *Mercy corps.* Accessed 21 May 2024. www.mercycorps.org.

Mercy Corps. 2024a. *Who we are.* Accessed 23 May 2024. https://europe.mercycorps.org/en-gb/who-we-are.

Mercy Corps. 2024b. *Advancing adolescence.* Accessed 23 May 2024. https://europe.mercycorps.org/en-gb/research-resources/advancing-adolescence.

Meyer-Demott, M, Jakobsen, M, Wentzel-Larsen, T and Heir, T. 2017. 'A controlled early group intervention study for unaccompanied minors: Can expressive arts alleviate symptoms of trauma and enhance life satisfaction?' *Scandinavian Journal of Psychology*, *58*: 510–518. doi:10.1111/sjop.12395.

Moutsou, I, Georgaca, E and Varaklis, T. 2023. 'Psychotherapeutic and psychosocial interventions with unaccompanied minors: A scoping review'. *Healthcare*, *11*: 1–20.

Nikut. 2024. *Introduksjonskurs: Finn Den Kreative Lederen I Deg.* Accessed 3 May 2024. https://nikut.info/.

Ncube-Millo, N, and Denborough, D. 2007. 'Tree of Life, mainstreaming psychosocial care and support: A manual for facilitators'. Regional, Psychosocial Support Initiative.

Norweigan Centre for Violence and Traumatic Stress Studies. 2020. *Forced migration and refugee health.* Accessed 1 May 2024. https://www.nkvts.no/english/project/expressive-arts-therapy-for-newly-arrived-unaccompanied-minor-refugee-boys-in-transit-centers/.

Panter-Brick, C, Dajani, R, Eggerman, M, Hermosilla, S, Sancilio, A and Ager, A. 2018. 'Insecurity, distress and mental health: Experimental and randomized controlled trials of a psychosocial intervention for youth affected by the Syrian crisis'. *The Journal of Child Psychology and Psychiatry*, *59*(5): 523–541. doi:10.1111/jcpp.12832.

Panter-Brick, C, Eggerman, M, Hadfield, K and Dajani, R. 2020. 'Measuring the psychosocial, biological and cognitive signatures of profound stress in humanitarian settings: impacts, challenges and strategies in the field'. Conflict and Health, *14*(40). doi: / 10.1186/s13031-020-00286-w

Pennebaker, J and Chung, C. 2006. 'Expressive writing, emotional upheavals and health'. In H Friedman and R Cohen Silver, *Foundations of health psychology*, 263–284. Oxford University Press.

Pennebaker, J and Ferrell, J. 2013. 'Can expressive writing change emotions? An oblique answer to the wrong question'. In D Hermans, B Rime and B Mesquita, *Changing emotions*, 183–186. Psychology Press.

Perry, B and M Szalavitz. 2006. *The boy who was raised as a dog and other stories from a child psychiatrist's notebook.* Basic Books.

REPSSI. 2016. *Tree of life: A workshop methodology for children, young people and adults.* REPSSI.

REPSSI. 2022. *Psychosocial wellbeing for all children.* Accessed 5 May 2024. https://repssi.org/.

Ruini, C and Mortara, C. 2022. 'Writing technique across psychotherapies – From traditional expressive writing to new positive psychology interventions: A narrative review'. *Journal of Contemporary Psychotherapy, 52*: 23–34. doi:10.1007/210879-021-09520-9.

Sarkadi, A, Ådahl, K, Stenvall, E, Ssegonja, R, Batti, H, Gavra, P, Fangström, K and Salari, R. 2018. 'Teaching recovery techniques: Evaluation of a group intervention for unaccompanied refugee minors with symptoms of PTSD in Sweden'. *European Child and Adolescent Psychiatry, 27*: 467–479.

Schaefer-McDaniel, A. 2024. 'Conceptualizing social capital among young people: Towards a new theory'. *Children, Youth and Environments*, 14(1): 153-172.

Slatcher, R and Pennebaker, J. 2006. 'How do I love thee? Let me count the words'. *Psychological Science, 17*(8): 645–735. doi:10.1111/j.1467-9280.2006.01762.

Smith, P, Dyregrov, A and Yule, W. 2023. *Teaching recovery techniques for ages 8+ children and war.* Children and War Foundation.

Solhaug, A, Røysamb, E and Oppedal, B. 2023. 'Changes in life satisfaction among unaccompanied asylum-seeking and refugee minors who participated in teaching recovery techniques (TRT)'. *Child and Adolescent Psychiatry and Mental Health, 17*(50): 1–13.

Spaas, C, Said-Metwaly, S, Skovdal, M, Langer Primdahl, N, Smith Jervelund, S, Hilden, P, Andersen, A, et al. 2023. 'School-based psychosocial interventions' effectiveness in strengthening refugee and migrant adolescents' mental health, resilience and social relations: A four country cluster randomised study'. *Psychosocial Intervention, 32*(3): 177–189.

Stark, M, Quinn, B, Hennessey, K, Rutledge, A, Hunter, A and Gordillo, P. 2019. 'Examining resilience in adolescent refugees through the tree of life activity'. *Journal of Youth Development, 14*(2): 130–152. doi:10.5195/tyd.2019.692.

Stiles, D, Alaraudanjoki, E, Wilkinson, L, Ritchie, K and Brown, K-A. 2021. 'Researching the effectiveness of tree of life: An Imbeleko approach to counseling refugee youth'. *Journal of Child and Adolescent Trauma* 14: 123–139. doi:10.1007/s40653-019-00286-w.

The World Bank. 2024. *Databank: World development indicators.* Accessed 1 May 2024. https://databank.worldbank.org/source/world-development-indicators.

The World Bank. 2024. *Training at Dulwich Centre.* Accessed 9 May 2024. https://dulwichcentre.com.au/training-in-narrative-therapy/.

Truijens, F, Zühlke-van Hulzen, Z and Vanheule, S. 2017. 'To manualise or not to manualise: Is that still the question? A systematic review of empirical evidence for manual superiority in psychological treatment'. *Journal of Clinical Psychology, 75*(3):329–343.

Urnes Johnson, S, Hoffart, A and Havik, O. 2016. 'A survey of clinical psychologists' attitudes toward treatment manuals'. *Professional Psychology: Research and Practice, 47*(5): 340–346.

Walther, S and Fox, H. 2012. 'Narrative therapy and outsider witness practice: Teachers as a community of acknowledgement'. *Educational and Child Psychology, 29*(2): 8–17.

White, M. 2006. 'Responding to children who have experienced significant trauma: A narrative perspective'. In M White, *Narrative therapy with children and their families,* 85–97. Dulwich Centre Publications.

Yavna, K, Sinelnichenko, Y, Zhuravel, T and Yule, W. 2024. 'Teaching Recovery Techniques (TRT) to Ukrainian children and adolescents to self-manage post-traumatic stress disorder (PTSD) symptoms following the Russian invasion of Ukraine in 2022 – The first 7 months'. *Journal of Affective Disorders, 351*: 243–249.

Yogo, M and Fujihara, S. 2008. 'Working memory capacity can be improved by expressive writing: A randomized experiment in a Japanese sample'. *The British Journal of Health Psychology*, *13*: 77–80.

Yohani, S. 2008. 'Creating and ecology of hope: Arts-based interventions with refugee children'. *Journal of Child and Adolescent Social Work*, *25*: 309–323. doi:10.1007/210560-008-0129-x.

Yule, W, Dyregrov, A, Raundalen, M and Smith, P. 2013. 'Children and war: The work of the children and war foundation'. *European Journal of Psychotraumatology*, *4*(1): 1–8. doi:10.3402/ejpt.v410.18424.

Chapter 7

Introduction to the Case Studies

Introduction

This chapter presents a comprehensive six-stage framework for supporting adolescent refugees through expressive arts approaches, clearly delineating which stages are appropriate for all practitioners to implement and which require specialised psychotherapy training. After addressing common concerns about implementing expressive arts approaches in refugee contexts, the chapter explores each stage in detail, providing both theoretical foundations and practical applications.

The six stages are presented as distinct phases for conceptual clarity. However, the The chapter emphasises that these stages are inevitably interconnected and overlapping, rarely following a linear progression in real-world practice with adolescent refugees.

Case examples illustrate how these approaches can be adapted for various settings and individual needs, with practitioners often encountering material that crosses between stages. The chapter concludes by examining the methodology used to construct the case studies presented in subsequent chapters, explaining how these narratives were developed from clinical experience while maintaining confidentiality and ethical considerations.

Six-Stage Framework for Therapeutic Support with Adolescent Refugees

The case studies in Chapters 8–12 embed expressive arts practice into a comprehensive framework with six interconnected stages.

Stages for Both Psychotherapists and Non-Psychotherapist Practitioners

(1) Stabilisation and relationship-building
(2) Psychoeducation
(3) Bearing witness

DOI: 10.4324/9781003430032-8

Stages Exclusively for Psychotherapists

(4) Trauma memory processing
(5) Integration of trauma memories
(6) Identity development

Each of these stages serves a distinct purpose in the healing journey while building upon the foundations established in previous phases. This structure integrates therapeutic skills, trauma-informed practice, and expressive arts strategies. While presented here as distinct stages, it remains adaptable to the non-linear nature of healing. This approach helps readers distinguish between general therapeutic practice and formal psychotherapy, clarifying roles and boundaries for different practitioners. All stages emphasise cultural sensitivity and adaptability, aligning with the cognitive, emotional, and social developmental stages of adolescence while recognising the complex healing needs of adolescent refugees.

Theoretical Foundations

This chapter combines elements from trauma-informed care, expressive arts therapy, and cross-cultural psychology. It recognises the unique challenges faced by adolescent refugees who must navigate both developmental transitions and cultural displacement simultaneously. By integrating established trauma recovery models with creative expression, this approach provides multiple pathways for healing that do not rely exclusively on verbal processing, making it particularly valuable for young people working across language barriers.

The six-stage structure acknowledges both the universal elements of trauma recovery and the specialised interventions that require clinical expertise. This distinction supports ethical practice amongst all support professionals while ensuring adolescent refugees receive appropriate care at each stage of their healing journey. Throughout all stages, the framework maintains a strengths-based perspective that recognises resilience alongside trauma, empowering young people as active participants in their own recovery.

As the stages are interconnected, support professionals will inevitably encounter material that needs to be addressed by psychotherapists. In such instances, they can still provide valuable support maintaining a safe environment, recommending personal development resources and referring adolescent refugees to psychotherapy services or community support groups where available. Throughout all stages, expressive arts play a crucial role in facilitating healing and communication. This structured approach ensures that each professional group operates within its scope of practice while providing comprehensive support to adolescent refugees. For some case studies, the same expressive arts practice will be continued through several stages, whereas for others, each stage will showcase a different practice to ensure that the reader is exposed to a variety of approaches.

Having established the theoretical framework for supporting adolescent refugees through expressive arts, it is important to address common hesitancies professionals may have about implementing these approaches in their practice.

'But I'm No Good at Art': Embracing the Use of the Expressive Arts with Adolescents Refugees

You might be a social worker supporting adolescent refugees through case management and connecting them with vital resources. Perhaps you are a social care worker supporting separated adolescent refugees in a residential setting as they navigate everyday life and strive for independence, a frontline humanitarian worker assisting families, or a teacher helping refugee youth adjust to a new educational environment. You could be an occupational therapist helping them develop skills for daily living and paid work, a therapist looking to introduce expressive arts and play into working with refugee adolescents, or any other professional supporting adolescent refugees. Regardless of your role, you may have reservations about incorporating expressive arts into your practice. Common concerns include: 'I'm not good at art, how can I use this approach?' 'I'm worried that they just won't engage with the materials,' or 'how do I know which approach to adopt?'

You are not alone in these concerns. Many professionals in this field have faced similar uncertainties when beginning their journey with the expressive arts. Interestingly, research conducted by George Land for NASA (National Aeronautics and Space Administration) found that rather than being indicative of a lack of innate talent, concerns around engaging in artistic expression in professional settings are the result of educational systems that prioritise rationality and conformity over creative exploration. He claims that non-creative behaviour is learned as soon as we start school. This systematic suppression of the natural creative instincts prevalent in early childhood is documented in his 1992 work with Beth Jarman (Land and Jarman 1992) and continues to impact us throughout our lives.

A good way to start on your new creative journey is by introducing simple tools like fidget toys and playdough into the spaces where you engage with adolescent refugees. Serving as an important introduction to the power of the expressive arts and play, you may be surprised at how effectively these materials can help young people alleviate their own anxiety (Schaeffer and Drewes 2014). They can also be instrumental in building the therapeutic relationship. The expressive arts techniques presented in these case studies are intended to enhance rather than replace your current skill set. By incorporating these creative and innovative strategies into their practice, all professionals who support adolescent refugees can enrich their existing approaches and provide them with more holistic support.

Detailed Framework: Six Interconnected Phases of Healing

This section outlines the six interconnected phases that comprise the comprehensive framework used in this book for adolescent refugee healing and growth. It establishes the conceptual foundation for the case studies presented in Chapters 8–12, offering guidance for navigating the complexities of the healing process. Each phase description below includes theoretical underpinnings and practical applications with expressive arts approaches.

While presented as distinct stages, it is important to emphasise that healing rarely follows a linear progression. These phases integrate therapeutic skills, trauma-informed practice, and expressive arts strategies, remaining adaptable to each individual's unique journey. Throughout all stages, cultural sensitivity and developmental appropriateness are essential, recognising the complex healing needs of adolescent refugees as they navigate both trauma recovery and the challenges of adolescent development. The following sections examine each phase in detail, highlighting how different expressive arts approaches can be implemented within each stage of the framework.

Stabilisation and Relationship-Building

Many adolescent refugees have experienced or witnessed conflict and extreme violence in their home countries (pre-flight) and during their escape to safety (flight). Some may never have known the feeling of safety. Therefore, the focus during the stabilisation stage is on helping the adolescent refugee feel safe in their new context, within their body and in their relationships, while exploring ways to calm their nervous system (Herman 1992; van der Kolk 2015). Cultivating a sense of security during this crucial initial stage lays the groundwork for the development of a trusting relationship within a supportive environment. Establishing this foundation enables deeper emotional healing to occur in subsequent phases of recovery, and expressive arts practice can play a vital role in this stabilisation phase.

One effective approach involves guided imagery combined with gentle movement, which helps refugee adolescents to reconnect with their bodies in a safe and controlled manner. Levine and Kline (2007) describe an effective technique where participants are guided to visualise a safe space while engaging in slow, rhythmic movements, fostering a sense of grounding and calm. Baker and Jones (2006) extend this concept to music and drumming, highlighting their rhythmic nature as particularly beneficial for refugee adolescents. Their study demonstrated that these non-verbal, musical activities offer a powerful means of emotional regulation and establishing a sense of safety in group settings. The rhythmic elements in both movement and music appear to be key in promoting grounding and emotional regulation among this population.

These practices not only contributed to creating a stabilising environment but also enhanced group cohesion. Notably, participants reported feeling more relaxed and connected to their peers following these sessions, underscoring the potential of music and rhythm in fostering a foundation of safety for refugee adolescents. In her own practice, the author found that as refugee adolescents begin to feel more grounded and secure, they become better equipped to engage with and benefit from psychoeducation, the next critical phase in their healing journey.

Psychoeducation

Psychoeducation is a powerful mental health tool that combines psychotherapeutic and educational interventions. This approach operates on the premise that individuals who understand why a particular approach may be helpful are more likely to engage with it and become empowered in their healing process (Walsh 2010). Psychoeducation delivers age-appropriate information that fosters understanding and provides choices through therapeutic collaboration and wellbeing activities, serving as a crucial step in empowering adolescent refugees by offering both psychological and practical support.

In the early stages of building therapeutic relationships with adolescent refugees, practitioners often encounter a 'thin' version of their stories (Kohli 2006). Despite this limited information, valuable psychoeducation support can still be provided by combining these details with knowledge of the common challenges faced by refugee adolescents. Practitioners can offer insights into trauma responses, helping young refugees understand that experiences like intrusive thoughts, flashbacks, and sleep disturbances are normal reactions to abnormal events (Whitworth 2016).

This foundational knowledge serves as a basis for introducing specific coping strategies. By explaining the rationale behind the different strategies, practitioners can effectively recommend and model practices to improve sleep quality, enhance concentration, and manage emotional responses (see Chapter 8). Additionally, practitioners can offer practical trauma-informed support by delivering and signposting information on educational opportunities, health systems navigation, social care access, language support, and other community resources.

To maximise effectiveness, it is crucial to deliver information in an age-appropriate way. Visual formats can be particularly helpful, supporting different learning preferences, enhancing comprehension, and improving memory retention (see Chapter 8). As the therapeutic relationship deepens and a fuller understanding of each individual's unique experiences and needs is built, this initial psychoeducational support lays the groundwork for more focused interventions.

This holistic approach equips adolescent refugees with knowledge about the potential impact of their experiences alongside practical tools for daily life, supporting their overall wellbeing and adaptation to their new circumstances. By establishing this foundation of understanding, a supportive environment is created for the next phase of bearing witness where adolescents may feel more comfortable sharing their 'thicker' stories and experiences (Kohli 2006), allowing for a deeper exploration of their journey and emotions.

Bearing Witness

Building upon the foundations of safety and psychoeducation, the next critical step in supporting refugee adolescents is bearing witness to their stories (Kohli 2006), while remembering that all stages are integrated within a dynamic system. This process helps strengthen the developing relationship, cultivating an environment where these young people feel secure enough to share fuller versions of their experiences. The act of bearing witness is crucial, as it acknowledges refugee adolescent experiences, promotes healing, and reinforces their sense of identity and belonging. All professionals working with refugee adolescents can play a vital role in this process by authentically bearing witness to these narratives and validating diverse means of expression.

Jalonen and Cilia La Corte (2017) emphasise the importance of understanding the psychosocial context when bearing witness to refugee adolescents' experiences. This aligns with Bronfenbrenner's socio-ecological framework, which highlights the dynamic interplay between individuals and their multiple environmental systems, underscoring the importance of a supportive, coordinated approach (Bronfenbrenner and Morris 2006). By considering this broader context while bearing witness, professionals can better comprehend and validate the complex narratives shared by these young people.

Blackwell (2005) advises practitioners to maintain a balanced approach, avoiding both detachment and over-involvement, to prevent alienating or disempowering refugee adolescents. He stresses the importance of allowing them to express overwhelming experiences rather than focusing solely on consoling them. Recent neuroscience research (e.g. van der Kolk 2015; Schore 2012) validates and builds upon Winnicott's (1965) concept of the practitioner 'holding' the individual through emotional understanding and Bion's (1965) principle of 'containing' their often-unbearable projected feelings.

Jalonen and Cilia La Corte (2017) apply a maritime metaphor to illustrate the practitioner's role, likening them to a seaworthy vessel with a stabilising keel and robust hull capable of weathering intense emotional storms. This imagery underscores the importance of the practitioner as a steadfast, containing presence throughout the healing journey. By maintaining this equilibrium and supportive stance, practitioners can effectively bear witness to the experiences of refugee adolescents, guiding their path towards healing and integration.

While the first three stages can be facilitated by a range of professionals with appropriate training, the following three phases require specialised psychotherapeutic expertise to ensure safe and effective trauma processing.

Psychotherapist-Specific Phases

The following three phases should be conducted exclusively by qualified psychotherapists with appropriate training in trauma work. Other practitioners who identify these needs in adolescent refugees should refer them to appropriate professional services.

Trauma Memory Processing

Trauma memory processing is a fundamental aspect of healing that addresses the psychological, emotional, and physiological impact of traumatic experiences (Levine 2008, 2015; van der Kolk 2015). It enables adolescent refugees to express their emotions, begin grieving for their losses, and start the process of working towards integrating their traumatic experiences into a coherent personal narrative. Expressive arts activities play a crucial role in this process. Activities such as drawing (Annous et al. 2022), creating and listening to music (Bensimon et al. 2008), and sculpting with clay (Malchiodi 2020) have been shown to facilitate the externalisation and processing of traumatic memories. These non-verbal pathways provide a safe medium for expressing difficult emotions and experiences.

Within a supportive environment, adolescent refugees can learn to reframe their traumatic memories through creative expression. For example, an adolescent refugee might initially depict scenes of fear or sadness through drawing, painting, or collaging (see Chapters 5, 8, 9, 14). They can then be encouraged to add symbols of safety and hope, transforming these memories into a coherent personal narrative (Malchiodi 2021). This process not only facilitates trauma processing but also reinforces previously acquired self-soothing techniques from the stabilisation phase. Additionally, it helps normalise their experiences as natural responses to their circumstances rather than indications of personal deficiency – a concept introduced during the psychoeducation stage.

By combining creative expression with cognitive reframing, adolescent refugees can gradually transform traumatic memories into elements of a resilient personal narrative. This method strengthens emotional regulation, cultivates a sense of agency, and promotes the integration of traumatic experiences into the broader life story. Ultimately, it sets the stage for post-traumatic growth, enabling these individuals to find new meaning and strength beyond their traumatic experiences. As refugee adolescents progress through this process, the next crucial step involves a more comprehensive integration of trauma memories, building upon the foundations laid during the earlier phases.

Integration of Trauma Memories

The integration of memories from potentially traumatic events into a coherent narrative is crucial for healing adolescent refugees. This process transforms fragmented, distressing recollections into a more structured and meaningful account of experiences, reducing the emotional impact of traumatic memories while promoting individual stability and increasing self-acceptance. Peter Levine's therapeutic 'titration' technique facilitates this integration process by pacing and modulating memory integration. This approach gradually introduces potentially triggering topics, allowing the adolescent to engage and withdraw as needed, thus prioritising their safety and reducing the risk of overwhelm (Levine 2015).

The approach presented here combines expressive arts methods with body-based grounding and stabilisation techniques, creating a holistic framework for integrating traumatic experiences. This approach draws on the work of Malchiodi (2021), who illustrates how activities such as drawing, painting, sculpting, making music, and engaging in drama enable individuals to view their traumatic experiences from different perspectives and integrate them into their broader life narratives. It helps adolescent refugees to develop a coherent narrative of their experiences while empowering them to cultivate new coping strategies and construct a more positive life narrative.

As adolescent refugees are supported to integrate their trauma memories, they often gain the mental and emotional capacity to address fundamental questions of identity and belonging. This process initiates a personal reframing that extends beyond their past and current challenges. However, this journey unfolds uniquely for each individual, with some requiring more time before engaging fully with identity exploration. Respecting this varied pace is essential. Ensuring a supportive environment where refugee adolescents can safely navigate their changing perceptions of self when they are ready to do so is crucial for their ongoing healing and development.

Identity Development

Identity development is a key task of adolescence, as young people navigate the complex process of understanding who they are and how they fit into the world (Ferrer-Wreder and Kroger 2020). For refugee adolescents, this process is particularly challenging as they bear the double burden of forced displacement and the transition from childhood to adulthood. During this period, they are often faced with the task of developing an identity that integrates both their ethnic heritage and their connection to their host country, embracing feelings of belonging, and developing emotional connections to both communities (Hayes and Endale 2018). The successful formation of this integrated cultural identity is vital for ensuring a smooth cultural transition and has been shown to positively impact the adjustment and wellbeing of refugee adolescents (Nguyen and Benet-Martinez 2013).

Expressive arts play a crucial role in this process, enabling adolescents to explore different aspects of their identity, share their unique experiences, and build a cohesive self-concept while supporting emotional healing and empowering them to embrace their individuality and cultural heritage. Through creative expression of identity issues related to migration and cultural minority status, adolescent refugees can adapt to their new environment while maintaining connections to their roots, developing a more confident and integrated sense of identity as they transition into adulthood.

A range of expressive arts approaches has proven effective in supporting identity development among refugee adolescents. Rousseau et al. (2005) describe how drama workshops provide adolescent refugees with a safe space for self-expression, support, and validation through the ritual nature of dramatic play. Participants explore diverse values and hybrid identities, construct meaning, and grieve the losses associated with forced migration. Through storytelling, they begin to recognise the intersections between their host and home country identities.

Meyer-Demott et al. (2017) further illustrate the power of the expressive arts by highlighting the role of movement in exploring refugee adolescent identities. In their group sessions, participants form a circle, introduce themselves, and perform movements related to activities they enjoy (e.g. riding a horse, playing soccer, flying a kite). The group then mirrors these movements, reinforcing each individual's uniqueness while promoting acceptance of differences. Another valuable technique, documented by Rubesin (2016), involves the use of a collective 'I Am' poem as an identity-based creative writing prompt.

These diverse approaches empower adolescent refugees by emphasising capacities strengthened through adversity, encouraging creative resistance, and cultivating supportive peer networks. Through these expressive arts practices, refugee adolescents can further explore and integrate the multiple facets of their evolving bicultural identities. This process enhances their resilience and sense of belonging in new contexts while honouring their cultural heritage, ultimately supporting their successful adaptation and wellbeing in their host countries. With this comprehensive framework established, it is important to understand how the case studies in subsequent chapters were constructed to illustrate these principles in practice.

Construction of the Case Studies

Each case study features a composite character constructed from the author's clinical notes compiled over six years of therapy sessions with 42 adolescent unaccompanied minor refugees. Individual sessions took place over periods ranging from several months to a year depending on individual needs. By creating these composites, the author preserves their anonymity while capturing both common and unique experiences, ensuring the character's multi-dimensionality. Each case study begins by detailing the refugee adolescent's context, background, and trauma responses, viewed through Urie Bronfenbrenner's socio-ecological framework. This framework recognises the complex range of social interactions impacting individuals at various levels (Bronfenbrenner 1979; Bronfenbrenner and Morris 2006).

The case studies are informed by research in neuroscience (how our brain and nervous system work), interpersonal neurobiology (how our brains grow and change through interactions with others), and traumatology (the study of the impact of trauma on individuals). They draw on van der Kolk's (2015) comprehensive integration of these fields to explain trauma's complex effects on the brain and the body. These concepts are made accessible through simple visual explanations which provide psychoeducation for practitioners to help adolescent refugees to normalise, understand, and connect with their feelings.

After presenting the background of each composite character, each case study is divided into two sections. The first section, relevant for all those supporting adolescent refugees, focuses on stabilisation, relationship-building, psychoeducation, and bearing witness. The second section, designed for psychological therapy professionals, concentrates on trauma memory processing, the integration of trauma memories, and identity development. Throughout both sections, examples from a wide range of expressive arts are provided, illustrating the versatility of these approaches. Each case study will give a different weight to the sections depending on the presenting issue (and this will be made clear in the introduction to each case study). It is important to reiterate that while the case studies present these stages sequentially, in practice, they are often interconnected and overlapping. Given the complexity of the therapeutic process, these case studies can only describe small segments of what is typically a much longer and more nuanced journey. Chapters 8 to 12 will demonstrate how this six-stage framework is applied to support adolescent refugees through various challenges and healing journeys.

Conclusions

This chapter has presented a comprehensive six-stage framework for supporting adolescent refugees through expressive arts approaches. By distinguishing between stages appropriate for all practitioners and those requiring specialised psychotherapy training, it provides clear guidance for a range of professionals. The framework's emphasis on cultural sensitivity, developmental appropriateness, and the non-linear nature of healing recognises the complexity of refugee adolescents' experiences.

The case studies in subsequent chapters will demonstrate this framework in action through diverse scenarios. Chapter 8 illustrates how psychoeducation can be delivered through visual metaphors; Chapter 9 explores emotional connection through safe space, visualisation, and collaging. Chapter 10 demonstrates identity work with music and storytelling; Chapter 11 showcases trauma processing through body-based approaches; and Chapter 12 examines cultural integration through community arts. Each case study highlights different combinations of the six stages, reflecting the individualised and non-linear nature of healing work with adolescent refugees.

Through these practical applications, readers will gain insight into how expressive arts can facilitate healing, promote resilience, and honour cultural identity among this population.

References

Annous, N, Al-Hroub, A and El Zein, F. 2022. 'A systematic review of empirical evidence on art therapy with traumatised refugee children and youth'. *Frontiers in Psychology, 13*: 1–15. doi:10.3389/fpsyg.2022.811515

Baker, F and Jones, C. 2006. 'The effect of music therapy services on classroom behaviours of newly arrived refuge students in Australia – a pilot study'. *Emotional and Behavioural Difficulties*, *11*(4): 249–260. doi:10.1080/13632750601022170

Bensimon, M, Amir, D and Wolf, Y. 2008. 'Drumming through trauma: Music therapy with post-traumatic soldiers'. *The Arts in Psychotherapy*, *35*: 34–48. doi:10.1016/j.aip.2007.09.002.

Bion, W R. 1965. Learning from experience. William Heinemann.

Blackwell, D. 2005. *Counselling and psychotherapy with refugees.* Jessica Kingsley Publishers.

Bronfenbrenner, U. 1979. *The ecology of human development: Experiment by nature and design.* Harvard University Press.

Bronfenbrenner, U and Morris, P. 2006. 'The bioecological model of human development'. In R M Lerner and W Damon, *Theoretical models of human development: Handbook of child psychology*, vol. 1. Wiley.

Ferrer-Wreder, L and Kroger, J. 2020. *Identity in adolescence,* 4th edn. Routledge.

Hayes, S and Endale, E. 2018 'Sometimes my mind, it has to analyse two things': Identity development and adaptation for refugee and newcomer adolescents'. *Peace and Conflict: Journal of Peace Psychology*, *24*(3): 283–290.

Herman, J. 1992. *Trauma and recovery: From domestic violence to political terror.* Basic Books.

Jalonen, A and Cilia La Corte, P. 2017. *A practical guide to therapeutic work with asylum seekers and refugees.* Jessica Kingsley Publishers.

Kohli, R. 2006. 'The sound of silence: Listening to what unaccompanied asylum-seeking children say and do not say'. *British Journal of Social Work*: 707–721. doi:10.1093/bjsw/bch305

Land, G and Jarman, B. 1992. *Breakpoint and beyond: Mastering the future today.* Harper Business.

Levine, P. 2015 *Trauma and memory: Brain and body in search for the living past: A practical guide for understanding and working with traumatic memory.* North Atlantic Books.

Levine, P. 2008 Healing trauma: *A pioneering program for restoring the wisdom of your body.* Sounds True.

Levine, P and Kline, M. 2007. *Trauma through a child's eyes: Awakening the ordinary miracle of healing.* North Atlantic Books.

Malchiodi, C. 2021. Creative interventions with traumatised children. Guilford Press.

Malchiodi, C. 2020. *Trauma and the expressive arts therapy: Brain, body and imagination.* Guilford Press.

Meyer DeMott, M, Jakobsen, M, Wentzel-Larsen, T and Heir, T. 2017. 'A controlled early group intervention study for unaccompanied minors: Can expressive arts alleviate symptoms of trauma and enhance life satisfaction?' *Scandinavian Journal of Psychology*, *58*(6): 510–518.

Ngyen, A.-M.D., and Benet-Martinez, V. (2013). 'Biculturalism and adjustment: A meta-analysis'. *Journal of Cross-Cultural Psychology*, 44(1):122-159.

Rousseau, C, Gauthier, M-F and Lacroix, L. 2005. 'Playing with identities and transforming shared realities: Drama therapy workshops for adolescent immigrants and refugees'. *The Arts in Psychotherapy*, *32*(1): 13–27.

Rubesin, H. 2016. 'The stories we share: Reflections on a community-based art exhibit displaying work by refugees and immigrants'. *Journal of Applied Arts and Health*, 7(2): 159–174.

Schaeffer, C and Drewes, A. 2014. *The therapeutic powers of play: 20 core agents of change.* John Wiley and Sons.

Schore, A. 2012. *The science of the art of psychotherapy.* W.W. Norton & Company.

van der Kolk, B. 2015. *The body keeps the score: Brain, mind and body in the healing of trauma.* Penguin Books.

Walsh, J. 2010. *Psychoeducation in mental health.* Oxford Academic. doi:10.1093/oso/9780190616250.001.0001

Whitworth, J. 2016. 'The role of psychoeducation in trauma recovery: Recommendations for content and delivery'. *Journal of Evidence-Informed Social Work*: 442–451. doi:10.1080/23761407.2016.1166852

Winnicott, D. 1965. The maturational processes and the facilitating environment: Studies in the theory of emotional development. International Universities Press.

Chapter 8

Daahir's Story

Developing a Mental Health Toolbox and Healing Trauma through the Expressive Arts

Introduction

This chapter presents the first case study of the book which focuses on Daahir, a 15-year-old male unaccompanied minor refugee from a country in sub-Saharan Africa. It provides an overview of the challenges often faced by young refugees who have experienced trauma and demonstrates how the expressive arts used within Bronfenbrenner's ecological systems framework can facilitate the healing process. This framework helps us understand how various interconnected environmental layers influence and shape the recovery process, allowing us to explore the complex interplay between Daahir's internal experiences and the multiple external systems he interacts with, from his close relationships to broader societal influences. The expressive arts approaches featured throughout this case study provide powerful tools for healing and self-discovery, offering non-verbal means of expression and processing which are particularly valuable for individuals who have experienced trauma and may struggle with verbal communication. The case study is structured into two main sections.

Section 1: All Professionals Working with Refugee Adolescents

- Relationship-building and stabilisation using the safe space activity
- Providing psychoeducation
- Bearing witness to the refugee adolescent's experiences

Section 2: Psychological Therapy Professionals

- Trauma memory processing
- Integration of traumatic memories
- Supporting identity development

By providing a comprehensive overview of the entire therapeutic process and offering equal attention to all stages, this case study allows readers to gain insights

DOI: 10.4324/9781003430032-9

into the unique challenges faced by unaccompanied minors. It also presents practical, culturally sensitive strategies for supporting their mental health and wellbeing. As the first detailed case study in this book, Daahir's story sets the stage for understanding the complex, multifaceted nature of therapeutic work with refugee adolescents. It demonstrates how a holistic, creative approach, grounded in ecological systems theory, can effectively address the diverse needs of these young people as they navigate the challenges of forced displacement.

Daahir's Experiences: Pre-flight, Flight, and Post-flight

At the age of 15, Daahir embarked on a solitary journey to Europe from his war-torn home country in Africa where he belonged to a persecuted minority group. As the eldest of six siblings, he was the only one his family could afford to send to Europe with people smugglers. His journey to Europe was fraught with danger, spanning seven countries and including six months in prison where he was routinely beaten. After his family paid for his release, Daahir continued his perilous journey, culminating in a harrowing Mediterranean Sea crossing where he survived a capsized dinghy and witnessed many drownings, including those of young children.

After six months in mainland Europe, Daahir was smuggled to Ireland in a lorry, arriving in a country he had never heard of and had mistaken for the UK. Upon claiming asylum, he underwent an immediate assessment by the Social Work Team for Separated Children Seeking Asylum and was assigned a social worker. His initial meeting, conducted in a busy open-plan office, left him feeling unsafe and reluctant to share his full story. After two weeks in emergency accommodation, Daahir was relocated to a residential unit for unaccompanied minors where Laura was assigned as his social care worker and keyworker.

All Professionals Working with Refugee Adolescents

Relationship-Building and Stabilisation using a Mental Health Toolkit

Relationship-Building

Careful preparations were made to ensure that Daahir's arrival at the residential unit and his first meeting with Laura would be characterised by clear communication and an environment which was conducive to building trust. Laura coordinated with Daahir's social worker beforehand to select an appropriate interpreter based on Daahir's ethnicity and gender preferences. Initially, Daahir had expressed concerns about interpreter confidentiality, and Laura addressed these worries by explaining the strict confidentiality measures in place, clarifying exactly what this meant for their interactions. Reassured, Daahir agreed to proceed with the interpreter. To ensure that the meeting ran smoothly, Laura briefed the interpreter on confidentiality protocols and arranged post-meeting debriefings for both Daahir and the interpreter (see Chapter 13 for guidance on working with interpreters).

Creating a safe and welcoming environment was of utmost importance from the start. Daahir's initial meeting with Laura took place in a secure, confidential space – a crucial consideration given the abuse and betrayed trust he had experienced during displacement. This safe setting, often overlooked in other services for refugee adolescents, proved vital for Daahir, helping him feel physically safe and welcomed in the residential unit. During their first encounter, Laura cultivated a collaborative atmosphere using inclusive language and maintaining direct engagement with Daahir, despite the presence of the interpreter and his social worker. Her use of the collaborative 'we' to show that issues would be tackled together was particularly effective.

Cultural sensitivity which embodies Bronfenbrenner's microsystem is crucial when building a therapeutic relationship with a refugee adolescent. Recognising this, Laura approached her interactions with Daahir with open-mindedness and cultural curiosity. She created a safe, culturally sensitive environment and formed a strong, supportive relationship, establishing a positive microsystem that would serve as a foundation for Daahir's healing and growth. Laura engaged with communities from Daahir's cultural background to gain a deeper understanding of their traditions and practices, attending events and interacting with members of his community who had been living in Ireland for a number of years.

This engagement highlighted the profound cultural significance of names, prompting Laura to pay particular attention to pronouncing Daahir's name correctly. This consideration was especially meaningful to Daahir, who had previously felt as though his identity had been dismissed when other service providers incorrectly pronounced or anglicised his name. Laura also acknowledged Daahir's use of multiple names, a practice rooted in his culture as protection against authorities, rebel groups, and perceived threats from evil spirits. By respecting these cultural nuances, Laura further strengthened the microsystem she was building with Daahir, creating a foundation of trust and understanding essential for their developing therapeutic relationship.

By respecting these cultural nuances and embodying a hospitality attitude (Jalonen and Cilia La Corte 2017), Laura established a foundation of trust and understanding essential for their developing relationship. Her empathic, collaborative approach created an environment in which Daahir felt respected, understood, and safe – key elements in building a positive therapeutic relationship with refugee adolescents. This culturally sensitive foundation not only facilitated their initial interactions but also paved the way for effective therapeutic work in the future while demonstrating the importance of cultural competence in working with diverse populations.

Stabilisation: Developing a Mental Health Toolkit for Daahir

During Daahir's initial weeks in the residential unit, Laura observed his withdrawn behaviour and how he struggled with emotional regulation. She also noticed that he had difficulties remembering things and often found it hard to concentrate. Daahir confided in Laura that he was haunted by the events which had happened during the journey from his home country. Recognising these challenges, Laura prioritised developing a mental health toolkit for Daahir, based on Lahad's (1992) BASIC Ph model of coping and resiliency, later refined by Lahad et al. (2013).

Lahad's model, designed for assessing and developing coping skills and building resilience in the wake of natural and man-made disasters, identifies coping resources across six dimensions: Belief, Affect, Social, Imagination, Cognition, and Physical pathways. Laura and Daahir collaboratively constructed the toolkit focusing on strategies most likely to provide Daahir with additional support when needed. As a result, Daahir could metaphorically open up the toolkit and see what might help him at any particular moment. This collaborative approach to developing Daahir's mental health toolkit aligns with Bronfenbrenner's mesosystem, as it involves the interaction between different microsystems in Daahir's life, including his relationship with Laura, his peers, and his cultural background.

Daahir chose to build his toolkit in his phone's notes app, finding it the most accessible resource when feeling anxious or hopeless. While younger children often prefer creating a physical toolkit, adolescents typically opt for digital versions on their phones. Daahir found it beneficial to photograph items which he identified for his toolkit and add these images to his phone's notes. Visual cues resonate more strongly with trauma survivors than written or spoken words as our brains process images more efficiently. Moreover, images can help anchor individuals in the present moment, a particularly valuable benefit for those who have experienced trauma. Daahir's toolkit included the following components which helped him to stabilise and stay grounded.

Regulating the Body Using Breathing Techniques

Deep breathing is a powerful tool for managing anxiety and stress. To maximise its effectiveness, individuals need to understand how and why it works – this is where psychoeducation comes in. The combination of practical techniques and educational approaches exemplifies how stabilisation methods and understanding work together to support psychological wellbeing. Laura, Daahir's keyworker, applied this integrated approach when teaching him deep breathing techniques. She not only showed Daahir how to perform deep breathing but also explained its physiological effects, demonstrating the close connection between coping strategies and comprehending their impact.

In her explanation, Laura introduced Daahir to the concept of the autonomic nervous system. She described how stress activates the sympathetic nervous system, triggering the 'fight or flight' response. In contrast, deep breathing stimulates the parasympathetic nervous system – often called the 'rest and digest' system.

Laura explained that when Daahir practises deep breathing, especially during exhalation, his body responds in the following ways:

- His blood pressure lowers
- His heart rate decreases
- His pupils constrict

By providing both the technique and science behind it, Laura empowered Daahir with a comprehensive tool for managing his anxiety and stress. Building on this foundation, Laura introduced Daahir to a specific deep breathing exercise known as the **7/11** technique. This method provides a structured approach to deep breathing, making it easier for Daahir to implement in his daily life:

The **7/11** Breathing Technique practised by Daahir:

1. Breathe in for a count of 7
2. Breathe out for a count of 11

It is important to note that Laura showed Daahir how to use deep 'diaphragmatic breathing,' ensuring that his stomach expanded when he breathed in, rather than his chest rising. As Daahir continued to practise these techniques with Laura's guidance, he found he could more effectively manage stress and anxiety in his daily life. He particularly appreciated how this technique gave him a sense of control during moments of heightened stress. Figure 8.1 is the image which he put into the notes section of his phone:

Each case study will present a different deep breathing technique, all of which can be used interchangeably.

Cultural Comforters

Daahir uploaded pictures of an inspirational verse from the Qur'an, his prayer mat, his hometown, and a cat he had befriended there. He considered uploading pictures of the family he had left behind but felt that he was not ready to do that yet as he found it too upsetting. Daahir also decorated a stone using acrylic paint pens with his favourite quotation from the Qur'an which he then kept in his pocket. He found that holding it and taking it out when he was feeling anxious provided comfort.

Nourishing Items

Daahir kept a hot water bottle in his room which he would fill and cuddle when he was feeling low. He uploaded pictures of all these items to the toolkit on his phone to remind himself to use them when needed. Daahir also ensured that he always had access to an electronic version of the Qur'an on his phone.

7/11 Breathing

- Find a comfortable position either sitting or lying down

- Rest one hand on the centre of your upper chest

- Put your other hand on your stomach, just below your ribcage

- Breathe in slowly through your nose whilst counting to 7, focusing on filling your lower lungs. You should feel your stomach rise against your hand, while your chest stays mostly still.

- Breathe out by gently contracting your stomach muscles, feeling your belly lower whilst counting to 11. Your chest should remain relatively motionless.

Figure 8.1 7/11 Breathing.

Source: Ellen Sanders.

Calming and Grounding

When Laura first met Daahir, he was struggling to manage and express his anger in a healthy and constructive way. According to Sunderland (2016), the root causes of anger in adolescents often mask deeper feelings of hurt, sadness, or fear, and it is therefore important to address these underlying emotions to prevent destructive behaviours. Daahir needed a safe outlet for his anger, so Laura and himself explored various healthy ways in which he could express anger and frustration.

Daahir discovered that writing down his feelings was particularly effective. He kept a private journal in his native language, finding that handwriting gave him a greater sense of empowerment than typing. In their book, 'Opening it up by writing it down,' James Pennebaker and Joshua Smyth highlight the psychological and health benefits of expressing emotions through writing (Pennebaker and Smyth 2016).

Friends and Other Human Supports

Daahir also added the phone numbers of several of his friends to his toolkit – people he could call when he was feeling low, as well as emergency helpline numbers. Daahir and Laura also worked on the wording for text messages which he copied and pasted into the toolkit so that he always had them ready if he was unable to think of what to say to his friends when he was feeling low. With Daahir's permission, Laura informed the other staff in the residential unit that Daahir had the toolkit in the notes section of the phone so that they could direct him to it when they felt he might benefit from it.

Psychoeducation

Psychoeducation formed the foundation of Laura's approach in supporting Daahir during the stabilisation phase of his healing process by providing scientific explanations of the importance of deep breathing techniques. This approach allowed Daahir to understand the underlying principles of the coping strategies he was learning. Laura's role was vital in providing Daahir with a comprehensive understanding of how psychological trauma affects thoughts, emotions, and physical responses. By breaking down complex concepts into accessible explanations, she enabled Daahir to draw connections between his past experiences and current challenges. Laura first emphasised that a trauma or stress response is a normal reaction to an abnormal event. She explained that the responses illustrated in Figure 8.2 are typical, while the traumatic experience itself is not normal. Daahir kept this visual in his phone as a reminder that his responses were normal and that he was not 'going crazy.' It also served to reinforce the importance of engaging with his stabilisation techniques.

Recognising Daahir's specific difficulties with memory and concentration, as well as his interest in understanding his own emotional experiences, Laura focused on these aspects of his cognitive and emotional functioning. This approach aligned with typical adolescent development which often involves increased self-reflection and the desire to understand one's internal experiences (Meeus 2019). Laura explained where important cognitive and emotional processes were situated in the brain and was then able to connect Daahir's personal experiences to the underlying neurobiology (see Figure 8.3).

Using clear analogies and simple, accessible explanations, Laura described how trauma affects key brain areas:

- The amygdala, the brain's alarm system, activates quickly when danger is perceived. After a traumatic event, this alarm can get stuck in the 'on' position, causing feelings of nervousness even in safe situations.
- The hippocampus, which acts as a memory storage cabinet, can be disrupted by scary events, resulting in memories that are too overwhelming to file neatly away. This can cause them to feel jumbled or to resurface unexpectedly.
- The prefrontal cortex, the brain's control centre, helps with thinking and emotional regulation. Traumatic events can overwhelm this centre, making it harder to focus or manage feelings. However, Laura explained that the prefrontal cortex can be strengthened through practices like calm breathing, engaging in good sleep hygiene, taking regular exercise, and learning new skills.

Effects of trauma

It's normal to experience strong emotions and feelings after a traumatic event. These can include:

Emotional disconnection and distance

Feeling separated from the event, others, and your own self

Disbelief and bewilderment

Struggling to accept the reality of what occurred

Fear

Of death, solitude, inability to manage, or recurrence of the event

Helplessness

Experiencing a lack of control over the situation

Guilt or shame

For failing to prevent the incident, faring better than others, or not responding or coping adequately

Sadness

For what has been lost or taken away

Isolation

Feeling that non-one understands or can help

Euphoria

Relief at survival and security

Anger and frustration

Regarding the incident or its perceived injustice

Reliving the incident

Through nightmares, intrusive memories, or intrusive thoughts

Changes in relationships

Some people may appear detached or unsupportive, while others might seem overly concerned and protective

Figure 8.2 Effects of Trauma.

Source: Ellen Sanders.

By explaining neurobiological processes in accessible terms, Laura effectively bridged Bronfenbrener's exosystem (scientific knowledge about trauma) with Daahir's microsystem (his personal experiences). This approach empowered Daahir to better navigate his recovery journey by connecting abstract concepts to his lived experiences. Laura then introduced practical stabilisation tools based on these principles. She and Daahir explored the 7/11 breathing exercise together, learning how to regulate the nervous system. Additionally, Laura introduced mandala colouring as a meditative practice. Mandalas, sacred circular geometric designs symbolic in Buddhist and Hindu cultures (see Figure 8.4), offer a non-verbal outlet for processing emotions and promoting mindfulness, further supporting Daahir's healing process.

Laura explained how these methods directly apply the neurobiological principles they had discussed, helping to calm the nervous system and provide a non-verbal outlet for processing emotions. Laura showed Daahir examples of mandalas and explained their centuries-old use across various cultures for meditation and healing. She emphasised how the act of colouring these patterns induces a state of mindfulness, which can help regulate the brain areas they had discussed.

Laura then demonstrated how to synchronise rhythmic breathing with the colouring process, creating a powerful, multi-sensory experience of self-regulation.

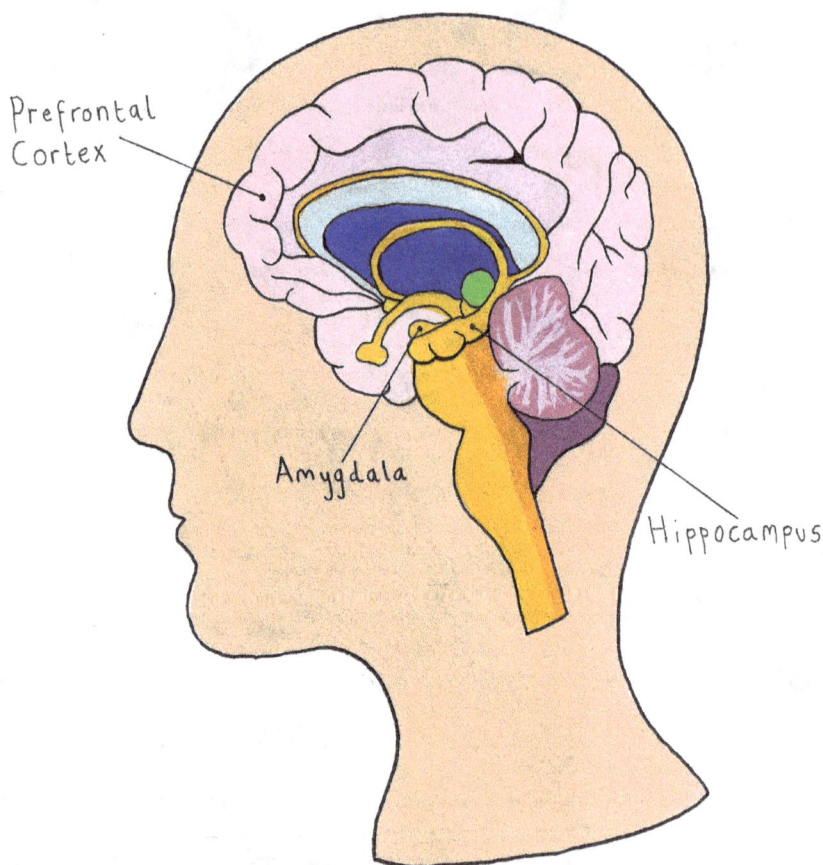

Figure 8.3 The Brain and Traumatic Stress.

Source: Ellen Sanders.

She explained that this combination of activities could help calm intrusive thoughts, reduce anxiety, and ground Daahir when he felt overwhelmed by traumatic memories or stress. By engaging in these practices regularly, Daahir could not only manage immediate stress responses but also build long-term resilience, reinforcing the healthy coping mechanisms they had discussed.

Bearing Witness

Given Daahir's early openness to creative expression, Laura introduced the strengths-based 'Tree of Life' intervention as an effective way for him to share his story and be witnessed in the process (see Chapter 6). Originally developed

Figure 8.4 Mandala Examples.
Source: Ellen Sanders.

to support vulnerable young people in Zimbabwe, this intervention is now used globally with children, adolescents, and adults, individually and in groups. This approach uses the tree and its constituent parts as metaphors to represent different aspects of an individual's life. Aligning with storytelling traditions, this approach helps adolescents to externalise their narratives and create psychological distance for their experiences. This is particularly beneficial for refugee adolescents like Daahir because it:

1. reduces feelings of overwhelm by offering a more objective perspective on their life story and;

2. provides a culturally sensitive framework for expressing complex emotions and experiences.

The intervention enhances feelings of belonging in the host country while respecting diverse cultural viewpoints, family structures, and traditions. Initially designed for clinicians, it has been adapted for broader professional use through appropriate training. Daahir created his personal Tree of Life, with each element symbolising a part of his journey:

> Roots: origins, ancestry, and culture
> Ground: current place of residence
> Trunk: skills and abilities
> Branches: hopes and dreams
> Leaves: important people
> Fruits: gifts received (material and non-material)

This process enriched Daahir's narrative, emphasising supportive relationships, talents, and aspirations rather than focusing on loss and trauma. It provided a safe space for him to address challenges and celebrate his unique story, with Laura witnessing and validating his experiences (see Figure 8.5).

Creating the tree allowed Daahir to rediscover himself, recognise his agency, and take ownership of his life story. Often, individuals are defined by their experiences, a concept known as 'thin description' (Jacobs 2018). By drawing the tree, Daahir could 'thicken' or enrich his narrative, highlighting positive aspects that might otherwise be overlooked due to a focus on problems (Azarova et al. 2018). Through this process, Daahir reconnected with his whole identity, including its positive aspects, and considered his challenges without risking re-traumatisation. He felt seen, acknowledged, and validated by Laura's attentive witnessing of his experiences. For those interested in using this approach, REPSSI (2016) provides a comprehensive rationale and clear instructions.

Psychological Therapy Professionals

Trauma Memory Processing

Recognising Daahir's struggle with emotional regulation after his traumatic experiences, his therapist, Rosie, ensured that she had a range of materials available in the therapy room which included coloured pencils, paints, markers, and clay. Daahir was drawn to the tactile nature of the clay, and Rosie guided him through a brief grounding exercise, encouraging him to feel its coolness and malleability. She then invited him to create a physical representation of a trauma memory that had been troubling him, explaining that there was no right or wrong way to do this.

As Daahir worked with the clay, Rosie observed his process, noting how he initially created small, tightly formed balls before gradually moulding them into more abstract shapes. She encouraged him to notice any physical sensations or

Figure 8.5 Daahir's Tree of Life.

Source: Ellen Sanders.

emotions that arose as he manipulated the clay, particularly those associated with the traumatic memory so that they could address them with grounding techniques. After a while, Rosie invited Daahir to share his reflections on his creation if he felt comfortable doing so.

Responding to her genuine curiosity, Daahir explained that the smaller, more compact shapes represented the intense feelings of fear and helplessness he experienced during the traumatic event. He described how one shape symbolised the paralysing fear he felt when hearing gunshots near his home, while another represented the helplessness of being unable to contact his family during their forced separation. Daahir explained that the larger, more fluid forms symbolised moments of resilience and survival. One of the shapes represented the strength he found in comforting younger children during their dangerous journey, while another symbolised the hope he felt upon safely reaching the refugee camp.

Rosie then introduced a technique called 'transformative sculpting' (Bat Or 2010). She asked Daahir to choose one of the shapes representing a difficult aspect of the traumatic memory and slowly transform it into something that felt more manageable or empowering. As Daahir reshaped the clay, Rosie guided him to focus on his breathing and the sensations in his body, helping him to connect the physical act of transforming the clay with the internal process of reframing and integrating the traumatic memory.

Throughout the session, Rosie maintained a calm, accepting presence, validating Daahir's experiences and emotions related to the traumatic event. She encouraged him to take breaks when needed and to express any discomfort or resistance he felt during the process. At the end of the session, Rosie and Daahir discussed how the clay work could relate to his healing journey. They explored how Daahir might apply the idea of 'reshaping' to his traumatic memories when they felt overwhelming, identifying specific coping strategies he could use to help manage flashbacks or intrusive thoughts in his daily life. This hands-on metaphorical approach allowed Daahir to externalise and process his traumatic memory in a safe, contained manner, while also practising emotional regulation skills that he could apply outside of therapy.

While Daahir chose to verbalise his experience, it is important to recognise that not all individuals feel comfortable or ready to discuss their creative expressions in detail. Rosie always explains to the refugee adolescents she works with that there is no obligation to explain or interpret their work. She affirms that the creative process itself is a powerful tool for healing and self-discovery, with therapeutic value extending beyond verbal expression. The focus required to physically manipulate the clay and the externalisation of internal experiences all contribute to bringing unconscious material into conscious awareness, an embodied process which can be healing without the need for verbal interpretation.

Integration of Trauma Memories

As Daahir's healing journey progressed into the integration of the trauma memories, Rosie introduced several expressive arts techniques, each chosen to address different aspects of this integration process and grounded in the safety of the secure base of the therapeutic relationship. One particularly effective method was story-telling using symbols, for which Rosie provided Dahir with a set of symbol cards featuring various images, patterns, and abstract designs. She invited him to select cards that resonated with his inner experiences, focusing on feelings and sensations rather than actual events. This symbolic approach allowed Daahir to express the complex, often fragmented nature of his traumatic memories in a safe and con-tained environment. Through this medium, Daahir was able to integrate the chaos of fleeing his home country, the fear he experienced during his migration journey, and the confusion related to navigating life in a new culture.

Recognising that trauma is often stored in the body, Rosie also guided Daahir through exercises that allowed him to express his experiences through physical movement. This helped him to release tension held in his body and to connect with emotions that were difficult to verbalise. As he moved, Daahir sometimes found words or images emerging, which he and Rosie would then explore further through art or discussion. Music became another tool for memory integration. Rosie intro-duced Daahir to the concept of creating soundscapes that represented his emotional journey. Using various instruments and digital tools, Daahir created compositions that captured the intensity, rhythm, and tonal qualities of his experiences. This auditory expression provided a new dimension through which he was able to pro-cess his memories, allowing him to engage with them in a non-verbal, sensory way.

Throughout this process, Rosie maintained a stance of compassionate witness, validating Daahir's experiences and emotions without judgement. She helped Daahir to recognise the strength and resilience he demonstrated in surviving his traumatic experiences, thereby cultivating a sense of empowerment and agency. As Daahir engaged with these various expressive arts techniques, he began to notice a shift in how he related to his traumatic memories. While they remained a part of his history, they began to feel less fragmented and overwhelming. He developed a greater capacity to hold the complexity of his experiences – acknowledging the pain and loss while also recognising his resilience and growth.

Through this multi-modal, expressive arts approach, embedded within a strong therapeutic relationship, Daahir was able to gradually integrate his traumatic mem-ories into a more coherent sense of self. Furthermore, Rosie emphasised that the integration of trauma memories is an ongoing process, and she encouraged Daahir to continue using expressive arts as a tool for self-regulation and processing outside of their sessions. Drawn particularly to creating music, Daahir continued to com-pose and play at home, empowering himself with strategies to manage future chal-lenges and to continue his healing journey beyond the confines of formal therapy.

Identity Development

As Daahir progressed in his therapy, Rosie recognised the critical importance of supporting him in developing an identity that embraced both his African herit-age and his new life in Ireland. For Daahir as an unaccompanied minor, this task held special significance. He was striving to find a sense of belonging and continuity while navigating the profound changes in his life. To facilitate this process, Rosie introduced a series of expressive arts activities designed to explore and integrate different aspects of Daahir's identity. These activities illustrated the interaction between Bronfenbrenner's macro- and microsystems, as Daahir integrated elements from his broader cultural context (macrosystem) into his personal identity (microsystem), creating a unique synthesis that reflected his evolving sense of self.

One especially powerful exercise was the creation of a 'personal flag.' Rosie provided Daahir with a large piece of paper, paints, markers, and different craft materials and invited him to design a flag that represented different aspects of his identity – his African roots, Muslim faith, refugee journey, and his new experiences in Ireland. Daahir divided his flags into sections, each symbolising a part of his complex identity. He incorporated symbols from his own flag to represent his homeland and used Islamic calligraphy to depict his faith, which had been a source of strength throughout his journey. The section representing his life in Ireland included the green, white, and orange of the Irish tricolour interwoven with African patterns, symbolising his emerging bicultural identity. Large swathes of blue paint tinged with red, representing his very difficult journey across the Mediterranean, were woven into both sections. By adding a picture of the flag to the notes section of his phone, Daahir expanded his toolkit of coping strategies and reminders of strength, fostering ongoing personal growth and resilience.

Music also played a significant role in Daahir's identity development. Rosie encouraged him to create a personal soundtrack, incorporating both traditional Somali music and contemporary music which he heard in Ireland. This musical fusion became a powerful metaphor for Daahir's evolving identity, demonstrating the harmonisation of his different cultures. He added it to his invisible toolkit as he found that listening to it helped to ground him when he was missing his family and struggling with feelings of non-belonging.

Rosie maintained a supportive and curious stance throughout this process, always validating Daahir's experiences and emotions. She helped him to recognise the strength inherent in his bicultural identity, framing it as a unique asset rather than a source of confusion or conflict. As Daahir engaged with these expressive arts techniques, he began the slow process of developing a more integrated sense of self, starting to see his identity as incorporating elements of both cultures rather than having to make a choice between them. This was a slow process with frequent challenges and setbacks, but overall, this shift allowed him to feel more grounded in his present life while maintaining a strong connection to his roots.

Through this expressive arts-based approach to identity development, embedded within a strong therapeutic relationship, Daahir was able to move towards a more coherent and flexible sense of self. Throughout the process, Rosie encouraged Daahir to reflect on how these different aspects of his identity coexisted and influenced each other. She helped him to see that, rather than abandoning his roots, his new life meant that he was adding new dimensions to his identity. Rosie emphasised to Daahir that identity development is an ongoing, lifelong process, and she encouraged him to continue exploring and expressing his evolving sense of self beyond their sessions.

Conclusions

Daahir's journey through therapy illustrates the power of expressive arts in supporting unaccompanied minors through the complex processes of relationship-building, stabilisation, psychoeducation, trauma memory processing, and integration and identity development. His case study demonstrates how a culturally sensitive, multi-modal approach can effectively address the unique challenges faced by unaccompanied minors arriving in Ireland. Through the collaborative efforts and skilled guidance of professionals like Laura and Rosie, combined with the use of the expressive arts, Daahir gradually built resilience, processed traumatic memories, and developed a more integrated sense of self. This holistic approach, grounded in a strong therapeutic relationship, not only helped Daahir to navigate his immediate challenges but also equipped him with valuable tools for ongoing healing and growth.

Viewing Daahir's journey through Bronfenbrenner's ecological systems theory highlights how his healing process was influenced by and in turn influenced various interconnected systems. From the microsystem of his therapeutic relationships to the macrosystem of cultural differences between his home country and Ireland, each layer played a crucial role in Daahir's recovery and growth. This systemic perspective underscores the importance of holistic, culturally sensitive approaches in supporting unaccompanied minors like Daahir. Daahir's story underscores the value of flexible creative interventions in supporting the mental health and wellbeing of unaccompanied minors as they adapt to life in their host countries.

References

Azarova, V, Law, H, Hughes, G and Basil, N. 2018. 'Celebrating heritage: A mixed-method approach to explore the experiences of refugee children and young people in the evaluation of Tree of Life Groups'. *Psychotherapy Section Review*, *61*: 50–67.

Bat Or, M. 2010. 'Clay sculpting of mother and child figures encourages mentalization'. *The Arts in Psychotherapy*, *37*: 319–327.

Jacobs, S. 2018. 'Collective narrative practice with unaccompanied refugee minors: "The tree of life" as a response to hardship'. *Clinical Child Psychology and Psychiatry*, *23*(2): 279–293. doi:10.1177/774424

Jalonen, A and Cilia La Corte, P. 2017. *A practical guide to therapeutic work with asylum seekers and refugees*. Jessica Kingsley Publishers.

Lahad, M. 1992. 'Story-making in assessment method for coping with stress: Six part story-making and BASIC Ph'. In S. Jennings, *Dramatherapy: Theory and practice*, vol. 2, 150–154. Routledge.

Lahad, M, Shacham, M and Ayalon, O. 2013) *The 'Basic PH' model of coping and resiliency*. Jessica Kingsley.

Meeus, W. 2019. *Adolescent development: Longitudinal research Into the self, personal relationships and psychopathology.* Routledge.

Pennebaker, J and Smyth, J. 2016. *Opening up by writing it down: how expressive writing improves health and eases emotional pain.* The Guilford Press.

REPSSI. 2016. *Tree of Life: A workshop methodology for children, young people and adults.* REPSSI. www.repssi.org.

Sunderland, M. 2016. *What every parent needs to know: Love, nurture and play with your child.* Penguin, Random House.

Chapter 9

Nabeel's Story
Learning to Feel Again

Introduction

This case study documents Nabeel's healing journey towards learning to feel again. Nabeel's emotional shutdown resulted from traumatic events experienced before and during forced displacement, and her recovery from trauma, like Daahir's, is a dynamic process with interacting and overlapping phases which create a complex tapestry of emotional rediscovery. This non-linear experience of emotional healing aligns with the intricacies of human experiences and interactions captured in Bronfenbrenner's ecological systems theory, introduced in Chapter 1 and applied throughout the case studies.

Consistent with our approach across all of the case studies, we explore Nabeel's journey using the two section structure outlined in Chapter 7, while recognising that these phases often nterweave and overlap. We explore how interconnected environmental layers contribute to Nabeel's gradual reconnection with her emotions, understanding her healing as complex interactions between internal experiences and external systems. Throughout this process, I observe a subtle balance of progress and reflection, marked by incremental shifts in awareness – often felt physically – alongside periods of consolidation.

Nabeel's journey reflects the intricate interplay between her close relationships (microsystem), broader social contexts (mesosystem and exosystem), and overarching cultural influences (macrosystem). Each stage of her recovery demonstrates the complex interaction between Nabeel and her multifaceted ecosystem, from nurturing intimate connections to recognising societal factors that shape her experiences. The chronosystem, representing the dimension of time and significant life events, underlies the entire process, influencing how Nabeel's experiences across all systems shape her ongoing recovery. As she navigates these interconnected layers, Nabeel gradually reclaims her capacity to feel, ultimately rediscovering the rich spectrum of emotions suppressed by trauma.

Nabeel's Experiences: Pre-Flight, Flight, and Post-Flight

Aged 14, Nabeel was kidnapped in her home country in sub-Saharan Africa by a terrorist organisation and repeatedly raped by its members. After almost six

DOI: 10.4324/9781003430032-10

months, she managed to escape and fled the country with the help of a people smuggler. Arriving in the host country as an unaccompanied minor at 16, Nabeel reported 'feeling dead inside,' unable to feel any emotions. This case study focuses on Nabeel's healing journey several months after her arrival in the host country. Addressing Nabeel's emotional numbness and initiating her healing process during this period is crucial, as it will better prepare her to manage her emotional needs. The expressive arts are used within the context of Bronfenbrenner's ecological systems framework to help Nabeel explore and express her suppressed emotions, facilitating a deeper connection with herself and her surroundings.

Section 1: All Professionals Working with Refugee Adolescents

Relationship-Building and Stabilisation Using the Safe Space Activity

Ivor Browne's concept of the 'unexperienced experience' and the 'frozen present' characterises situations where individuals endure potentially traumatic events without fully experiencing them, blocking out the pain of the trauma to continue functioning (Browne 2008). This 'frozen' traumatic experience continues to affect the individual in the present, and Nabeel's case clearly illustrated this phenomenon. Her journey of learning to feel again began with two crucial steps: building relationships and identifying a secure internal sanctuary.

For unaccompanied minors like Nabeel, trauma is not confined to past experiences but is compounded by ongoing challenges, creating a complex interplay of historical and present-day stressors. In this context, relationship-building formed the foundation of her healing process. Through consistent, empathetic interactions, a trusting relationship gradually formed with her caregivers, providing Nabeel with a stable base to explore her emotions and begin the stabilisation process.

At the core of the stabilisation and relationship-building phase was the safe space activity, enhanced here through the expressive arts. This psychological haven offered Nabeel a refuge from overwhelming emotions, fostering a sense of safety within her relationships. By encouraging Nabeel to use art materials to create her imagined safe space, she externalised and reflected on this inner landscape. Designed to be protective, comforting, and tranquil, this mental sanctuary allowed her to:

- temporarily distance herself from distressing feelings;
- begin to cope with her ongoing traumatic stress; and
- establish a basis for progressively reconnecting with her emotions.

This creative process deepened Nabeel's engagement with the healing journey, allowing for a more profound exploration of her emotions and experiences while strengthening her connections with her support network.

The safe space exercise was not merely an escape but a strategic tool for stabilisation and for deepening Nabeel's relationships with her caregivers in the residential unit. It enabled Nabeel to regulate her emotional experiences, gradually building her capacity to engage with long-suppressed feelings. This approach recognised that healing from trauma, especially for those with ongoing stressors, requires a delicate balance between confronting emotions and having an effective method for self-soothing, all within the context of supportive relationships. This reflects Bronfenbrenner's microsystem, where immediate interactions play a crucial role in development and healing.

The 'Create a Safe Space' stabilisation exercise began with careful preparation in Nabeel's bedroom in the residential unit, which she identified as her most comfortable and private space. To ensure uninterrupted time, Nabeel would inform the staff of her intention to engage in this calming activity, an act that itself built trust and communication. Nabeel started each session with a paced breathing exercise (see Gerbag et al. 2021 for examples of breath-based mind-body interventions in mass disaster situations). This involved breathing in for four seconds and out for six seconds, always ensuring the out-breath was longer than the in-breath. She focused her attention on her breath, inhaling gradually through her nostrils and exhaling slowly through pursed lips, making a gentle swoosh sound. If her mind wandered, she gently redirected her focus back to counting and breathing.

The breathing exercises described throughout this book are interchangeable, offering flexibility in the stabilisation process across various situations. As Nabeel struggled to imagine a safe place on her own, Louise, her keyworker in the residential unit, helped her create a vivid, multi-sensory mental image. They wrote down the description together, using simple language to accommodate Nabeel's developing English skills:

Imagine a quiet forest. Big trees stand tall around you, making you feel safe. The sun shines through the leaves, making spots of light on the ground. The air feels fresh and cool. You can smell the earth and trees. It's a good smell that makes you feel calm. When you walk, the ground is soft under your feet. You hear birds singing in the trees. Some are close and some are far away. You can also hear a small stream of water nearby which makes a gentle sound. The tree bark feels rough when you touch it. If you look closely, you might see some berries growing. They taste sweet if you try them. In this forest, you feel peaceful. Everything around you – what you see, hear, smell, touch and taste – helps you feel safe and calm.

To consolidate Nabeel's connection to her safe space, Louise encouraged her to bring it to life, offering her a variety of art materials. Nabeel chose soft pastels to create a visual representation of her forest sanctuary. As she carefully selected colours that matched her mental image, Nabeel found herself becoming deeply immersed in the calming atmosphere of her safe space. This tangible creation not only reinforced the vivid details of her mental refuge but also provided a physical anchor she could turn to whenever she needed reassurance. Louise encouraged her to take a picture of it, and she pasted it into the notes section of her phone.

To anchor this safe space in Nabeel's mind, Louise helped her choose a cue word that represented this peaceful forest. They settled on the word 'serenity,' which Nabeel felt captured the essence of her safe space. Nabeel recorded herself reading the description on her phone for easy access. Louise also encouraged Nabeel to develop a version in her native language, reinforcing the connection to this mental sanctuary and demonstrating cultural sensitivity. This collaborative process not only deepened their bond but also empowered Nabeel in her healing journey.

The practice of creating and regularly accessing this vivid, multi-sensory safe space provided Nabeel with a powerful tool for self-soothing and emotional regulation. It became a regular part of Nabeel's routine of integrating stabilisation into her daily life. She would revisit and refine her safe space using her cue word to quickly access this mental refuge when needed, and over time, both the paced breathing and the safe space visualisation became second nature to Nabeel and helped her to gradually build resilience, making it easier to face her challenges.

Psychoeducation through Metaphor

A metaphor expresses one thing in terms of another, creating an implied comparison (Meier 2012). Rather than directly describing aspects of an individual's life, metaphors provide an alternative, symbolic representation that facilitates a deeper exploration of thoughts, feelings, and experiences, and for people from different backgrounds, metaphors can bridge linguistic and cultural gaps, making them particularly valuable in therapeutic contexts. By offering a way to understand complex experiences, metaphors serve as powerful therapeutic tools which can support individuals who struggle to express their emotions.

In the context of psychoeducation, metaphors emerged as particularly effective tools when engaging with adolescent refugees (Baraitser 2014). These figurative explanations enhance therapeutic engagement, improve understanding of psychological concepts, and foster hope and agency within the developing support worker–refugee relationship (Golden and Lanza 2013). By making complex psychological ideas more accessible, metaphors provide a framework for understanding internal experiences. This approach is especially valuable for refugee adolescents like Nabeel, who may struggle to both understand and express their feelings due to limited emotional vocabulary, language barriers, or cultural differences (Ware 2023).

Louise frequently employed metaphors to help Nabeel grasp complex concepts. Geldard et al. (2020), in their proactive approach to counselling adolescents, emphasise that metaphors are more meaningful when they reflect the interests of the adolescent. Incorporating this principle into her practice, Louise drew upon Nabeel's strong connection with water and nature to compare her emotional state to a frozen river:

Imagine your feelings are a river. Right now, that river is frozen solid. The ice protects you from the rush of emotions underneath, which might feel over-whelming. The expressive arts are gentle sunlight, slowly melting the ice. As the ice thaws, you'll start to feel the flow of emotions again, but in a way that's man-ageable and safe. Just as a thawing river nourishes the land around it, allowing your emotions to flow again will help you grow and heal.

This nature-based metaphor not only helped Nabeel understand her current emotional state but also provided a hopeful vision of the healing process. Such metaphors can be particularly effective with adolescents from diverse cultural back-grounds, as natural phenomena are often universally understood and can provide a non-culturally specific basis for exploring complex emotional states. While this particular metaphor resonated strongly with Nabeel, Louise identified the potential to deepen understanding by drawing on different aspects of Nabeel's experience and knowledge to develop other metaphors.

Recognising Nabeel's familiarity with digital devices, Louise introduced a tech-nology-based metaphor to expand her understanding of the neurological impact of trauma. She invited Nabeel to imagine her brain as a sophisticated computer controlling her body and feelings and likened the brain's 'emergency response' during frightening events to a computer's security system going into high alert. Just as a computer might lock down access to protect sensitive data, Louise explained that during this emergency state, the brain's emotional management centre initiates a partial shutdown for protection. This safeguard, she clarified, can lead to emo-tional numbness and restricted memory access. While this protection is the brain's attempt to protect brain function, Louise noted that it can lead to difficulties in experiencing or expressing emotions over time, similar to a computer's prolonged security lockdown limiting normal operations.

These diverse metaphors provided Nabeel with accessible frameworks for understanding her emotional experiences and the impact of trauma, facilitating understanding and laying the groundwork for the therapeutic process of bearing witness to her experiences. This process aligns with Bronfenbrenner's mesosys-tem, where connections between different microsystems (such as therapy and daily life) influence overall development. The frozen river metaphor illustrated the slow thawing of emotions, while comparing the healing process to updating computer software reinforced its feasibility and instilled hope. Louise suggested that through talking with trusted individuals, engaging intentionally with the expressive arts, and learning new coping strategies, Nabeel could progressively regain control over her emotional responses. Additionally, Louise took care to adapt the language used for the metaphors to align with each adolescent refugee's language learning stage, making this approach flexible across varying levels of language proficiency.

Bearing Witness through Collaging

Bearing witness was the next crucial step in the thawing of Nabeel's frozen experiences (Browne 2008). To nurture this process and help Nabeel gradually soften the boundaries surrounding her suppressed feelings, Louise introduced collaging, an activity which allowed Nabeel to express her experiences and emotions non-verbally in Louise's warm and accepting presence. Collaging can be particularly helpful for individuals who may be hesitant to engage with traditional art media. It requires no specific artistic skills and relies on pre-existing images, offering a low-pressure, accessible entry point into creative expression and emotional exploration. Through her empathetic approach, Louise created a safe space for Nabeel to engage in collaging without fear of judgement, allowing her to communicate aspects of her experiences that defied verbal articulation.

Louise gathered magazines with images of various cultures, landscapes, people, and animals. This carefully curated collection of visual resources provided Nabeel with a wide range of imagery to draw from as she engaged with this powerful tool for bearing witness to her experiences. The collaging process began with Louise inviting Nabeel to create a series of collages representing different phases of her journey: her life before displacement, the challenging period of flight, and her current experiences in the host country.

As Nabeel explored the images, carefully selecting and arranging them on paper, she began to externalise her narrative in a tangible, visual form. This process allowed for Nabeel's gradual reconnection to her suppressed feelings, with chosen images serving as symbols or metaphors for complex emotions and memories. Throughout the collaging sessions, Louise maintained a supportive and attentive presence, offering gentle encouragement and bearing witness to Nabeel's unfolding story. This interaction exemplifies the importance of the microsystem in Bronfenbrenner's model, where direct relationships significantly impact an individual's growth and healing.

The act of choosing and placing images provided Nabeel with a sense of control over her emotional narrative, empowering her to share at her own pace. As each collage took shape, Louise's role as a compassionate witness grew increasingly vital, as she offered a non-judgemental presence while Nabeel engaged with her own narrative through the visual medium. The collages evolved into powerful visual testimonials of Nabeel's emotional reconnections, serving not only as a means of expression throughout the creative process but also as enduring reminders of Nabeel's experiences, strengths, and resilience. Through this creative process, Nabeel safely externalised aspects of her journey non-verbally, while Louise offered supportive acknowledgement of her experiences.

Section 2: Psychological Therapy Professionals

Continuing Collaging to Process and Integrate Trauma Memories

Recognising the effectiveness of collaging in bearing witness to Nabeel's experiences and facilitating emotional reconnection, Julia, Nabeel's psychotherapist, decided to incorporate this approach into the trauma memory processing and integration phases of the healing process. The continuation of this approach ensured consistency in Nabeel's healing journey while enabling a smooth transition into deeper therapeutic work. Over a series of sessions, collaging assumed a more focused role in processing and integrating traumatic memories associated with Nabeel's flight from her home country, while also nurturing her capacity for emotional attunement. Upon completion of this process, Nabeel offered her reflections on the collaging experience. These reflections are woven into the description of each stage, providing a window into Nabeel's experience of the process and offering valuable insights into her journey of healing and rediscovery.

Julia guided Nabeel through the following process:

1. **Setting the scene:** Julia provided Nabeel with a large piece of paper, magazines, scissors, and glue. She explained that Nabeel could use any images that drew her attention, even if she was not sure why. Nabeel reflected: 'When Julia laid out the materials, I felt a mixture of curiosity and apprehension. There were so many images to choose from, and I wasn't sure what I was supposed to do with them. But as I had already made a collage with Louise, it felt familiar and somehow comforting.'

2. **Image selection:** As Nabeel looked through the magazines, she was drawn to the following images without necessarily understanding their significance:
   - An abstract swirl of blues and greys
   - A bird's nest
   - A child looking up at her mother
   - A maze
   - A pair of hands cupped together
   - A closed door

   'As I flipped through the pages, certain images seemed to jump out at me. I didn't always know why I was choosing them, but they somehow felt important. It was as if a deeper part of me was guiding my choices, though I couldn't explain why.'

3. **Collage creation:** Julia encouraged Nabeel to arrange and glue the images onto the paper in any way that felt right to her. Nabeel worked silently, fully absorbed in the process. 'Arranging the images on the paper felt both challenging and freeing. I found myself moving them around, trying to make sense of how they fit together. It was like I was piecing together parts of my story, even though I couldn't quite explain it in words.'

4. **Reflection:** Once the collage was complete, Julia invited Nabeel to sit back and observe her creation. She asked Nabeel to share any thoughts, feelings, or memories that arose as she looked at the collage. 'Looking at my finished collage was overwhelming at first. There were all these images laid out in front of me, and it brought up a lot of unfamiliar feelings. I couldn't quite explain it, but it felt like there might be pieces of my journey there. Some parts were hard to look at but others were comforting.'

5. **Exploration:** Julia gently guided Nabeel through an exploration of the symbolism of each image. As they discussed the collage, Nabeel began to uncover deeper meanings. She reflected: 'I started to see connections I hadn't noticed before. The maze seemed to represent my feelings of confusion and fear during my journey, while the bird's nest and mother and child images stirred up thoughts of safety and the home I'd left behind. It was surprising how much meaning was hidden in these pictures. Each image seemed to tell a part of my story in a way I hadn't expected.'

6. **Emotional processing:** As Nabeel discussed the images, she began to connect with the emotions associated with her traumatic experience. Julia provided support and validation throughout this process, helping Nabeel to safely experience and process these feelings 'Talking about the images brought up a lot of difficult feelings. There were moments when I felt overwhelmed, but Julia's presence made me feel safe enough to explore these emotions. It was hard, but also somehow a relief to finally feel these feelings.'

7. **Trauma memory integration:** Building on the emotional processing, Julia guided Nabeel through the process of integrating her traumatic memories into a coherent narrative. This involved helping Nabeel connect the fragmented pieces of her experience represented in the collage into a more complete story. 'As we started to piece together my experiences, it felt like solving a puzzle. Julia helped me see how different parts of my journey were connected. It was challenging to face some memories but seeing them as part of a bigger picture made them feel less overwhelming. I began to understand how my past experiences influenced my present feelings and reactions.'

Julia encouraged Nabeel to create a timeline using the images, helping her to establish a sense of continuity in her experiences. This process helped to transform fragmented, emotionally charged memories into a more coherent, manageable narrative. 'Arranging the images in a timeline was revealing. I could see how one event led to another, and how my feelings changed throughout my journey. It helped me to make sense of why I felt certain ways at different times. Some gaps in my memory started to fill in, and I felt like I was regaining control of my story.'

8. **Resilience identification:** Julia explored the collage with genuine curiosity, her gaze drawn to the abstract swirl Nabeel had mentioned earlier. 'I'm curious about this swirl,' she said softly. 'There seem to be some lighter touches

in there. What do you make of those?' As Nabeel reflected on Julia's gentle prompt, she felt something shift. 'Her curiosity got me looking at it in a new way. I found myself wondering if those lighter bits might represent moments of clarity in all the confusion. It was enlightening – made me realise I might have more strength than I'd thought.'

9. **Closure:** To conclude the session, Julia asked Nabeel to give her collage a title. After some thought, Nabeel chose 'My journey through the storm,' acknowledging both the difficulties she faced and her resilience in overcoming them. 'Choosing a title for my collage felt important. "My journey through the storm" seemed to capture both the hardships I'd faced and the strength I'd found along the way. Looking at my completed collage, I felt a mixture of sadness for what I'd been through and pride for how far I'd come.'

This approach, carried over multiple sessions, allowed Nabeel to engage with her traumatic memories in a non-verbal, visually expressive manner, providing a new avenue for witnessing, processing, and integrating these experiences within the safety of the therapeutic relationship. This process illustrates the interplay between Bronfenbrenner's microsystem (the therapeutic relationship) and chronosystem (the temporal aspect of healing), showing how different layers of the ecological system contribute to recovery over time. By combining the gentle, witnessing approach introduced by Louise with more focused trauma processing techniques, Julia was able to help Nabeel gradually confront and make meaning of her traumatic experiences. The collage served not only as a tool for expression and exploration during the session but also as a tangible reminder of Nabeel's journey towards healing and resilience.

Creating Mixed Media Self-Portraits to Explore Identity

Building on the insights gained from the collaging activities, Julia introduced Nabeel to a creative, multi-dimensional approach to exploring identity. This approach aligned with Bronfenbrenner's ecological systems theory, encouraging Nabeel to consider how different aspects of her environment, from immediate relationships to broader cultural influences, shaped her evolving sense of self. Julia presented Nabeel with the concept of creating a self-landscape. 'Imagine your identity as a world you can touch and explore,' Julia explained. 'We're going to build a landscape that represents who you are on the inside and how you interact with your surroundings.' The process of crafting this self-landscape unfolded over several sessions, each reflecting aspects of Bronfenbrenner's nested systems:

1. **Conceptualisation:** Julia provided Nabeel with modelling clay and asked her to close her eyes and imagine her inner feelings and experiences. Julia prompted gently, 'how would you show your feelings and experiences using shapes and textures?' As Nabeel thought about this, she shaped the clay with her hands, making abstract shapes and contours. 'I started with rolling hills

and a winding river,' Nabeel shared later. Julia reflected on how Nabeel's creation mirrored Bronfenbrenner's theory: the hills represented the challenges and opportunities in various environments influencing Nabeel's development, while the river symbolised the interconnectedness of these different contexts in her life.

2. **Foundation building:** Julia introduced a variety of materials: cardboard, wood pieces, wire, and a sturdy base. Nabeel began constructing the framework of her self-landscape. 'I used the wire to create the river's path,' Nabeel explained. 'It flowed through the whole landscape, showing how my experiences in one area of life influence and shape my identity.'

3. **Adding layers and texture:** Julia offered an array of materials: fabric, paper, small objects, paint, and natural elements like pebbles and leaves. Nabeel carefully selected items to add depth and meaning to her landscape. 'I covered some hills with soft fabric that reminded me of home,' Nabeel said. 'But I left others bare and rocky to show the challenges I've faced. The river got smoother as it went along, like how I'm finding more peace now. It's interesting to see how these different parts of my life work together. The soft hills are like my family and friends who support me. The rocky ones are like school or work, which can be hard sometimes. The river connects them all, just like how what happens in one part of my life affects the others.'

4. **Symbolic elements**: As the self-landscape took shape, Julia encouraged Nabeel to incorporate symbolic elements. Nabeel added a small mirror at a point where the river widened into a calm pool. 'It shows times when I think about myself,' she explained. 'And how I'm learning to understand myself better in this new place.'

5. **Reflection and integration:** Throughout the process, Julia and Nabeel explored the emerging landscape and its meanings. 'Creating this world helped me see how all parts of my experience connect,' Nabeel reflected. 'The difficult terrains, the peaceful valleys, they're all part of who I am.'

The final self-landscape stood as a unique, multi-dimensional representation of Nabeel's identity. Unlike the flat collages of previous sessions, this piece occupied physical space, allowing Nabeel to interact with it from different angles. 'It's like I can explore my own inner world,' Nabeel reflected. 'From some viewpoints, I see the challenges I've overcome. From others I see growth and hope. It reminds me that there are always different perspectives on my experiences.' This multi-dimensional self-landscape approach provided a novel way for Nabeel to explore and express her identity, building upon her engagement from the start, pushing her self-expression into new realms – both tangibly and metaphorically. The tactile, spatial nature of the landscape allowed for a deeper, more holistic exploration of self, reflecting the complex, multi-faceted nature of identity development in the context of Bronfenbrenner's ecological systems.

Conclusions

Through a journey of expressive arts activities, from creating a safe space and exploring metaphors to collaging and mixed media self-landscapes, Nabeel gradually reconnected with her suppressed emotions and rediscovered her sense of self. These creative processes, addressed in sections for both general professionals working with adolescent refugees and specialised psychological therapy professionals, served as a bridge between her inner world and external reality, allowing her to safely explore and express feelings that had long been frozen. The progression from visualising a safe forest sanctuary and understanding her emotional state through the frozen river metaphor, to creating two-dimensional collages and finally a three-dimensional self-landscape, mirrors Nabeel's evolving capacity to engage with the complexity of her experiences and emotions.

References

Baraitser, M. 2014. *Reading and expressive writing with traumatised children, young refugees and asylum seekers: Unpack my heart with words.* Jessica Kingsley Publishers.

Browne, I. 2008. *Music and madness.* Cork University Press.

Geldard, K, Geldard, D and Yin Foo, R. 2020. *Counselling adolescents: the proactive approach for young people,* 5th edn. Sage Publications Ltd.

Gerbag, P, Brown, R, Mansur, S and Steidle, G. 2021. 'Innovative programs support recovery and resiliency in adult and child survivors of mass disasters'. In S Okpaku, *Innovations in global mental health,* 1557–1579. Springer. doi:10.1007/978-3-030-57296-9_130

Golden, A and Lanza, E. 2013. 'Metaphors of culture: Identity construction in migrants' narrative discourse'. *Intercultural Pragmatics, 10*(2): 295–314. doi:10.1515/ip-2013-0013

Meier, S. 2012. *Language and narratives in counseling and psychotherapy.* Springer Publishing Company.

Ware, V-A. 2023. 'Metaphor in conflict transformation: Using arts to shift perspectives and build empathy'. *The European Journal of DEevelopment Research, 35*(4): 914–937.

Chapter 10

Anastasiya's Story

Being Supported to Cope with Sleep Disturbances and Nightmares

Introduction

Sleep disturbances represent a significant challenge for adolescent refugees, often manifesting as both a symptom of trauma and a barrier to adaptation in their new environment. This chapter examines effective strategies for supporting adolescent refugees experiencing sleep disturbances and nightmares, through the case study of Anastasiya, a 15-year-old Ukrainian refugee living in Ireland with her mother. Through her story, we explore how sleep difficulties can be effectively addressed and transformed from a source of distress into opportunities for healing and growth.

I begin by detailing Anastasiya's migration journey from Ukraine to Ireland, providing context for her experiences as a refugee adolescent. Next, I explore the foundations of sleep health, including an overview of sleep mechanisms and how stress and trauma can impact sleep patterns. I then apply the modified two-section framework from Chapter 7:

1. Section 1, aimed at all professionals supporting refugee adolescents, focuses on sleep literacy, understanding sleep processes, sleep hygiene, healthy sleep practices, and sleep-inducing creative rest and relaxation practices, illustrated through Anastasiya's experience with her school chaplain, Miriam, who demonstrates and practises these techniques with her.
2. Section 2 follows Anastasiya's journey with her psychotherapist, Natasha, who introduces her to nocturnal journaling and collaborates with her on dream processing strategies. These methods complement and build upon the foundational sleep education and relaxation techniques provided by Miriam. By offering deeper insights into unconscious processes, these more advanced approaches provide additional tools to help her improve the quality of her sleep and reduce nightmares.

This integrated approach focuses on immediate sleep difficulties while empowering Anastasiya to develop sustainable sleep habits.

DOI: 10.4324/9781003430032-11

From Kyiv to Dublin: Anastasiya's Journey of Displacement and Adaptation

When the invasion of Ukraine began in February 2022, Anastasiya and her mother were forced to make the difficult decision to flee their home city of Kyiv. Anastasiya's father, like many Ukrainian men aged 18–60, was called up for military service and had to stay behind. After hastily packing some essential belongings, Anastasiya and her mother joined the masses of people crowding onto trains heading west, enduring a long and uncomfortable journey to Lviv. From there, they boarded an overcrowded bus to the Polish border. A trip that would normally take a few hours stretched into days as they waited in long queues of vehicles and people trying to cross the border.

After a long wait at the border crossing filled with uncertainty and fear, Anastasiya and her mother finally entered Poland on foot, leaving their familiar world behind. They spent several days in a refugee reception centre before being allocated flights to Ireland. Upon arrival in Ireland, Anastasiya and her mother were granted temporary protection and accommodated in a refugee reception centre in Dublin, the capital city.

Anastasiya's strong English language skills, acquired at school in Ukraine and enhanced through watching YouTube videos, a common method of learning English often reported by the young people we support, enabled her to start at her local secondary school just three weeks after arriving. However, the trauma of their sudden departure and the stress of adjusting to a new country began to significantly affect her psychological wellbeing. Shortly after Anastasiya started school, one of her teachers noticed that she was constantly falling asleep in class, and after class the teacher gently asked if she was OK. Anastasiya confided that she was struggling with disrupted sleep and nightmares.

Recognising her need for support, the teacher introduced Anastasiya to the school chaplain, Miriam. In educational settings, chaplains provide pastoral and spiritual support to students. In Anastasiya's case, the chaplain's role became crucial in addressing her sleep difficulties through psychoeducation and rest and relaxation practices. Miriam offered a compassionate and stable presence as Anastasiya navigated her sleep challenges and the broader difficulties of adapting to her new life in Ireland.

Understanding Sleep: A Scientific Foundation

Sleep health is a crucial yet frequently overlooked aspect of refugee adolescent wellbeing. As professionals working with this population, it is essential to address sleep-related issues early on. A good understanding of sleep mechanics and the importance of consistent sleep to overall good health and wellbeing can significantly enhance our ability to support adolescent refugees to cope and thrive in their new environment. To effectively support adolescent refugees with sleep-related challenges, it is firstly important to familiarise ourselves with the basic structure and patterns of sleep see Hanson 2006 for a comprehensive overview.

The Hypnagogic State: The Gateway to Sleep

Before we can understand the stages of sleep, it is important to recognise how we transition into sleep. The hypnagogic state represents this crucial transitional phase, bridging wakefulness and sleep, and is characterised by distinctive sensory experiences (Ghibellini and Meier 2023). During this period, individuals typically experience:

- visual imagery: fleeting scenes, geometric patterns, or fleeting facial imagery;
- auditory intrusions: perceived voices, musical fragments, or sudden loud noises; and
- bodily sensations: illusory feelings of falling, floating, or involuntary limb movement.

This transitional state has been shown to trigger intrusive thoughts or memories associated with past experiences (McCarthy-Jones et al. 2011). Understanding this phase is therefore crucial for professionals working with adolescent refugees.

Sleep Cycles and Stages

Once an individual moves through the hypnagogic state, they enter the sleep cycle proper. Sleep occurs in repeating cycles throughout the night, each cycle lasting approximately 90–120 minutes (Walker 2017). Each cycle progresses through distinct stages, ranging from light sleep to deep sleep and finally to Rapid Eye Movement (REM) sleep. These stages can be broadly categorised into REM and Non-REM (NREM) sleep, each serving unique and vital functions for physical and mental restoration (see Sullican et al. 2021, for more detailed descriptions).

Light Sleep N1 and N2

The journey through each sleep cycle begins with light sleep stages, known as N1 and N2. During these stages, the heart rate slows, the body temperature drops, and brain waves begin to change. Light sleep makes up about 50% of our total sleep time and is vital for memory consolidation, particularly of facts, new words, and instructions. Although people in light sleep can be easily awakened, these stages help transition the body into deeper, more restorative sleep.

Deep Sleep N3

As the cycle progresses, we enter deep sleep, also known as slow-wave sleep, where the brain produces characteristic slow delta waves. This profound stage of rest serves as the body's primary restoration period. During these crucial hours, multiple healing processes occur simultaneously – tissues repair themselves, the immune system strengthens, and bones and muscles are rebuilt. Meanwhile, the brain engages in its own maintenance, flushing out accumulated toxins to maintain cognitive health. This cleansing process coincides with the release of growth hormone, which supports overall cell regeneration throughout the body. Notably, these restorative processes are most active in the first half of the night, when deep sleep predominates.

REM Sleep

The final stage in each cycle is REM sleep, when the most vivid dreaming occurs. The brain becomes highly active, while the body experiences temporary paralysis to prevent acting out our dreams. REM sleep is critical for emotional processing, creativity, and complex learning. It helps the brain make new connections, consolidate emotional memories, and prepare for future challenges. REM periods typically become longer as the night progresses, with the majority occurring in the latter part of sleep.

Understanding these sleep cycles and stages provides vital context for professionals working with adolescent refugees, particularly when addressing sleep disturbances that may be connected to trauma, anxiety, and adjustment challenges.

The Impact of Stress and Trauma on Refugee Adolescent Sleep Patterns

For refugees who have experienced trauma, disturbances can occur in any of these sleep stages (Jou and Pace-Schott 2022). Adolescent refugees are particularly vulnerable due to the combination of their developmental stage and trauma experiences. As explored in Chapter 2, the adolescent brain undergoes significant changes, including shifts in sleep patterns and circadian rhythms (Tarokh et al. 2019). This natural biological transition, combined with the stress of displacement, trauma, and adapting to a new environment, makes adolescent refugees especially susceptible to sleep issues (Rae 2023). As their developing cognitive and emotional systems are less equipped to handle trauma-induced stress, this can potentially lead to more severe disruptions across all sleep stages.

These sleep disruptions manifest in various ways, affecting both sleep quality and duration. Many adolescent refugees find themselves lying awake, their minds racing with worries and intrusive thoughts related to their experiences. When sleep does come, it can be fragmented and restless, with awakenings often triggered by nightmares – a common occurrence among trauma-exposed refugee youth – which disrupts the natural progression of sleep cycles (Harb and Schultz 2020). These disturbances typically result in chronic sleep deprivation, with some adolescents experiencing early-morning wakefulness and an inability to fall back to sleep. The trauma-related factors contributing to these sleep disturbances can be categorised as follows:

1. **Physiological arousal**: Trauma can lead to a state of hyperarousal, with increased activity in the amygdala and decreased activity in the medial pre-frontal cortex. This imbalance can inhibit sleep onset and maintain a state of vigilance incompatible with restful sleep (van der Kolk 2015).
2. **REM sleep alterations**: Trauma can fragment or reduce REM sleep, which is crucial for emotional processing and memory consolidation (Socci et al. 2020).
3. **Nightmares and intrusive memories**: Traumatic experiences often manifest as recurring nightmares or intrusive thoughts during the hypnogogic state, impeding sleep initiation (Giannakopoulos and Kolaitis 2021).
4. **Circadian rhythm disruption**: The stress of displacement and adapting to a new environment can disrupt the body's natural sleep-wake cycle (Agorastos and Olff 2021).
5. **Bidirectional relationship**: While trauma can cause sleep disturbances, poor sleep can also exacerbate trauma symptoms and hamper recovery, creating a self-perpetuating cycle (Germain 2013).
6. **Individual variations**: Sleep disturbances vary based on trauma type, age at trauma exposure and individual resilience factors (Richter et al. 2020).

Understanding these factors allows professionals to better support adolescent refugees like Anastasiya in addressing their sleep issues while recognising that although sleep disturbances are a normal response to abnormal circumstances, they can be improved with appropriate supports.

Section 1: For All Professionals Supporting Refugee Adolescents

Psychoeducation

Sleep Literacy for Adolescent Refugees

Sleep literacy is the knowledge and understanding needed to make informed decisions about sleep habits and recognise when sleep difficulties need attention (Feldman and Slavish 2024). To make explanations about sleep age-appropriate and engaging for refugee adolescents, we suggest using a metaphorical narrative tailored to their experiences. By sharing this information in an accessible way, you can help to demystify sleep issues, normalise their experiences, and empower them with knowledge to improve their sleep quality. This approach not only addresses immediate sleep concerns but also contributes to their overall resilience and ability to cope with significant life changes.

The text in the next section gives one example of how to explain fundamental sleep concepts to adolescent refugees. This should be adapted to align with the developmental stage and linguistic competence of the young person you are supporting. By using age-appropriate explanations, you can help refugee adolescents to understand their sleep patterns, fostering a sense of control and promoting more restorative sleep habits. This understanding can reduce worry and provide useful strategies to improve their sleep quality as they adjust to life in their new country. Remember, the goal is to help them better comprehend their sleep experiences, thereby empowering them to manage their sleep more effectively during this significant life transition.

Understanding Sleep: A Journey of Healing for Refugee Adolescents – Suggested Explanation

Sleep can be seen as a restorative power that helps our bodies and minds recover each night. But when you've been forced to leave your home and adjust to a new culture, language and way of being, this natural recovery system might not work as well as it did before. That's completely normal, and I want to help you understand why.

We are going to explore the science of sleep and how it is affected by the big changes and challenges you've faced. Whether you've travelled far from home, experienced traumatic situations, or are simply trying to adapt to a new environment, your sleep patterns might have changed. This isn't your fault – it's your body's way of coping with everything you've been through. Many young people in situations like yours might get used to sleeping differently, while others might want help to sleep better. Everyone's experiences are different.

By learning how sleep works and understanding your own sleep needs, you can start to improve its quality. Think of it as getting to know a new friend – the more you understand them, the better you can get on together. As we explore how sleep works and how stress affects it, remember that there's always a reason behind what you're experiencing. No matter how mixed up your sleep seems right now, there's always a chance to improve it.

One powerful tool in this journey is awareness. Like a skilled gardener tending to a plant, paying attention to our sleep patterns can nurture positive change. By carefully observing how we're currently sleeping without judgement, we can begin to understand the roots of our sleep issues. This gentle cultivation of awareness can be healing in itself, gradually guiding us towards healthier sleep habits. Just as a gardener learns to read the needs of their plants, you can learn to interpret and respond to your own sleep patterns.

Our goal is to help you understand your sleep better, so you don't have to worry about it as much. We'll look at why your experiences might be affecting your sleep and what you can do about it. This knowledge can be a powerful tool as you get used to life in your new country.

The Four Stages of Sleep: A River Journey – Suggested Explanation

Now that we have discussed the importance of understanding your sleep, we are going to explore its different stages. Imagine your sleep is like a journey down a peaceful river. This river has four distinct parts, each with its own purposes to help your body and mind rest and recover.

(1) *The Shallow Waters Stage 1: As you first step into the river, the water is shallow. This is like the beginning of your sleep. You're starting to relax, but you can still easily step back onto the shore wake up if needed.*

(2) *The Gentle Current Stage 2: As you move further into the river, the current becomes steady and carries you along. Your body is more relaxed now, and it's a bit harder to get back to shore.*

(3) *The Deep Pool Stage 3: Now you've reached a deep, still part of the river. Here, the water supports your whole body and you feel heavy and very relaxed. This is where your body does most of its repairing and healing.*

(4) *The Dream Rapids REM sleep: Finally, you reach a part of the river with gentle rapids. The water moves faster here and you might see some interesting things float by – these are your dreams. Your mind is very active in this part, even though your body is still resting.*

Just as a river has different sections that you pass through as you float along, you naturally journey through these different parts of the sleep river several times each night. Each time you float through the river, it's like a new cycle of sleep. Each part of the river helps clean, refresh, and prepare you for the next day.

Remember, even when life feels stormy, trying to give yourself time to float down this sleep river can help you feel more rested and stronger. It's a journey that helps your body and mind heal and grow, no matter where you are or what challenges you face.

By understanding these stages of sleep, you can begin to appreciate the importance of giving yourself enough time to complete this nightly journey. Each stage plays a vital role in helping you process your experiences, recover from stress and prepare for the challenges and opportunities of a new day in your new country. While understanding the sleep stages is crucial, it is equally important to develop practical strategies for achieving a restful sleep. While understanding sleep stages through the river metaphor provides insight, successfully navigating this journey requires proper preparation.

For adolescent refugees like Anastasiya, establishing good sleep habits is particularly important when adjusting to a new environment.

Basic Sleep Hygiene: Building Healthy Sleep Habits

Research has shown that maintaining good sleep hygiene is especially important for trauma-exposed youth as it can help regulate disrupted sleep patterns (Richter et al. 2020). Miriam worked with Anastasiya to develop basic sleep hygiene practices that could help create a more stable foundation for sleep, and the following principles proved to be helpful for Anastasiya:

Creating a Sleep-Friendly Environment

Research indicates that environmental factors significantly impact sleep quality in displaced populations (Simsek and Tekgul 2019). However, even in temporary or shared accommodation, the following small adjustments can have a positive impact:

- Using an eye mask to block out light
- Having a special blanket or comfort item for sleep
- Keeping the sleeping area as quiet and cool as possible

Developing a Consistent Routine

Studies of displaced populations have shown that maintaining regular sleep-wake patterns can help restore the circadian rhythms which have often been disrupted by forced displacement (Richter et al. 2020). Working collaboratively with Anastasiya, Miriam developed sustainable pre-sleep rituals that could be maintained regardless of circumstances:

- Trying to go to bed and wake up at similar times each day.
- Creating a wind-down period of 30 minutes before bed using calming activities, such as the expressive arts activities described in the section on sleep-inducing expressive arts practices.
- Taking a pragmatic approach to technology use by enabling night mode on the phone before bedtime, acknowledging that complete avoidance of phones is unrealistic for adolescents.

Managing Food and Drink

Research has demonstrated the relationship between dietary habits and sleep quality (Godos et al. 2021). While access to food and drink may be limited in different contexts, Anastasiya found these guidelines helpful:

- Avoiding caffeinated drinks in the afternoon and evening.
- Having a light snack before bed if hungry when possible.

- Not going to bed too full or too hungry.
- Keeping a water bottle nearby for the night.

Physical Activity and Light Exposure

Studies show that exposure to natural light and regular physical activity can help regulate sleep patterns (Yamanaka et al. 2015). Miriam encouraged Anastasiya to:

- get some form of physical activity during the day, even if just walking to school;
- spend time outside during daylight hours when possible;
- do gentle stretching before bed; and
- limit vigorous exercise in the evening.

Screen Use and Social Connection

While digital devices can disrupt sleep through blue light exposure (Touitou et al. 2016), they also provide vital social connections for refugee youth. Anastasiya worked with Miriam to find balance by:

- engaging in video calls with family in Ukraine at times that would not disrupt sleep;
- switching her phone to night mode in the evening;
- setting herself boundaries around news checking, especially before bed; and
- using meditation, visualisation, and relaxation apps.

When exploring visualisation apps, Miriam and Anastasiya worked together to develop personalised exercises that felt meaningful and culturally resonant. Miriam recorded these co-created visualisations as voice notes, allowing Anastasiya to maintain a sense of connection between sessions through the familiar comfort of her voice, while also honouring their trusting relationship.

When Sleep Will Not Come

Evidence-based strategies for managing sleeplessness were adapted for Anastasiya's situation (see Walker 2017, for an in-depth exploration of these approaches(:

- If unable to sleep after 20 minutes, getting up and doing a quiet activity until feeling sleepy.
- Using breathing techniques (see Chapter 15 for the locations of all breathing exercises throughout the book).
- Having a 'worry time' earlier in the evening to process concerns.
- Remembering that occasional sleepless nights are normal, especially when adjusting to change.

While establishing these fundamental sleep practices helped create structure for Anastasiya, the complexity of her trauma experiences required additional therapeutic approaches. The next phase of intervention moved beyond basic sleep hygiene to explore how creative engagement could support emotional processing and pre-sleep calming. Anastasiya discovered the power of the expressive arts for managing the psychological barriers to restful sleep and ultimately supporting her journey towards better sleep patterns.

Sleep-Inducing Rest and Relaxation Practices Incorporating the Expressive Arts

When incorporated into bedtime routines, expressive arts activities can prepare the mind and body for restful sleep, serving as a powerful tool to transition from the stress of the day to a state of calm, conducive to sleep. This approach was particularly beneficial for Anastasiya, who struggled with pre-sleep anxiety and intrusive thoughts. Incorporating the expressive arts into rest and relaxation practices before bed helped her to do the following:

1. Process the day's events: expressive arts activities provide a non-verbal outlet to reflect on and release the emotions and experiences of the day, reducing the mental clutter that might otherwise interfere with sleep.
2. Shift focus from worries: creative engagement can redirect attention away from anxious thoughts, helping to break cycles of rumination that often intensify at bedtime.
3. Induce relaxation: the rhythmic and repetitive nature of many creative activities e.g. colouring or listening to music can have a meditative effect, lowering heart rate and promoting physical relaxation.
4. Create a sense of safety: engaging with familiar artistic materials and processes can foster feelings of comfort and security, which are crucial for quality sleep, especially in unfamiliar or challenging environments.
5. Establish a consistent sleep routine: Incorporating expressive arts into a nightly ritual signals to the body and mind that it is time to wind down, enhancing the effectiveness of other sleep hygiene practices.

Miriam worked closely with Anastasiya to introduce and adapt the following techniques, tailoring them to her specific needs and preferences. Through their collaborative efforts, they developed a personalised bedtime routine that effectively addressed Anastasiya's pre-sleep anxiety and intrusive thoughts.

1. Mindful colouring
     Miriam introduced Anastasiya to mindful colouring, a technique that involves focusing on the present moment while engaging in the repetitive and soothing act of colouring. This practice helps quiet the mind, reduce anxiety, and promote relaxation. Miriam provided Anastasiya with Mandala patterns

(see Chapter 9) and nature scenes, which Anastasiya found particularly calming.

2. Sleep playlist creation

Together, Miriam and Anastasiya curated a personalised sleep playlist. This technique involves selecting and arranging calming music, nature sounds, or guided relaxations to create a soothing auditory environment conducive to sleep. Anastasiya discovered that soft instrumental music and gentle rain sounds were most effective for her.

3. Worry dolls

Miriam and Anastasiya created worry dolls. This technique involves crafting small figures and symbolically transferring worries to them before sleep. Anastasiya found comfort in the ritual of 'giving away' her concerns, allowing her mind to rest more easily.

4. Dream landscape visualisation

Miriam guided Anastasiya in developing a dream landscape visualisation. This technique involves imagining a peaceful, safe place in detail, engaging all the senses. Anastasiya created a mental image of a serene forest glade, which she could revisit nightly to help her transition into sleep. This visualisation is a specific application of the Safe Space technique described in Chapter 8, demonstrating how visualisation can be effectively used to create a mental sanctuary for relaxation and sleep preparation.

5. Butterfly hug

Miriam introduced Anastasiya to the butterfly hug technique, a self-soothing method developed by Lucina Artigas while working with survivors of Hurricane Pauline in Acapulco, Mexico, in 1998 (Artiglas and Jarero 2014). This simple yet effective technique involves crossing one's arms over the chest and alternately tapping the upper arms with the hands. The rhythmic bilateral stimulation is believed to activate both hemispheres of the brain, potentially mimicking the natural bilateral stimulation which occurs when our brains are processing and consolidating memories during REM sleep. This helps to process emotional experiences and reduce anxiety.

Miriam carefully guided Anastasiya through the correct application of the butterfly hug, emphasising the importance of finding a comfortable pace and pressure. The ease of self-administration made this technique particularly valuable for Anastasiya who incorporated it into her nightly routine and found it especially helpful during moments of heightened stress or when intrusive thoughts threatened to disrupt her sleep. The technique's versatility and discretion allowed Anastasiya to use it in various settings, providing a quick and effective way to induce a sense of calm and safety whenever needed.

6. Progressive muscle relaxation with body mapping

Miriam taught Anastasiya progressive muscle relaxation combined with a body mapping exercise. The relaxation component involves systematically tensing and relaxing different muscle groups, with Anastasiya imagining the tension as a specific colour e.g. red for tightness and then visualising it fading to a calming blue or gentle warmth as she released each muscle group. After completing the full relaxation sequence, she would then transfer her experience on to a body outline drawing, using different colours or shading to record where she had experienced the most tension. This visual mapping enhanced the body awareness aspect of traditional progressive muscle relaxation, allowing Anastasiya to track patterns in her physical tension over time and more easily identify the areas contributing to her sleep difficulties.

By incorporating these expressive arts-based relaxation techniques into her bedtime routine, Anastasiya was able to develop personalised tools for managing her pre-sleep anxiety and creating a sense of safety and calm. These practices offered her a bridge between the stress of her day and the restfulness of night, helping her to transition more smoothly into sleep. Through consistent use of these creative methods, Anastasiya found herself better equipped to process her daily experiences, quiet her racing thoughts, and cultivate the peaceful state of mind necessary for restorative sleep in her new environment.

Bridging Foundational Support and Therapeutic Work

While the foundational sleep hygiene practices and relaxation techniques introduced in Section 1 can significantly improve sleep quality, additional therapeutic support may be beneficial when adolescents experience:

- persistent nightmares;
- ongoing difficulty with emotional regulation around sleep;
- strong trauma-related content in nighttime experiences; and
- limited improvement from the foundational interventions.

Section 2: For Psychological Therapy Professionals

Dream Awareness and Nocturnal Journaling: Anastasiya's Journey

The relationship between daytime experiences and nighttime processing is especially significant for adolescent refugees navigating traumatic experiences and adjusting to their new cultural context. This connection encompasses all sensory experiences – the sounds of a new language, unfamiliar smells, different textures and tastes of their new environment – all of which can manifest in dreams. Memory and emotional processing are fundamentally linked to sensory input, with research showing that memories triggered by smell and sound evoke the most intense recollections, playing a vital role in processing traumatic experiences (Holzinger et al. 2021). The emergence of these memories in their dreams often creates a complex interplay between their past and present lives. Understanding this relationship between waking experiences and dream content becomes crucial for therapeutic support and healing through approaches such as nocturnal journaling.

Understanding Dreams: From Ancient Wisdom to Modern Science

The connection between our waking lives and our dreams has fascinated humans for centuries (Pick and Roper 2011). While early civilisations interpreted dreams as divine messages and predictors of future events, Aristotle c. 350 BC later proposed that dreams were continuations of our waking thoughts and experiences occurring in an altered state of consciousness (Coolidge 2023). A major shift in dream theory came with Freud's work, which suggested that dreams present our thoughts and desires in disguised, symbolic forms, incorporating sensory elements – visual images, sounds, physical sensations, tastes, and smells – that connect to underlying memories and emotions (Freud 1953, translated by J Strachey).

Modern research has challenged, validated, and built upon these historical perspectives. Studies reveal varying degrees of influence between waking life and dream content, particularly in processing emotional experiences. Vallet et al. (2017) found that 83% of dreams incorporated waking life elements, while Eichenlaub et al. (2019) identified one in three dreams referencing current concerns. Malinowski and Horton (2014) demonstrated that dreams not only reflect recent experiences but also serve crucial cognitive and emotional functions, especially in processing significant life changes. Neuroimaging studies have revealed overlapping brain activation patterns during waking activities and related dream content, with multiple sensory systems engaging simultaneously (Scarpelli et al. 2021).

The interplay between conscious awareness and unconscious processing emerges as fundamental to dream formation and interpretation (Eudell-Simmons and Hilsenroth 2007). Dreams facilitate a unique dialogue between our conscious mind – the realm of active thoughts and immediate awareness – and our unconscious mind, which shapes our psychological processes below awareness. Research suggests that even unremembered dreams contribute to psychological processing (McNamara 2023). This understanding of dreams as a bridge between conscious and unconscious mental processes informs therapeutic approaches like the Nocturnal Journal that helps to integrate waking experiences with dream content for psychological healing.

The Nocturnal Journal: A Bridge between Waking and Dreaming

For refugee adolescents navigating the complexities of forced displacement, the relationship between waking and dreaming takes on particular significance. Their sensory world undergoes fundamental disruption – from the cadence of a new language to unfamiliar environmental sounds, smells, and textures. These sensory shifts often manifest in their dreams, creating a complex interplay between past and present experiences. Drawing on both historical dream work practices and contemporary trauma-informed approaches, the Nocturnal Journal emerged as a therapeutic tool that combines systematic documentation with creative expression. This approach allows refugee adolescents to track their sleep patterns while exploring the deeper meanings of their dreams, offering an adaptable pathway to process their experiences of displacement and cultural transition.

How the Nocturnal Journal Works

Natasha introduced Anastasiya to nocturnal journaling as a therapeutic tool for understanding her nighttime experiences. She emphasised the importance of recording not just visual memories but all sensory aspects of sleep patterns, dream content, and waking mental states. It helped Anastasiya to track her sleep quality over time, identify recurring patterns in her dreams, and gradually understand how her daily experiences shaped her nighttime world. This approach created opportunities for meaning-making and emotional processing in a safe, contained way, supporting her journey towards healing and resilience (San Antonio and Gorelick 2020).

The journal typically includes elements from these two main areas:

Sleep Aspects

- Times and experiences around sleep, going to bed, waking up, disruptions
- Environmental details, room temperature, sounds, smells, physical comfort
- Factors affecting sleep
- Ways of managing sleep difficulties

Dream Aspects

- Dreams remembered
- Feelings and sensations from the dreams
- Connections to daily life
- What helped with dream recall

While these elements offer a starting point, each person naturally develops their own way of recording what matters most. Approaches vary – from focusing on sensory details, to exploring emotions, to expressing experiences through drawings rather than words. The key is finding a natural way to capture these experiences that helps connect daytime and nighttime worlds.

To support dream recall, Natasha suggested both mental and sensory preparation before sleep. Along with having Anastasiya silently repeat: '*Tonight, I remember my dreams. I have excellent dream recall*' she encouraged her to notice and record the sensory details of her bedroom – the feel of her pillow, the sounds from outside, the temperature of the room – to heighten her sensory awareness.

Example from Anastasiya's Journal

> *6ᵗʰ October 2023*
> *My new room tonight:*
> *Too warm*
> *Rain on window sounds different from home*
> *New pillow very soft not like my old one*
> *Mattress very hard*
> *Clean sheets smell different not like mama's washing*
> *Strange voices speaking English outside*
> *Did some colouring with Mandalas to help me feel calm before bed. Went to bed at 10.30pm but couldn't sleep for a long time – thinking about war at home. Worried about my friends.*
> *Finally fell asleep around midnight. Woke briefly at 2.20am but remembered Miriam and Natasha's special breathing. Helped me sleep again.*
> *Woke up at 6.40am. Remember dream very clearly:*
> *I was in my old school in Kyiv, but everything was mixed up. All the signs had English words. Teachers were speaking Ukrainian and English together – I couldn't understand. My friends were there but their talking sounded like singing. Felt strange but not scary. Like it was OK to be half here, half there.*
> *Things I remember:*
> *Footsteps made echoes in corridor, like before school in Kyiv*
> *My classroom had that special smell – chalk and cleaning products*
> *Sun coming through our big windows, making warm light*
> *Taste of my mint gum*
> *What made sleep hard:*
> *First week at a new school*
> *Missing home and friends*
> *Hard to understand what people are saying*
> *New room feels different*
> *New bed feels strange*
> *Everything smells different*
> *Colouring helped. Breathing exercises helped too.*

Therapeutic Applications and Clinical Insight

Working with Journal Content

Through consistent journaling and therapeutic conversations with Natasha, Anastasiya began noticing connections between her daily experiences and her dreams. Natasha encouraged her to explore how sensory experiences from her new environment were woven into her dreams, often blending with familiar sensations from home. This sensory bridging helped Anastasiya understand how her mind was processing the transition between her old and new life.

Using her growing sensory awareness, Anastasiya developed a multi-sensory approach to representing her dreams, using colouring pencils to capture both visual elements and sensations – soft blues for cool temperatures, rough textures for anxiety, wavy lines for musical sounds. Her mini collages incorporated textured materials that captured both visual and tactile elements of her dreams, helping her process experiences that were too difficult to express in words alone. As their therapeutic engagement deepened, meaningful patterns emerged. Anastasiya's dreams often featured scenes where languages merged or transformed – Ukrainian felt familiar and comforting, while English embodied strangeness and uncertainty. In her dreams, both languages often merged into musical sounds, reflecting her experience of moving between two cultures. Natasha helped Anastasiya explore these connections, drawing on the research discussed earlier which shows that dreams significantly relate to recent experiences (Malinowski and Horton 2014).

The Nocturnal Journal evolved into a powerful tool for Anastasiya to maintain agency during her displacement. By systematically documenting her dreams and sleep patterns, Anastasiya developed a structured approach to understanding her experiences, providing a critical sense of control when much of her life felt uncertain. This documentation process allowed her to identify patterns and triggers, particularly in her anxiety dreams, enabling her to make conscious choices about her adjustment process rather than feeling overwhelmed by it.

Multi-Modal Approaches to Dream Processing

Building on this systematic documentation, Natasha helped Anastasiya understand that anxiety dreams, while distressing, can serve important adaptive functions (Samson et al. 2023). Using Holzinger et al.'s 2021 Dream–Sense–Memory approach, she encouraged Anastasiya to recount her anxiety dreams in the present tense while focusing on sensory elements. This created a safe distance from which to explore the emotional content and engage with three key therapeutic processes: cognitive rehearsal for real-world challenges, emotional processing in a secure environment, and memory consolidation of important details.

As their therapeutic relationship deepened, Natasha guided Anastasiya to explore her anxiety dreams more comprehensively. When working with Anastasiya's recurring dreams about getting lost on the way to school, they began by identifying key landmarks and breaking the route into smaller, manageable stages. Building on this practical approach, they moved into expressive arts techniques which offered new ways to work with more complex dream material. She encouraged Anastasiya to represent her recurring nightmares through claywork and drawing, providing another bridge between the dream world and conscious processing, allowing her to explore her experiences in a safe, contained way.

During one session, Anastasiya drew an image of herself standing alone in front of her old school in Kyiv, surrounded by shadowy figures. When discussing the drawing, Natasha encouraged her to notice the sensory memories associated with the scene – the sounds of her footsteps in the empty schoolyard, the familiar smell of the building, the air temperature. Through guided exploration, Anastasiya was supported to begin filling in the gaps with less frightening images, discovering that she could her agency to reshape the nightmare's narrative. This process of engaging with all her senses helped her feel more grounded and in control, while bringing frightening dream experiences into consciousness reduced their emotional impact (Walker and van der Helm 2009).

Through the combined use of the Nocturnal Journal and expressive arts techniques, Anastasiya gradually learned to understand her dreams as tools for processing her refugee experience. Her recurring dreams about English exams, where she felt unprepared and unable to understand questions, motivated her to dedicate more time to language practice. These practical insights, combined with her work on navigation challenges, demonstrated how dream content could guide concrete actions. Natasha explained how dreams incorporate sensory experiences from both past and present environments, helping Anastasiya to recognise these connections in her own dream content. This understanding, coupled with creative expression and sensory awareness exercises, strengthened her overall resilience and ability to cope with significant life changes.

For psychological therapy professionals working with refugee adolescents, this multi-layered approach to dream work offers valuable insights. Understanding how dreams reflect the integration of past and present experiences helps therapists guide young people through their adjustment process. Encouraging open discussion about anxiety dreams can normalise the experience while highlighting their adaptive potential. Dream content can be used to identify specific concerns and develop practical preparation strategies, transforming nighttime anxieties into daytime readiness. This approach better equips young people to face the challenges in their new environments while maintaining connections to their past.

Conclusions

Through complementary interventions from Miriam and Natasha, Anastasiya's journey demonstrates the effectiveness of integrating practical supports with therapeutic work. Miriam's guidance in sleep literacy, hygiene practices, and expressive arts-based relaxation techniques created a solid foundation for restorative sleep, while Natasha's specialised work using nocturnal journaling and dream processing opened up additional pathways for emotional healing. By contextualising her experiences within forced displacement, cultural adaptation, and adolescent development, this creative multi-layered approach transformed Anastasiya's relationship with sleep from a source of anxiety to an opportunity for healing. This integrative strategy demonstrates how sleep-focused interventions can strengthen overall resilience as adolescent refugees adapt to life in their new country, offering valuable insights for supporting the complex sleep needs of refugee youth.

References

Agorastos, A and Olff, M. 2021. 'Sleep, circadian system and traumatic stress'. *European Journal of Psychotraumatology, 12*: 1–7. doi:10.1080/20008198.2021.1956746

Artiglas, L and Jarero, I. 2014. 'The butterfly hug'. In M. Luber, *Implementing eMDR early mental health interventions for man-made and natural disasters: Models, scripted protocols and summary sheets*, 127–130. Springer Publishing Company.

Coolidge, F. 2023. *The science of dream interpretation.* Academic Press.

Eichenlaub, J-B, van Rijn, E, Phelan, M, Ryder, L, Gaskell, M, Lewsi, P, Walker, M, Blagrove, M. (2019) 'The nature of delayed dream incorporation ('dream-lag effect'): Personally significant events persist, but not major faily activities or concerns'. *Journal of Sleep Research*, 28(2). doi.org/10.1111/jsr.12697.

Eudell-Simmons, E and Hilsenroth, M. 2007. 'The use of dreams in psychotherapy: An integrative model.' *Journal of Psychotherapy Integration, 17*(4): 330–356. doi:10.1037/1053-0479.17.4.330

Feldman, E and Slavish, D. 2024. 'Initial development of a sleep health literacy scale'. *Sleep Health: Journal of the National Sleep Foundation*: 1–8. doi:10.1016/j.sleh.2024.08.001

Freud, S. (1953) *The interpretation of dreams* (J.Strachey, Trans.). Hogarth Press (Original work published 1900)

Germain, A. 2013. 'Sleep disturbances as the hallmark of PTSD: Where are we now?' *American Journal of Psychiatry, 17*(4): 372–382.

Ghibellini, R and Meier, B. 2023. 'The hypnagogic state: A brief update'. *Journal of Sleep Research, 32*(1): 1–16. doi:10.1111/jsr.13719

Giannakopoulos, G and Kolaitis, G. 2021. 'Sleep problems in children and adolescents following traumatic life events'. *World Journal of Psychiatry, 11*(2): 27–34.

Godos, J, Grosso, G, Castellano, S, Galvano, F, Caraci, F and Ferri, R. 2021. 'Association between diet and sleep quality: A systematic review'. *Sleep Medicine Reviews, 57.* doi:10,1016/j.smrv.2021.101430

Hanson, S. 2006. 'Sleep physiology'. In H Colten and B Altevogt, *Sleep disorders and sleep deprivation: An unmet public health Problem*, 33–55. National Academies Press.

Harb, G and Schultz, J-H. 2020. 'The nature of post-traumatic nightmares and school functioning in war-affected youth'. *PLoS One, 15*(11): 1–12.

Holzinger, B, Nierwetberg, F L C and Mayer, L. 2021. 'DreamSenseMemory – a Gestalt-based dream-work approach embracing all our senses'. *Research in Psychotherapy: Psychopathology, Process and Outcome, 24*: 122–129.

Jou, Y and Pace-Schott, E. 2022. 'Call to action: Addressing sleep disturbances, a hallmark symptom of PTSD, for refugees, asylum seekers and internally-displaced persons'. *Sleep Health, 8*(5): 593–600.

Malinowski, J and Horton, C. 2014. "Evidence for the preferential incorporation of emotional waking-life experiences into dreams". *Dreaming, 24*(1): 18–31.

McCarthy-Jones, S, Barnes, L, Hill, G, Marwood, L and Moseley, P. 2011. 'When words and pictures come alive: Relating the modality of intrusive thoughts to modalities of hypnagoci/hypnopompic hallucinations'. *Personality and Individual Differences, 51*: 787–790.

McNamara, P. 2023. *The neuroscience of sleep and dreams.* Cambridge University Press.

Pick, D and Roper, L. 2011. *Dreams and history: The interpretation of dreams from Ancient Greece to modern psychoanalysis.* Routledge.

Rae, T. 2023. *Understanding and supporting refugee children and young people: A practical resource for teachers, parents and carers of those exposed to the trauma of war.* Routledge.

Richter, K, Baumgartner, L, Niklewski, G, Peter, L, Kock, M, Kellner, S, . . . Buttner-Teleaga, A. 2020. 'Sleep disorders in migrants and refugees: A systematic review with implications for a personalised medical approach'. *European Association for Predictive, Preventive and Personalised Medicine EPMA, 11*: 251–260.

Samson, D, Clerget, A, Abbas, N, Senese, J, Sarma, M and Lew-Levy, S. 2023. 'Evidence for an emotional adaptive function of dreams: A cross-cultural study'. *Nature, Scientific Reports, 13*(1): 6530. doi:10.1038/s41598-023-43319-z

San Antonio, D and Gorelick, N. 2020. 'Making space for the adolescent unconscious: A case-based reflection on practice. *International Journey of Psychology and Counselling*: 13–21. doi:10.5897/IJC2019.0562

Scarpelli, S, Bartolacci, C, D'Atri, A, Girgini, M and De Gennaro, L. 2021. 'Investigation on neurobiological mechanisms of dreaming in the new decade'. Brain Sciences, 11(2), 220.

Simsek, Y and Tekgul, N. 2019. 'Sleep quality in adolescents in relation to age and sleep-related habitual and environmental factors'. *Journal of Pediatric Research*, 64: 307–313. doi:10.4274/jpr.galenos.2019.86619

Socci, V, Rosi, R, Talevi, D, Crescini, C, Tempesta, D and Pacitti, F. 2020. 'Sleep, stress and trauma'. *Journal of Psychopathology, 26*: 92–98. doi:10.36148/2284-0259-375

Sullican, S, Carskadon, M, Dement, W and Jackson, C. 2021. 'Normal human sleep'. In M Kryger, T Roth and C Goldstein, *Principles and practice of sleep medicine*, 7th edn., 16–26. Elsevier.

Tarokh, L, Short, M, Crowley, S, Fontanellaz-Castiglione, C. and Carskadon, M. 2019. 'Sleep and circadian rhythms in adolescence'. *Current Sleep Medicine Reports, (5)*,:181–192.

Touitou, Y, Touitou, D and Reinberg, A. 2016. 'Disruption of adolescents' circadian clock: The vicious circle of media use, exposure to light at night, sleep loss and risk behaviours'. *Journal of Physiology – Paris, (110)*: 476–479. doi:10.1016/j.jphysparis.2017.05.001

Vallet, R, Chatard, B, Blagrove, M and Ruby, P. 2017. 'Characteristics of the memory sources of dreams: A new version of the content-matching paradigm to take mundane and remote memories into account'. *PLoS ONE, (12)*10: 1–19. doi:10.1371/journal.pone.0185262

van der Kolk, B. 2015. *The body keeps the score: Brain, mind and body in the healing of trauma.* Penguin Books.

Walker, M. 2017. *Why we sleep: The new science of sleep and dreams.* Penguin Random House.

Walker, M and van der Helm, E. 2009. 'Overnight therapy? The role of sleep in emotional brain processing'. *Psychological Bulletin, (13)*55: 731–748.

Yamanaka, Y, Hashimoto, S, Takasu, N, Tanahashi, Y, Nishide, S, Honma, S and Honma, K. 2015. 'Morning and evening physical exercise differentially regulate the autonomic nervous system during nocturnal sleep in humans'. *American Journal of Physiology, (30)*99: 1112–1121.

Chapter 11

Creative Connections
Omar's Journey from Isolation to Community through Football-Themed Group Youth Work and Individual Psychotherapy

Introduction

The story of 14-year-old Omar, who fled Somalia with his 19-year-old sister Amira, illustrates how initial group-based youth work followed by individual psychotherapy created a progressive pathway for healing, with football serving as both a shared activity and metaphorical framework across both interventions. Through youth group activities that used football as both a social connector and a way to understand support networks, Omar began to rebuild his sense of belonging, which then enabled him to engage in deeper therapeutic work where football-based metaphors provided a medium for processing trauma and reconstructing his identity in a new environment.

Through the lens of Bronfenbrenner's ecological systems theory, this case study explores how youth worker Dylan and psychotherapist Mohammed sequentially supported Omar's recovery and development. Dylan first used football-themed creative activities and metaphors in a youth club group setting to help Omar map and expand his existing support systems. Building on this foundation of trust and identity, Mohammed then engaged Omar in individual therapeutic work around trauma processing and identity development, continuing to use football as a 'transcultural portal' through both physical play and symbolic representation. This sequential approach demonstrates how creative interventions can bridge linguistic and cultural barriers while supporting trauma recovery in refugee adolescents.

Omar's Experiences: Pre-flight, Flight, and Post-Flight

Omar and Amira fled Somalia when anti-government rebels attacked their village, separating them from their family during the violence. Growing up in a close-knit rural community, they had been surrounded by a supportive network of extended family and neighbours. Omar's daily life centred around helping with the family's goats and doing small jobs in the local market to help feed the family, as his dad's chronic health condition prevented him from working.

Before the conflict, Omar had happy memories of playing football with his friends in the late afternoons between the garanwa trees on the red, dusty

DOI: 10.4324/9781003430032-12

ground near his home. These spontaneous games offered precious moments of enjoyment and fostered deep feelings of belonging within his community. However, once the conflict started, the dangers of venturing outside forced Omar to remain inside apart from when desperately searching for food in the nearby bush or sharing what little they could find with their neighbours. His role shifted to helping his mother and Amira care for his younger siblings. Both Omar and Amira had quietly nurtured dreams of education, but the abrupt loss of their normal lives, their roles, relationships, and aspirations, combined with the growing uncertainty about their family's fate, profoundly impacted their sense of identity and purpose.

Omar and Amira's 16-month journey to safety took them through many countries. Along the way, they relied on transient connections with other people fleeing their countries and support from volunteers for survival. Amira shouldered the new burden of protecting her brother, which altered their sibling dynamic as she worked to balance this responsibility while staying emotionally strong. Throughout their displacement, Omar found moments of unity and normality through playing football with other young refugees in refugee camps. These spontaneous football games transcended language barriers, offering brief moments of connection amid the chaos.

Upon arrival in Ireland at ages 15 and 20, the siblings were placed together in a refugee reception centre. Noticing Omar's withdrawal into himself and his social isolation, the centre manager connected him with a local youth club where he joined a group for refugee youth led by Dylan, a gentle and patient youth worker with extensive experience working with displaced young people. The group sessions followed a structured approach, beginning with stabilisation activities to help members feel safe, moving through psychoeducation work to understand available supports, and gradually creating space for bearing witness to each other's journeys through creative expression. Their shared passion for football naturally emerged as one way to build connections alongside other creative approaches. Although initially hesitant, Omar gradually began to engage with these opportunities to rebuild his social world, supported by both Dylan and his peers in the group.

Omar's subsequent referral to Mohammed for psychotherapy opened another pathway to healing. Building on the football connections that had emerged naturally in the youth group setting, Mohammed created a therapeutic space where football could serve as a 'transcultural portal' for processing deeper emotional experiences.

This complementary support approach, combining Dylan's group-based creative work to build practical support networks followed by Mohammed's deeper individual therapeutic process, bridged Omar's internal world with external possibilities, leading to his engagement with the local football team. This marked a crucial step in rebuilding his capacity for trust and belonging, demonstrating how the combination of group youth work and individual therapy could support his journey towards reconnection.

Section 1: Building Connections through Group Youth Work

Following Omar's arrival at the refugee reception centre, his connection to the local youth club by the centre's manager proved to be a crucial turning point. The club ran specialised group sessions for refugee youth, creating a space where young people could begin building their social connections while processing their experiences through creative activities. All members of the group shared a passion for football, which naturally emerged as one way to build connections alongside other creative approaches. Under Dylan's facilitation, these sessions were carefully structured to accommodate varying levels of comfort and engagement, recognising that each young person's journey towards connection would follow its own time-line. The group setting offered unique opportunities for peer support and shared understanding, while still allowing space for individual expression and healing.

Stabilisation and Relationship-Building

When Dylan first introduced creative activities at the youth club, he recognised how the varying comfort levels of different group members required a flexible approach. The space was intentionally arranged to include both quiet corners for individual work and open areas for movement-based activities, allowing all group members to choose their level of engagement. The sessions evolved naturally over several weeks, beginning with simple grounding activities that the group members could engage with at their own pace. In one corner of the room, participants could access clay and playdough for tactile engagement. Omar initially gravitated towards this activity, often sitting quietly with others who shared his preference for hands-on materials. Drawing materials were always available on tables near the windows, where some group members found comfort in creating simple patterns and designs. A textile station offered various fabrics and materials for sensory exploration, while a dedicated space for gentle movement activities allowed the group to incorporate their shared interest in football through simple warm-up exercises and footwork practice with soft footballs.

As sessions progressed, Dylan observed how the group naturally attended to each other's comfort levels. When Omar hesitated to join more active exercises, other group members would moderate their energy, creating a more welcoming atmosphere for him. The football elements emerged organically: the gentle passing of a soft ball during check-ins, the incorporation of basic football movements into grounding exercises, and quiet conversations about favourite teams while working with art materials.

Dylan maintained flexibility throughout the sessions, allowing each young person to regulate their engagement based on their emotional state and energy levels. Some days, group members might gather around the art materials, working quietly in shared company. Other days, they might engage in more active exercises, with football often serving as a bridge between individual activities and group interaction. This careful balance of structure and freedom helped create an environment where young people like Omar could gradually move from observation to participation at their own pace.

Through this stabilisation phase, the shared rhythm of regular sessions and consistent activities helped build a sense of safety and predictability. The group's common interest in football provided natural moments of connection, while the variety of creative options ensured that everyone could find ways to feel comfortable and grounded within the space.

Understanding Support Networks through Creative Psychoeducation

Research has shown that empowering adolescent refugees to recognise their existing support networks while facilitating the development of new ones yields significant psychosocial benefits. By increasing the visibility and accessibility of both formal and informal support systems, this process reduces isolation and enhances resilience (Schwartz and Rhodes 2016). Building on the foundation of trust and stability established in the early sessions, Dylan introduced visual tools to help the group understand both support networks and their own responses to displacement. Using their shared interest in football as a starting point, he created activities that would help them recognise common responses to their experiences while learning about support services and developing coping strategies.

Visual Resource Mapping

Over several sessions, Dylan guided the group through creating a comprehensive visual system for understanding community resources. The process began when one group member mentioned that he did not know where to access English language support. This initiated broader conversations about navigating services in their new community and managing the feelings that came with seeking help. Dylan responded by introducing his 'team support map' activity. Together, the group created a large diagram on a magnetic dry-wipe board on the wall, dividing it into different zones like a football pitch. The familiar format immediately engaged the young people, with several offering suggestions about how to organise different types of support.

In the first session, they focused on placing photographs, held in place by magnets, of local places including the community centre, the library, different sports facilities, and the youth club, onto the football pitch. Several members recognised places which they had seen but had been hesitant to enter. They shared feelings of uncertainty and anxiety about approaching new services, which helped normalise these common responses. This led to exploring practical strategies, with group members suggesting approaches such as visiting new services with a friend from the youth club, writing down questions before appointments, or practising conversations in advance. These strategies became part of their personal toolkits, with Omar noting in his phone: 'For new places – buddy system with Ahmed from football, deep breaths like Dylan showed us, remember others feel nervous too. Numbers for youth club and reception centre saved under favourites.'

The following week they added simple symbolic drawings representing different types of support using universally recognisable symbols – a red cross for medical help, a book for education, a handshake for social support, and sports equipment for sports groups. Omar had a natural ability for suggesting clear, simple symbols that everyone could understand, helping bridge language barriers within the group. The symbols included representations for emotional and psychological support services – including the youth counselling service, cultural support groups, and the school wellbeing team – making these resources more visible and accessible. Finally, using coloured string to connect related services, they created a pattern similar to the passing movements drawn on a football tactics board. This visual metaphor resonated strongly with the group, leading to conversations about how different services could work together like players on a team.

Understanding Support Networks

Building on the enthusiasm for the support pitch diagram, Dylan developed the activity further through an interactive exercise he called 'Team tactics in motion' which evolved naturally over three sessions:

- In the first session, Dylan laid out a green training mat marked with football pitch lines. Group members could physically move around this space, positioning themselves in different 'zones' representing various types of support – close support like family and specialist services such as healthcare in the forward line. Initial hesitation quickly gave way to engagement as the adolescent refugees began suggesting additional zones and sharing their experiences with different types of support, including ways they helped each other cope with difficult days.
- The second session saw the group adding connections between positions using coloured string. When someone stood in the 'medical support' zone, others would help create string connections to related services like counselling or youth groups. This collaborative process often led to participants sharing useful information with each other about services which they had discovered.
- In the final session, participants developed personalised 'invisible toolkits' – digital visual guides stored in the notes section of their phone, which mapped out their support networks and coping strategies. Using a combination of text and images, each young person identified their key supports for various situations and documented strategies that helped build their resilience. This activity naturally evolved into peer support, with group members enriching each other's toolkits by suggesting additional resources and sharing effective coping mechanisms (see Chapter 8 for a detailed exploration of developing mental health toolkits.)

Throughout these activities, football provided a familiar framework that helped make abstract concepts of support more concrete and accessible. The shared understanding of football tactics and teamwork created a common language through which the group could explore and understand the complex network of supports available to them, while normalising their experiences and building practical coping skills.

Bearing Witness

Building on the trust and connections developed through these team-based activities, Dylan introduced eco-mapping as a way for the group to explore their journeys and support networks more deeply. Originally developed by Hartman (1978) to visualise social supports and relationships, eco-maps have been effectively adapted for creative work with adolescent refugees by using physical objects and symbols as an alternative to traditional paper diagrams (Hoare 2022). This creative approach offers a tangible way to explore the multiple interconnected environmental systems that Bronfenbrenner (1979) identified as central to human development and makes the mapping process more engaging and culturally responsive, particularly when working with young people from diverse backgrounds.

Moving from the team format to more personal creative expression, Dylan thoughtfully arranged the space with the following range of materials for each participant:

- a range of coloured fabrics for backgrounds;
- different coloured threads for representing connections;
- a wide selection of magazine images for symbolic representation; and
- cardboard for mounting selected magazine images.

The group members gathered around the materials. Initially quiet as they explored them, some immediately reached for images that caught their eye, while others like Omar took time to consider their choices. The shared process of selection and creation soon led to conversations about the significance of different symbols within their various cultures.

The eco-mapping process unfolded organically within the group setting. Omar's choice of a leopard, a powerful symbol in Somalia culture, resonated with several other members who began selecting their own culturally significant images. He positioned this central image on a light blue fabric that reflected his national flag, prompting others to share stories about their own national colours and symbols.

From these personal symbols, group members began developing intricate patterns of connection using coloured thread carefully pinned to their chosen fabric. Building on their experience with the team support maps, a shared colour-coding system emerged through group discussion:

- Red thread connected family members;
- Blue represented friendships;
- Gold linked places of emotional significance; and
- Green marked new connections in their host country.

The physical process of creating these maps within the shared space fostered natural moments of connection. As Omar traced patterns with his threads, linking memories of his father's shop and favourite football playing locations with gold thread, others in the group began sharing their own stories of significant places. The simple yet meaningful process of choosing colours and symbols and arranging the threads gave each young person agency over their memories while creating opportunities for shared understanding.

The tactile nature of the materials played a crucial role in supporting both individual expression and group connection. The texture of the fabric, the weight of the pins, and the flow of the threads helped participants remain grounded while exploring potentially difficult memories. When words felt challenging, group members could focus on the physical act of creating their maps, moving at their own pace while remaining part of the shared experience.

The eco-maps gradually evolved into complex visual representations of their journeys. Just as he had shown a natural ability for creating clear symbols in the earlier activities, Omar's systematic approach to representing his different microsystems inspired others in the group to develop their own meaningful systems of representation. Some members integrated football-related images – photos of matches played in refugee camps or symbols of teams that had helped them maintain a sense of continuity during displacement, echoing the football metaphors that had helped them understand support networks in earlier sessions. These choices often sparked gentle conversations about how sports had provided moments of connection throughout their journeys.

As trust deepened within the group, participants began adding new layers representing their present and potential future connections. Omar chose green thread to create fresh pathways from his central image – connecting to pictures symbolising his current support network: his sister Amira, youth worker Dylan, Robbie the night-time caretaker at the reception centre, and emerging friendships at the youth club. Seeing these new threads alongside the original patterns helped group members recognise that while their previous support networks had been disrupted, they could gradually build new connections while honouring their existing bonds.

This creative approach transformed the abstract concept of 'rebuilding networks' into something tangible. While each person worked on their individual eco-map, sharing the space allowed them to witness and support each other's process. When ready, participants shared their completed maps with each other, creating a powerful collective narrative of displacement, resilience, and hope. Through this process, Dylan observed how the shared experience of creative expression fostered natural connections between participants while respecting each person's unique pace of engagement.

As Omar's engagement with the group deepened through these creative processes, Dylan noticed that certain themes around loss and trust were emerging in his eco-map that might benefit from more focused therapeutic support. In consultation with the reception centre staff and Amira, Omar was referred to Mohammed, a psychotherapist experienced in working with refugee youth. Building on the role that football had played in the group setting – both as a shared interest and a metaphor for understanding support networks – Mohammed created a therapeutic space where football could serve as a transcultural portal for deeper emotional work. This integrated approach which built on Dylan's group-based creative work with Mohammed's deeper individual therapeutic process,would prove crucial in supporting Omar's journey towards healing and reconnection.

Section 2: The Therapeutic Journey: Football as a Portal for Trauma Processing, Memory Integration, and Identity Development

Trauma Memory Processing

Mohammed recognised that the football metaphors that had helped Omar understand support networks in the group setting could now serve as a pathway for processing deeper trauma. During their first meeting, Mohammed observed Omar's physical manifestation of trauma – eyes fixed firmly on the ground, body tense with hypervigilance. Yet when Omar spotted the football beneath a chair and tentatively reached for it, Mohammed recognised what Hoare (2020) terms a 'transcultural portal' – a means of connection that transcended linguistic and cultural barriers.

This connection was particularly meaningful given that football had provided continuity throughout Omar's displacement. From casual games in Somalia to spontaneous matches in refugee camps, it had now evolved into a tool for building relationships in the youth club setting and engaging with deeper therapeutic work around trauma and identity. Through this familiar medium, Omar could begin to regulate his nervous system and connect with Mohammed. The simple act of passing the ball back and forth in the therapy room became their first shared language, creating a safe foundation for the trauma processing work ahead.

As Omar's comfort with this form of interaction grew, the table football set in the therapy room became a contained space where he could begin mapping his journey. Working with the miniature figures, he was able to represent different aspects of his experience: the sudden disruption of his life in Somalia, the protective role his sister played during their flight, and moments of connection found in refugee camps. Using the football as a grounding object, Omar gradually expressed his experiences through metaphor: 'Sometimes you feel offside,' he explained while arranging the figures, 'like you're in the wrong position, running at the wrong time.' This metaphorical framework allowed him to express complex feelings about displacement and separation while maintaining emotional safety.

Building on the success of these metaphorical explorations, Mohammed introduced a sand tray alongside the table football game, recognising how this additional therapeutic medium could help Omar process trauma through both symbolic play and sensory engagement. The sand tray's contained space mirrored the holding environment of psychotherapy, while its tactile properties helped regulate Omar's nervous system during difficult narratives. Omar created three-dimensional scenes in the tray, incorporating both the miniature football figures and other symbolic objects, allowing him to actively reshape his narrative, smoothing away and rebuilding scenes as needed.

Omar's positive response to the sand tray reflected broader therapeutic principles that make this approach particularly valuable in trauma work. The tactile engagement with sand activates the body's natural capacity for self-soothing, while the creation of a miniature world provides psychological distance from overwhelming experiences. This distance allows those who engage to externalise their internal world and gain new perspectives on their experiences. The non-verbal nature of sand tray work also bypasses potential linguistic barriers and accesses implicit memories that may be difficult to verbalise, making it particularly valuable in transcultural therapeutic work.

In Omar's case, the sand tray became a powerful medium for expressing aspects of his journey that were too complex for words alone. He began incorporating natural elements such as stones and twigs to represent obstacles encountered during his displacement, while carefully positioned football figures came to symbolise moments of resilience and connection. The combination of familiar football metaphors with the therapeutic properties of sand work created a unique processing space where Omar could safely explore both past trauma and future hopes. Mohammed observed how Omar's increasing comfort with the medium paralleled his growing capacity to integrate difficult experiences, noting how he would sometimes reshape the sand surface multiple times before settling on a representation that felt true to his experience.

Drawing on these emerging expressions of his experience, each session built carefully on the previous one, allowing Omar to process his experiences at his own pace while staying within his window of tolerance – the optimal zone of arousal where he could process experiences without becoming overwhelmed or shutting down (Siegel and Payne Bryson 2012). Mohammed observed that combining the football metaphors with sand tray work created multiple pathways for emotional expression, particularly valuable when verbal communication felt overwhelming or inaccessible. The physical act of arranging figures in the sand or smoothing the surface provided emotional regulation while advancing the therapeutic work. This integration of approaches demonstrated how creative interventions could support trauma processing while maintaining emotional safety.

Integration of Trauma Memories

The therapeutic work evolved naturally from processing individual memories to helping Omar develop a more coherent narrative of his experiences. Following Peter Levine's titration principle (Levine 2010), which involves approaching difficult memories gradually while maintaining emotional regulation, Mohammed guided Omar through integrating his fragmented experiences into a more complete story. When directly processing memories felt too intense, Omar moved fluidly between different expressive modalities.

Mohammed introduced Omar to Matryoshka (Russian nesting) dolls to explore the layers of his journey (see Day and Day 2012, for creative ways to use these dolls in therapy settings). The set of five dolls created a physical metaphor for how each phase of his life remained present within him. At the core, the smallest doll held his early childhood in Somalia. Moving outward, each subsequent doll contained a crucial transition: the violent displacement from his home, his time in refugee camps, his arrival in Ireland, and finally his present self, represented by the largest doll that encompassed all the others. This nested structure mirrored how past experiences continue to live within us, shaping our present selves while remaining contained and potentially accessible. This nested structure mirrored how past experiences continue to live within us, shaping our present selves while remaining contained and potentially accessible. Omar carefully arranged these dolls on the football pitch mat which Mohammed had laid out, creating a physical representation of how these different versions of himself coexisted with his present identity. He photographed this arrangement, noting how the dolls could be opened and closed like chapters in his story, giving him control over when to explore different periods of his life.

Building on this metaphor of containing and revealing, Omar created a visual timeline around the edges of the football pitch mat, incorporating photographs, drawings, and written words. Each segment of the timeline aligned with different periods symbolised by the Matryoshka dolls, weaving together the nested elements of the story. Taking photographs of this evolving timeline allowed Omar to document his progress and reflect on how different elements of the story connected. Through this multi-modal approach, Omar could process his experiences at his own pace while staying emotionally regulated.

Omar's capacity for memory integration deepened through embodied storytelling (Letherby and Davidson 2015) which facilitated healing in multiple ways. First, it allowed access to implicit memories stored in the body that might be difficult to verbalise. Second, it offered a way to regulate emotional intensity through movement; and third, it helped integrate sensorimotor experiences with narrative memory. In one pivotal session, he physically enacted a football match from his childhood in Somalia, moving between positions on an imagined pitch while narrating memories of playing with his friends. His movements shifted noticeably as he described the day of the attack, his body lowering and his steps becoming uncertain, before demonstrating how he found moments of stability through spontaneous games in refugee camps. These embodied stories, combining movement with football metaphors, allowed him to integrate physical memories with his verbal narrative while staying within his window of tolerance.

This embodied expression became increasingly nuanced as Omar incorporated specific football movements that held meaning from different periods of his life. The quick footwork learned between the garanwa trees became a bridge to childhood memories, while defensive positioning developed during flight emerged in his movement sequences. Mohammed observed how Omar's body language shifted as he moved through these memories, flowing smoothly during happy recollections, becoming hesitant when approaching difficult memories, and then finding stability again through familiar football movements.

Identity Development

As Omar's memories became more integrated, his therapeutic work naturally progressed towards exploring and developing his evolving sense of identity. The Matryoshka dolls, which had helped him understand the layered nature of his experiences, became central to understanding his emerging sense of self. Mohammed observed how Omar began giving each nested doll deeper meaning: the smallest doll, representing his early childhood in Somalia, held memories of play and family connection; the next embodied his experience of displacement, revealing his emerging resilience in protecting his siblings; the following doll captured his time in refugee camps, where he developed resourcefulness in forging new connections; the fourth doll represented his arrival in Ireland; and the largest doll embodied his present self, containing all previous versions while embracing new dimensions of identity as a student, supportive friend, and cultural bridge-builder. The physical act of opening and closing these dolls allowed Omar to explore how each version of himself remained present and potentially accessible, contributing to his ongoing journey of self-discovery.

Through continued work with the sand tray, Omar began exploring how these different aspects of his identity interacted. He arranged the dolls in various configurations – sometimes partially nested, sometimes standing separately – exploring how different parts of himself emerged or retreated depending on the circumstances. His scenes grew more complex, depicting the coexistence of his multiple selves: the brave child who fled Somalia, the protective brother, the survivor in refugee camps, and his emerging self in Ireland. The ability to reshape and rework these scenes in the sand reflected his growing understanding that identity could be fluid and multifaceted while remaining coherent.

The embodied storytelling that had helped Omar process his memories evolved into a medium for exploring his present identity. His movements became more confident as he enacted different life roles: Amira's brother, his growing friendships at the youth club, and his place in the wider community. These physical expressions helped him to understand how his various roles and relationships could complement one another.

Mohammed observed Omar's deepening sense of self as he wove together his Somali heritage with his Irish identity. In the sand tray, he blended elements from both cultures – placing traditional Somali objects alongside symbols of his new life, creating scenes that embraced both worlds. The Matryoshka dolls in these scenes often represented how his cultural identity, like the nested dolls themselves, could contain multiple layers, each one enriching the whole.

Omar's growing confidence led him to mentor others in the community, particularly at the youth club where his journey began. This role demonstrated how therapeutic insights could translate into practical engagement across multiple ecological systems, strengthening his sense of agency and purpose. His transition from participant to mentor in group activities reflected his growing capacity to bridge past experiences with present opportunities while building pathways towards future possibilities. The photographs he had taken of his Matryoshka doll arrangements and sand tray scenes became touchstones in this process, reminding him of how far he had come and inspiring his vision for the future.

Conclusions

Omar's journey from isolation to connection illustrates the potential of a carefully structured, multi-modal approach to supporting adolescent refugees. The complementary relationship between group youth work and individual therapy created multiple pathways for healing and growth across different ecological systems. Dylan's creative group work provided a foundation of safety and preliminary support network development, while Mohammed's individual therapy enabled deeper processing of trauma and identity integration.

This case study highlights several valuable principles in creative therapeutic work with refugee adolescents: the power of establishing safety through predictable, culturally responsive activities; the effectiveness of working across multiple expressive modalities; and the importance of maintaining cultural continuity while supporting integration into a new environment. The variety of approaches, from tactile materials to embodied expression, offered Omar different channels for processing his experiences and building connections.

Omar's progression from initial stabilisation to becoming a mentor in the youth club setting demonstrates how therapeutic insights can extend into meaningful community engagement. His story illustrates how thoughtfully integrated creative interventions can help adolescent refugees rebuild their sense of self and community following displacement, supporting their capacity to thrive in new environments.

References

Bronfenbrenner, U. 1979. *The ecology of human development.* Harvard University Press.
Day, C and Day, R. 2012. *Matryoshka's in therapy: Creative ways to use Russian dolls with clients.* Book Creative Therapy.

Hartman, A. 1978. 'Diagrammatic assessment of family relationships'. *Social Casework*, *59*(8): 465–476.

Hoare, R. 2020. 'From global phenomenon to framework for living: using the beautiful game creatively to provide therapeutic care for unaccompanied male adolescents seeking asylum in Ireland'. *International Journal of Migration, Health and Social Care*, *16*(4): 373–387.

Hoare, R. 2022. 'Friends as family: Using composite psychotherapy case material to explore the importance of friendships for unaccompanied adolescent refugees coping with the challenges of resettlement in ireland'. *Journal of Refugee Studies*, *35*(3): 1160–1185.

Letherby, G and Davidson, D. 2015. 'Embodied storytelling: Loss and bereavement, creative practices and support. *Illness', Crisis & Loss*, *23*(4): 343–360.

Levine, P. 2010. *In An unspoken voice: How the body releases trauma and restores godness.* North Atlantic Books.

Schwartz, S and Rhodes, J. 2016. 'From treatment to empowerment: New approaches to youth mentoring'. *American Journal of Community Psychology*: 150–157. doi:10.1002/ajcp.12070

Siegel, D and Payne Bryson, T. 2012. *The whole-brain child: 12 proven strategies to nurture your child's developing mind.* Constable and Robinson Ltd.

Chapter 12

Ovie's Story

Voices beyond Silence: Collective Healing for Displaced Youth

Introduction

Sixteen-year-old Ovie travelled alone from West Africa to Ireland, marked by loss and trauma. As the son of a government official, his life was shattered when government rebels arrived in his village seeking revenge against his father, forcing the whole family to flee. After briefly finding refuge with his sister at their grandmother's house, he left to search for supplies and returned to discover the rebels had killed them. With his aunt's help, he began a harrowing journey across borders, enduring exploitation, including human trafficking.

Upon arrival in Ireland, Ovie was placed under the protection of the Irish Child and Family Agency (Tusla) in a supervised unit with other unaccompanied minors. In this new environment, he struggled with devastating losses, withdrew from others, had nightmares, and found it hard to trust or connect – natural responses to trauma. The care team patiently built trust and safety by using the grounding techniques from Chapter 5 and other case studies.

Initially reluctant, Ovie agreed after three months to join a therapeutic arts group for young refugees. He found pathways to healing through shared creative experiences and activities. The male-only group was designed to create a culturally sensitive space for male adolescent refugees to process their experiences. This approach recognised participants' cultural backgrounds and trauma, facilitating open expression and sharing.

Building on Chapter 11's case study of an expressive arts group facilitated by a youth worker, this chapter describes an expressive arts psychotherapy group that uses shared creative experiences to nurture therapeutic healing among adolescent refugees processing profound trauma and loss. Through Ovie's story, we witness how psychotherapeutic group work enables both individual processing and the development of supportive connections between refugee adolescents who understand each other's complex, often fragmented journeys.

Therapeutic Groups

Therapeutic groups play a vital role in trauma recovery, creating safe spaces where survivors can share and witness each other's experiences of both trauma and

DOI: 10.4324/9781003430032-13

survival (Herman 1992). Such groups draw healing power from the deep understanding that develops among participants recognising shared experiences. Group therapy offers refugee adolescents a strong platform for recovery and growth (Kira et al. 2012). Within such a supportive environment, young refugees find opportunities to normalise their responses to trauma and loss while diminishing their sense of isolation (Hutchinson et al. 2022). The combination of safety, mutual support, and emotional expression characteristic of these groups serves as a particularly powerful vehicle for processing profound losses (Jalonen and Cilia La Corte 2017).

Integrating expressive arts approaches within therapeutic groups provides refugee adolescents with non-verbal pathways for processing difficult experiences while honouring cultural expressions of loss (Bytyci and Zymberi 2023). Through flexible creative activities, therapists work together to help group members explore painful memories and emotions at their own pace, supported by peers who understand the complexity of forced displacement (Knettel et al. 2023). This combination of therapeutic containment, creative engagement, and group cohesion creates opportunities for both individual and collective meaning-making around experiences of loss.

Therapeutic Framework and Session Structure

Co-Facilitation

Working with refugee adolescents who have experienced profound trauma and loss in a therapy group setting requires careful attention to both individual and group needs. For this reason, the group was co-facilitated by psychotherapists Miriam and Ayesha, whose complementary skills and cultural knowledge enriched the therapeutic space. This model allowed one therapist to guide the group's flow and process while the other stayed attuned to individual responses, particularly when painful memories or emotions surfaced. Co-facilitation provided deeper therapeutic containment, modelled collaborative relationships, and ensured cultural sensitivity throughout the sessions. Furthermore, for group members like Ovie, who had experienced the rupture of trusted relationships, witnessing two therapists working together respectfully became an important part of the healing process.

Therapeutic Tools and Rituals

The therapeutic framework thoughtfully incorporated objects and rituals for regulation and grounding. The singing bowl, a traditional sound healing tool made of bronze or different metals, played an important role. Used in Buddhist meditation for centuries, singing bowls create gentle, resonant tones when struck or played with a wooden striker (called a mallet) (Seetharaman et al. 2024). Beyond marking the beginning and end of sessions, their sustained vibrations guide practitioners deeper into contemplation, helping maintain focus and inner stillness. Resonant tones and gentle vibrations can reconnect those who feel disconnected from their bodies. The sound draws attention outward, while the vibrations foster a sense of presence.

Natural objects like stones, shells, and pine cones were chosen for their grounding properties and potential as transitional objects. Winnicott's (1953) concept of transitional objects provides links between the therapeutic space and participants' daily lives. For young people facing disruption and loss, a tangible item between sessions could help them feel connected and grounded. Consistent opening and closing rituals, combined with these objects, create a predictable environment essential for trauma recovery.

The Sessions

Miriam and Ayesha developed a flexible therapeutic model carefully shaped for adolescent male refugees navigating profound loss and trauma. The single-gender composition reflected careful consideration of cultural sensitivities and therapeutic needs within this specific context, while acknowledging that preferences for group composition can vary among individuals and cultures. This model integrated Herman's (1992) trauma recovery model, group therapy approaches for refugees (Kira et al. 2012; Boyles et al. 2024), expressive arts approaches with young refugees (Bytyci and Zymberi 2023; Ramadan et al. 2024), and the clinical experience of the two psychotherapists, to create culturally responsive spaces for the verbal and non-verbal processing of loss. The one-and-a-half-hour sessions were structured with consistent opening and closing rituals that provided containment (Jalonen and Cilia La Corte 2017). The core focus of each session centred on collaborative meaning-making through creative expression and shared narratives.

Sessions were structured around the six-stage framework from previous case studies to support group members' needs. Each session built incrementally, moving from establishing safety to exploring loss and trauma, and finally to living with and honouring these experiences. Sessions remained flexible to accommodate cultural expressions of loss and respond to group dynamics and needs. The following sections detail this therapeutic framework across six sessions, using Ovie's journey to illustrate safety and connection.

Session 1: Stabilisation and Relationship-Building

Ovie paused at the therapy room doorway, absorbing the peaceful atmosphere Miriam and Ayesha had created. Soft classical music filled the room, with large cushions creating a welcoming circle around a low table. An LED candle softly illuminated shells, fir cones, and polished stones. A singing bowl sat beside them, its metal gleaming softly in the candlelight.

Miriam noticed his hesitation and welcomed him by name, inviting him to sit on a cushion wherever he felt comfortable, even apart from the circle. Other participants were settling in, some cross-legged on cushions, others with their backs against the wall for safety. Once everyone was settled, Ayesha lifted the singing bowl from the table. She gently explained they would start each session by passing the bowl around. 'You can make one sound or pass it along – whatever feels right today,' she said. She drew the striker around the bowl's rim, producing a clear tone that filled the room.

As the bowl circled, some participants made sounds while others passed it in silence. Ovie held it momentarily before passing it on. His silence was accepted by the therapists and group members. Miriam said: 'As we gather today, we carry memories of loved ones who cannot be here.' She allowed a moment of quiet acknowledgement before gently guiding the group into their next activity.

Miriam guided participants through gentle neck rolls and shoulder stretches, explaining how these movements help the body relax. 'Now we'll do some simple breathing together,' she said softly. 'When we breathe slowly, our body has a special way of helping us feel calm. Let's breathe in for four counts, hold for a moment, then breathe out for six counts.' As they practised together, she explained. 'Our body has two different modes. One for when we feel scared or stressed. And another for when we feel safe. This slow breathing helps switch on our safe mode. Making our heartbeat slower and our muscles relax. It's like pressing a gentle pause button for our body.'

Miriam gestured to a side table with arranged art materials. 'Now that we've connected with our breath and bodies, express your present feelings using these materials,' she explained, indicating the coloured paper, markers, crayons, and oil pastels. 'There's no wrong way to do this. Choose colours that match your mood, create patterns, or let your hand move across the page. Take your time.' Some began drawing immediately, while others, including Ovie, observed to feel secure in their new environment.

Miriam and Ayesha moved quietly through the space, attuned to subtle signals from participants. When someone glanced up seeking reassurance, they offered gentle nods or small gestures of acknowledgement. They maintained a respectful distance from those who were focused on their work and from those like Ovie who chose to observe, communicating through their presence that both participation and observation were equally valid choices. As the creative activity drew naturally to a close, Ayesha gently guided the group back into the circle.

Participants shared their names and interests in this safe space. Both therapists modelled this by sharing interests while maintaining boundaries. A young interpreter provided translation support, but the moments of silence between responses were equally valued. Participants discussed music, football, the gym, and cooking, creating a subtle web of connections.

Ayesha invited everyone to choose a natural object from the centre table. Ovie selected a polished stone, running his finger over it. These objects would link the therapy room's safety to the outside world, available for participants to touch to reconnect with their sense of calm. For young people like him, tangible items between sessions could help maintain a sense of connection and grounding.

Miriam and Ayesha guided the group in a final grounding exercise, inviting participants to hold their objects and take three deep breaths. They explained that just as these objects found safety in their hands, the group had also created a safe space together. These objects would be physical reminders of safety, available to touch or hold when participants wished to reconnect with the group's calm.

As three clear notes from the singing bowl marked the end of their time together, some participants slipped their objects into their pockets or continued to hold them – each object now more than a simple stone or shell, but a small anchor to this experience of safety. The therapists remained present and available as the adolescents prepared to leave, gently reminding them of the session time the following week.

This carefully crafted first session laid the foundation for the therapeutic journey ahead. Through predictable routines and gentle boundaries, it created a containing environment where young people carrying profound experiences of loss and displacement could begin to feel secure. This sense of safety would gradually enable them to explore their stories through creative expression and shared understanding.

Session 2: Strengthening Safety and Beginning to Share

This session built on the trust established in the first meeting. This session invites participants to explore tactile and interactive experiences through sand art, moving beyond initial grounding exercises and simple art materials. This shift from individual expression to shared spaces would test and strengthen the group's emerging security. Upon arriving for the second session, the familiar cushions and gentle music eased Ovie's anxiety. Several group members brought their chosen objects from the previous week, some already holding them as they settled into the circle. Ovie's singing bowl experiment produced a soft tone, receiving gentle nods of encouragement from participants and therapists.

Miriam introduced an activity to build on the safety from their first session and offer new expression opportunities. Cushions were moved to create space around two large tables covered with white paper. Ovie noticed the careful arrangement of shallow trays with coloured sand and small bottles of clear glue. The materials chosen reflected therapists' focus on creating sensory experiences to regulate the nervous system during trauma work.

Today we'll use sand and glue to create patterns, Miriam explained, demonstrating slowly. 'Watch how the glue creates different lines.' Varying pressure on the bottle produced delicate threads and broader pathways. 'Then we sprinkle sand over the glue,' she said, pouring sand over a section. She tapped off the excess to reveal the pattern beneath, her methodical movements offering a model of mindful engagement that Ovie found reassuring.

'You might like to create patterns that flow into each other,' she suggested, 'or keep your designs separate. There's no right or wrong way.' This emphasis on choice and autonomy was characteristic of the therapists' approach, recognising how experiences of forced migration often involved profound losses of control. Small cardboard trays were provided to catch the excess sand, which participants could then transfer back into the main trays. These practical aspects offered additional opportunities for mindful engagement.

Ovie observed that the repetitive process of glue, sand, and patterns created a meditative quality in the room. The shared tables facilitated connections as patterns intersected or participants requested different coloured sands. Maintaining individual autonomy, this balance of personal and collective experience was central to the therapeutic framework, allowing trauma to be processed both individually and within the group.

Some participants spontaneously shared memories evoked by the patterns they created: traditional textile designs, architectural details from past homes, or natural formations from familiar landscapes. Miriam and Ayesha listened attentively, reflecting on these memories while avoiding deep probing at this early stage. The young interpreter quietly ensured each story was understood.

When the sand art was finished, Ayesha invited the group to notice patterns in the artwork and their shared experiences. Some participants shared similarities in their journeys, while others silently absorbed the group's gradual trust. Ovie, though quiet, engaged by attentively listening to others' stories, occasionally touching the stone in his pocket. The therapists recognised that the tactile connection to the previous week's object offered extra security as the group moved towards deeper sharing.

The session ended with grounding movements. The group stood in a circle. Miriam guided them through neck rolls, shoulder rotations, and ankle circles. She encouraged participants to feel the solid floor beneath their feet, pressing down through their heels and toes. They took three deep breaths with arms overhead before letting their hands fall to their sides. Three notes from the singing bowl signalled the session's end, and the sand patterns served as reminders of their connections and healing journeys.

Session 3: Understanding Loss and Grief through Creative Expression

After establishing trust in Session 2, the group was ready to explore loss and grief. The third meeting would guide participants in understanding their responses to loss through movement and sound. This shift from sensory engagement to emotional exploration marked a key step in therapy.

For adolescents who have experienced forced migration, understanding the relationship between loss and grief is fundamental to their healing journey. Loss is the separation from home, family, culture, or anticipated futures, while grief is our natural emotional response to these losses. Refugee adolescents often face layered, intersecting experiences as they navigate multiple losses.

Contemporary grief research offers various perspectives for understanding these experiences. While Worden's 'Tasks of Mourning' (Worden 2009) and Kubler-Ross's 'Five Stages of Grief' (Kubler-Ross and Kessler 2014) have enriched our understanding, we now recognise that grief follows no predetermined path. The

'Dual Process Model' (Stroebe and Schut 1999) particularly resonates with refugee experiences, acknowledging how individuals may move fluidly between different aspects of grief while adapting to new circumstances. Consider a young person like Ovie, whose losses span multiple dimensions: the tangible (home and possessions), the relational (family members and community), aspects of identity (cultural connections, familiar roles), and anticipated futures (educational plans, expected life trajectories).

Each loss carries its own weight and meaning, while the grief responses to these losses can manifest in various ways – through physical sensations, emotional experiences, thought patterns, or behavioural changes. By acknowledging these varied manifestations of grief, we can support young people in honouring their experiences and recognising that healing unfolds not as a linear process, but as a dynamic process of adaptation and meaning-making.

When Ovie arrived for the third session, the room had been rearranged. Body-sized cutouts lay on the floor, surrounded by cushions in a wide circle. Small drums, shakers, and other percussion instruments were on a nearby low table. After the opening ritual with the singing bowl, Miriam introduced the exploration of personal grief responses. Each loss leaves a unique space in our lives, she explained gently. Grieving varies with each loss. Grief can be physical or emotional. It might affect our thoughts or behaviour. Today we'll explore different responses to loss.

Movement Mapping

Ayesha guided the group to understand that grief is a complex, embodied experience manifested physically. 'Grief is not only an emotional or cognitive experience,' she began. 'Our bodies express loss profoundly.' Ovie, who had been listening intently, felt the words resonate deeply. His own body seemed to carry memories of displacement – a tightness he had learned to carry but rarely acknowledged.

Ayesha invited participants to begin with simply noticing their breath and any areas of tension: 'When we experience significant losses,' she explained, 'our grief might show up in our bodies in different ways. We might notice tension, tiredness or changes in how we breathe or move. These are natural responses to loss.' Ayesha demonstrated how different losses might evoke different physical grief responses: heaviness in the chest when grieving separation from family members, tension across the shoulders when processing the loss of safety, or restlessness in the legs when dealing with the loss of familiar routines. As she spoke, Ovie carefully selected a cutout and began marking areas of tension with deep blue chalk – a visual map of his own journey through loss, the soft chalk leaving traces of his inner landscape.

Participants were then invited to explore their own experiences through movement, with the option to trace these expressions on their body cutouts. Some created patterns representing specific losses, while their choice of movement reflected their grief responses to these losses.

Sound Stories

Miriam introduced sound as a pathway for expressing loss and grief. She used various instruments to show how different sounds represented their experiences. A steady drumbeat might express the weight of lost home or family. She picked up a tambourine and shook it nervously. These rapid, trembling sounds may capture our anxiety over these losses. Miriam demonstrated how musical instruments could express both concrete losses and emotional responses.

Ovie recalled the rhythms of home – morning calls, the bustling marketplace, sounds now only in memory. His fingers traced a small shaker's outline, hesitant at first. The instrument felt strange yet familiar, like the life he was navigating. His movements were hesitant, barely whispering. Then, something shifted. The shaker spoke softly at first, then with growing intensity. A gentle rustle of loss or a sharp rhythm of unspoken frustrations. The sound captured the complexity of his journey – quiet grief, underlying resilience, and moments of overwhelming emotion.

Participants chose instruments. Miriam explained how cultures have used rhythm and sound to acknowledge communal losses and collective grieving. The group created a soundscape with the therapist's gentle rhythm containing their expression of loss and responses. Ovie's shaker became part of a shared narrative of healing and hope. Participants learned how individual grief responses coexist within communal holding.

Reflection and Integration

Ayesha guided the group back to the circle as the soundscape settled. 'Let's reflect on our losses and how we carry them,' she said. The quiet room echoed their shared expression. Participants started sharing cautiously. One recognised how a loss created tension in their shoulders, another how a rhythm captured inexpressible feelings. Ovie listened. The morning's explorations had awakened something in him. He was beginning to understand that his grief was a complex, changing landscape. Miriam moved among participants, helping them express their insights. 'Grief isn't conquered,' she said, 'but a journey we learn to navigate.' Each loss speaks its own language.

The group began to see their grief responses as deeply personal, yet fundamentally shared. Healing was not about eliminating pain, but about finding ways to acknowledge and integrate it. As the session drew to a close, Ayesha invited each participant to share a word or gesture that captured their experience. Some spoke softly, others moved slightly. Ovie's nod was almost imperceptible. A quiet acknowledgement of a journey begun. The three notes of the singing bowl marked the end of the session, a ritual of containment and hope.

Session 4: Embodied Memory and Relational Healing

Following the exploration of individual grief responses through movement and sound in Session 3, the fourth session moved towards examining the relational aspects of loss. This progression from personal to interpersonal experiences reflected the group's growing capacity to work with more complex dimensions of their journeys. Where previous sessions had focused on individual expressions of grief, this session would create spaces for understanding how loss affects our connections with others and our ability to form new relationships.

When Ovie arrived for the fourth session, the room had been transformed in a way that felt both familiar and different. Miriam and Ayesha had carefully designed the space to support the group's exploration of relational losses. Large pieces of fabric in muted, earthy tones were draped mindfully around the room, creating soft boundaries and intimate zones. Cushions were arranged to form smaller, interconnected circles, and natural light filtered through light fabric panels. The familiar singing bowl sat at the centre of a low table, now surrounded by a carefully curated collection of natural objects – weathered driftwood, smooth river stones, fragments of textiles with intricate patterns, and delicate shells that seemed to invite gentle exploration.

The therapists created an environment for a fluid approach to exploring memory and connection. Draped fabrics, cushions, and selected objects provided participants with various ways to express their experiences, both direct and metaphorical. Ovie observed the room, noting the changes but staying cautious. The therapists remained attentive to the group's energy, allowing participants to engage with the space as they felt comfortable.

Following the familiar pattern, the singing bowl journey around the circle allowed each participant to create or pass on a sound. Ovie, now more familiar with the group's rhythms, created a gentle, sustained tone that seemed to carry both hesitation and emerging strength. The sound resonated differently today; it was less tentative and more intentional. Miriam and Ayesha exchanged a subtle glance, noting Ovie's growing comfort within the group's supportive framework.

Miriam introduced the session's focus with her characteristic blend of gentleness and clarity. 'Today, we'll explore the connections we've lost and the connections we're creating,' she explained softly. Each participant was offered a large piece of neutral coloured canvas as a base, spread across their chosen space on the floor or on low tables. She placed small baskets containing fabric glue, safety pins, and thread beside each workspace.

'We'll use these fabrics to create a visual map of your relationships on your canvas,' she continued. 'You can choose whether to secure your fabrics permanently with glue, temporarily with pins, or leave them loose to move and adjust as you explore. When you feel your arrangement is complete, you can use your phone to photograph it if you'd like to keep a record of what you've created.'

She gestured to the variety of fabrics available. 'You might choose different fabrics to represent different people, places, or communities that have been important in your life. The way you arrange them can show how these relationships connect or how they have changed over time. Some might overlap; some might be placed far apart. There's no right or wrong way to do this.' Her words were an invitation rather than an instruction, leaving space for each participant to engage at their own pace.

Participants began selecting fabrics that spoke to their experiences. The therapists had chosen materials with intentional variety: rough, torn pieces that might represent painful separations; soft, flowing fabrics suggesting hope and resilience; textured cloths that invited touch and exploration. Some laid fabrics flat on the canvas like a landscape, pinning them in place, while others created layers or folds to show depth in relationships, securing them with small stitches or dabs of glue. A few participants twisted or knotted pieces to represent complicated connections, choosing to leave these arrangements loose and adjustable.

Ovie chose a deep blue fabric with frayed edges. A silent representation of his journey, he placed it carefully in the centre of his canvas, initially leaving it loose as he slowly added smaller pieces around it, creating a constellation of relationships, past and present. After some time arranging and rearranging, he chose to secure a few key pieces with safety pins, leaving others free to shift and move. When satisfied with his arrangement, he took out his phone and discreetly captured the image. Miriam and Ayesha moved quietly through the space, offering gentle acknowledgement and subtle support, ensuring each participant felt safe in their exploration.

After participants had photographed their fabric arrangements, Ayesha rose and softly addressed the group. 'Now we'll explore these relationships through movement,' she explained. 'Let's see how our bodies might express the stories we've created with fabric.' She guided the group through a movement exploration that echoed their mapping work. Participants began by standing, moving slowly between points in the room that represented different aspects of their fabric narratives. Sometimes they moved individually, sometimes creating temporary connections with others, mirroring how they had arranged their fabric pieces. The movements were fluid and improvised, allowing each person to express their internal landscape through physical exploration.

As the participants flowed back into their circle, a tangible shift in energy could be felt. Miriam invited reflection, speaking gently. 'Would anyone like to share what emerged for them through creating these visual maps of connection? The group sat together in comfortable silence for a moment before one participant gestured to the loose edges of his fabric piece.

'These remind me of connections that cannot be neatly contained,' he said softly, 'but they're still vital, still there.'

Another traced the overlapping layers in his work. 'The way these pieces layer helped me show how relationships exist across time and distance,' he shared. Through these shared observations, the group began to recognise how their individual experiences of loss and connection resonated with one another.

The session ended with their grounding ritual. As the bowl's notes ended, Ovie felt a profound shift, embodying both loss and the potential for new connections. In the bowl's resonance, he sensed the group shared a delicate balance between honouring loss and creating new connections, as their bodies held memory and hope.

Session 5: Creating Memory Holders

In the fifth session, participants created concrete spaces to hold their memories after exploring relational losses in Session 4. The shift from expressing to containing connections reflected the group's readiness for tangible representations of their experiences.

When Ovie arrived for the fifth session, the room had a different energy. Low tables were arranged for space and privacy. Each table had various containers. Participants could choose wooden boxes with lids, cardboard boxes for decoration, or various-sized natural baskets. Materials for personalising these memory holders were arranged nearby. The therapists gathered various items for decorating but knew simpler materials could also create meaningful memory keepers. Classic cardboard boxes and paper can hold memories when treated with care.

Following their established ritual, the singing bowl's journey round the circle allowed each person to create or pass on a sound. Ayesha observed their group's growing comfort with the ritual, the sounds now more confident yet still gentle. Ayesha gently introduced the session's focus. 'Memories need a special place to rest,' she explained. Today we'll create spaces to hold important memories of people, places, and times. Create sections in your container for memories, messages, and items that make you feel strong.

Participants moved thoughtfully towards the tables, each taking time to consider their choice of container. Some were drawn to boxes with separate compartments, others to simple containers they could customise. Ovie selected a wooden box with a smooth lid that opened on small hinges. Inside were three natural divisions that seemed to offer spaces for different kinds of memories.

Miriam demonstrated different ways she could work with their chosen containers. 'You might want to line certain sections with soft fabric for precious memories,' she suggested, showing how material could be carefully folded to create gentle spaces. 'Other areas could hold written messages, drawings, or objects that carry special meaning.' She showed how paper could be folded into small envelopes or pockets, perfect for holding written memories or messages.

As participants began working with their memory keepers, each found their own way of creating meaningful spaces. One young person lined a compartment with soft green fabric that reminded him of his grandmother's garden, placing within it a small paper flower he had crafted. Another created a series of tiny folded papers, each holding a message to family members far away. Several participants used the natural objects available – smooth stones, shells, small pieces of wood, marking them with symbols or words before placing them in their containers.

Ovie worked quietly with his box first, taking time to feel its smooth wooden surface and solid corners. The three compartments seemed to offer different possibilities, one smaller, two slightly larger. He began with the smallest section, carefully lining it with the same deep blue fabric he had used in previous sessions, folding it precisely so it covered every corner. In this space, he placed the stone from their first session. He had spent time during the week running his thumb over its surface, and now he took a white paint pen and marked it with a small symbol that looked like a traditional protection sign from his homeland.

In the second compartment, he created layers. First, he lined the base with a piece of reddish-brown fabric that reminded him of the earth at his grandmother's house. On this, he carefully positioned a small paper envelope where he had written memories of his sister, things he wanted to remember about her laugh, the games they used to play, and the way she would tease him about his serious face. The envelope was sealed as some memories needed to stay private.

The third compartment he approached differently. He chose a textured material in warm yellowish-orange tones, creating soft folds that formed smaller spaces within the larger section. This colour reminded him of the bright clothes his sister used to wear. Here he placed a bracelet she had made from thread, the only thing he had of hers, and left room for other objects he might want to add later. This space felt like it was for his ongoing journey, for memories still being made.

When Miriam passed by, she commented on how precisely he had created each section, how each choice of material and object seemed so carefully considered. She offered him a small piece of ribbon to secure the envelope if he wished. Ovie accepted it with a slight nod, each fold and loop made with a quiet reverence.

The therapists moved gently through the space, offering support when needed. When one participant seemed overwhelmed by memories, Ayesha sat quietly beside him, her presence grounding and reassuring. Miriam helped another participant figure out how to create a special compartment for holding particularly difficult memories, those not ready to be looked at yet but needing a safe place to rest.

As the session progressed, some participants began sharing the significance of their choices. One explained how different fabrics represented different family members. Another described how he had created a special space for memories of home. These sharings emerged naturally without pressure, with each person choosing what felt right to reveal. As their time together drew to a close, Miriam spoke softly about caring for these memory keepers. 'Like the memories they contain, these containers might need different things at different times,' she explained. 'Sometimes you might want to look inside often, other times they might need to stay closed for a while. There's no right or wrong way.'

The group gathered for their closing ritual; their memory keepers were placed carefully beside them. Together they took three deep breaths, the familiar rhythm now carrying new meaning. As the singing bowl's clear notes marked the end of their session, Ovie noticed how his box felt both light and significant in his hands, a tangible space where memories could rest, be honoured, and perhaps in time, be more fully understood.

Session 6: Weaving Past and Present – Honouring Our Journey

Moving from individual memory holders to collective meaning-making, the final session invited participants to weave their personal journeys into a shared narrative. This progression from containing to connecting memories marked the culmination of their therapeutic journey.

When Ovie arrived for the final session, the room reflected their shared journey. The singing bowl was centred in their circle, surrounded by familiar fabric, natural objects, art materials, and small percussion instruments. Each participant's memory keeper was on a low table near the circle, reminding them of their collective story. The singing bowl's journey around the circle held new meaning during their last ritual. Ovie observed that each sound reflected its creator's journey, with some producing strong tones and others gentle resonances of quiet transformation. He drew the striker around the bowl's rim, creating a tone that felt grounded and hopeful.

Ayesha started the session by saying, 'Each of us holds pieces of strength we've discovered along the way.' Indicating the art materials and natural objects arranged nearby, she continued: 'Today we'll weave these together, creating a collective tapestry of our journey.' She demonstrated how they could use fabric pieces, drawings, written words, or symbols to create individual sections that would connect to form a larger whole.

Participants began selecting materials, some returning to colours or textures that had become meaningful in previous sessions. Ovie chose several pieces of fabric: the deep blue that had become a constant in his work, a warm earth tone that spoke of roots, and a new gentle green colour that suggested growth. As he worked, he noticed how his movements had become more certain, his choices more deliberate.

The group worked individually and collectively, gradually connecting their pieces into a larger narrative. Some added messages of hope; others created patterns. One participant included traditional designs, while another wove protective symbols into the fabric. The young interpreter translated words and phrases, enriching their shared creation. Miriam invited participants to share what they would take forward from their time together. They could speak, add to the tapestry, or hold the space in silence. Some participants felt less alone, while others found new ways to hold their memories. A young person gestured to the tapestry's connections, softly discussing strength in shared understanding.

From his memory keeper, Ovie took out the white paint pen he had used to mark his stones. With careful movements, he added a small protection symbol to his section of the tapestry, then connected it with a flowing line to the symbols others had created. The gesture seemed to speak of both his individual journey and his growing sense of connection to the group. Ayesha then introduced their closing ritual. 'We've spent time creating safe spaces for her memories,' she explained, 'and now we'll create a way to carry our collective strength forward.' She invited each person to choose one final object – a stone, a shell, or a small piece of their working materials – to keep as a reminder of their shared journey. These would join the objects in their memory keepers, bridging their group experience with their ongoing lives.

Miriam addressed the practical aspects of continuing support. She explained how participants could maintain their connection with therapeutic services by providing cards with contact details for both therapists and explaining how they could access additional support if needed. 'Your journey continues beyond this room,' she said, 'and support remains available whenever you might need it.' The group moved into their final closing circle. Each memory keeper was placed in front of its owner, the collective tapestry spread in the centre. Miriam lifted the singing bowl one last time: 'As we make our final sound together,' she explained, 'let it carry both our acknowledgement and of all we've held here and our hopes for what lies ahead.'

The bowl's resonance filled the room, joined gradually by soft sounds from the percussion instruments that had supported their journey. Participants were invited to add their voices in whatever way felt right – through instruments, movement, sound, or silence. Ovie gently shook the same small instrument he had used in earlier sessions, its rhythm now steady and contained. As the sound gradually settled into silence, Ayesha spoke of how their individual stories had become part of a larger narrative of healing and hope. The collective tapestry would remain with the therapy service, she explained, joining other groups' creations as a testament to shared healing and growth.

The session ended with a simple farewell. Each participant gathered their memory keeper and chosen objects while exchanging quiet farewells. The therapists stayed present, offering support as the group prepared to leave. Ovie paused at the doorway, as he had in the first session. This time, the pause held a moment of quiet recognition. He carried tangible reminders of his journey in his memory keeper. He embodied new ways to experience life. In the room behind him, threads of his story are now part of a larger fabric of healing and hope.

This session embodied the core therapeutic principles guiding the group: safety, creative expression, and the healing of shared understanding. The therapists created a space to acknowledge profound loss and explore new possibilities for living with it. For young people like Ovie, this blend of creativity, cultural sensitivity, and group connection provided healing pathways that could extend beyond therapy into their lives.

Conclusions

Ovie's journey through the therapeutic group illustrates the transformative potential of culturally responsive, trauma-informed expressive arts therapy for refugee adolescents. His progression from initial hesitation to meaningful engagement demonstrates how carefully structured creative experiences can support both individual healing and collective resilience. The integration of theoretical understanding with practical therapeutic tools, from the grounding properties of natural objects to the symbolic power of creative expression, provides a framework for working with profound loss while honouring cultural identity and building new connections. This case study highlights the importance of creating therapeutic spaces that acknowledge both the weight of trauma and the capacity for healing, where refugee adolescents can process their experiences within a supportive community of shared understanding. As mental health practitioners continue developing approaches for supporting displaced youth, Ovie's story reminds us that healing emerges not just through individual transformation, but through the careful weaving together of personal narrative, cultural recognition, and collective support.

References

Boyles, J Ewart-Biggs, R, Horn, R and Lamb, K. 2024. *Groupwork with refugees and survivors of human rights abuses.* Routledge.

Bytyci, A and Zymberi, M. 2023. 'The art of healing in a transitory context: Groupwork with people seeking asylum in asylum centres in Kosovo'. In J Boyles, R Ewart-Biggs, R Horn and K Lamb, *Groupwork with refugees and survivors of human rights abuses: The power of togetherness,* 139–150. Routledge.

Herman, J. 1992. *Trauma and recovery: from domestic violence to political terror.* Basic Books.

Hutchinson, R, King, N and Majumder, P. 2022. 'How effective is group intervention in the treatment for unaccompanied and accompanied refugee minors with mental health difficulties: A systematic review'. *International Journal of Social Psychiatry*, 68(3): 484–499.

Jalonen, A and Cilia La Corte, P. 2017. *A practical guide to therapeutic work with asylum seekers and refugees.* Jessica Kingsley Publishers.

Kira, I, Ahmed, A, Wasim, F, Mahmoud, V, Colrain, J and Rai, D. 2012. 'Group therapy for refugees and torture survivors'. *International Journal of Group Psychotherapy*, 62(1). doi:101521ijgp201262169

Knettel, B, Oliver-Steinberg, A, Lee, M, Rubesin, H, Duke, N, Esmaili, E and Puffer, E. 2023. 'Clinician and academic perspectives on expressive arts therapies for refugee children and families: A qualitative study'. *International Journal of Migration, Health and Social Care*, 19(3/4): 260–272.

Kubler-Ross, E and Kessler, D. 2014. *On grief and grieving: finding the meaning of grief through the five stages of loss.* Simon and Schuster.

Ramadan, M, Hadfield, K, Ryan, M, Penpang, C, Bosqui, T and Nolan, A. 2024. 'The use of creative art therapy to address the mental health of refugee adolescents: A systematic review'. *Arts and Health*: 1–19. doi:10.1080/17533015.2024.239586

Seetharaman, R, Avhad, S and Rane, J. 2024. 'Exploring the healing power of singing bowls: An overview of key findings and potential benefits'. *Explore*: 39–43. doi:10.1016/j.explore.2023.07.007

Stroebe, M and Schut, H. 1999. 'The dual process model of coping with bereavement: Rationale and description'. *Death Studies, 23*(3): 197–224. doi:10.1080/074811899201046

Winnicott, D. 1953. 'Transitional object and transitional phenomena'. *International Journal of Psychoanalysis, 34*: 89–97.

Worden, J. 2009. *Grief counselling and grief therapy: A handbook for the mental health practitioner.* Springer.

Chapter 13

Working with Interpreters to Support Refugee Adolescents

Introduction

Supporting refugee adolescents requires effective communication across multiple contexts, from educational and residential settings to healthcare, legal, and therapeutic contexts. For adolescent refugees processing trauma and forced displacement while navigating complex systems in an unfamiliar language and simultaneously managing crucial developmental transitions of adolescence, skilled interpretation becomes essential not just for basic understanding, but for emotional safety and meaningful engagement.

Interpreters play multiple essential roles across these settings, serving as linguistic and cultural bridges between adolescent refugees and the various systems they must navigate. Their work ranges from facilitating daily communications in schools and residential settings to mediating complex legal procedures and healthcare interactions. Beyond simple language translation, interpreters help convey cultural nuances, explain unfamiliar systems, and create spaces where adolescent refugees feel understood and respected (Fennig and Denov 2021).

When considering these diverse interpreter roles, Bronfenbrenner's Ecological Systems Theory (1979) offers valuable insights into how interpreting support operates across multiple environmental levels. In the microsystem, interpreters facilitate direct communications in therapy rooms, classrooms, and healthcare settings, where the immediate quality of interpreting shapes refugee adolescents' access to support. Within the mesosystem, connections between these interpreting settings demonstrate how coordinated language assistance across services can create a more coherent support network. At the exosystem level, interpreter training programmes and service policies influence the quality of support available, while the macrosystem's broader cultural attitudes towards language and integration shape how interpretation services are valued and implemented.

This systems perspective is reflected in recent European guidelines that emphasise the importance of cross-sectoral cooperation when working with refugee youth (Henriques 2019). These guidelines recognise that effective interpreting support requires coordination across all system levels, from direct service provision to

DOI: 10.4324/9781003430032-14

policy frameworks. Such collaboration necessitates clear protocols around roles and responsibilities while maintaining focus on the young person's needs.

The role of interpreters becomes even more nuanced and complex in psychotherapy settings. As Hunt and Swartz (2017) highlight, even under ideal circumstances with highly trained interpreters, the therapeutic relationship requires careful consideration when conducted through an intermediary. While interpreters can serve as valuable cultural brokers bridging different worldviews, their presence fundamentally alters the therapeutic dynamic and requires the careful orchestration of roles, boundaries, and power dynamics. Yet despite these challenges, using interpreters remains vital for enabling the therapeutic processing of trauma and supporting identity development in refugee youth who cannot access services in their native language (Miller et al. 2005).

Throughout this chapter, we draw on the experiences of three adolescent refugees: Mira, a Syrian teen who fled with her family and accesses individual expressive arts therapy; Hassan, an Iraqi unaccompanied minor attending group psychotherapy who navigates linguistic challenges with his Sudanese-Arabic speaking interpreter; and Aran, a Kurdish adolescent receiving school-based support while living with his father and dealing with experiences of bullying. Their diverse journeys demonstrate how interpreted interactions involve complex cultural mediations and power relations, while highlighting the specific needs of adolescents navigating trauma, identity formation, and new social systems across different support contexts.

While expressive and creative approaches offer powerful channels for connection and understanding, effective interpretation remains crucial across therapeutic settings. As other chapters in this volume demonstrate, many of the expressive arts can help transcend linguistic barriers. Yet skilled interpreters continue to play an essential role in establishing therapeutic principles, providing psychoeducation, and ensuring young people can fully engage with their support systems. This integration of verbal and non-verbal approaches creates richer possibilities for refugee adolescents to express themselves and participate meaningfully in their healing journey.

Interpreting for Refugee Adolescents: The Reality of 'Ad Hoc' Provision

Despite the well-documented importance of professional interpreting services, the reality for most refugee adolescents is quite different (Fennig and Denov 2021). Rather than accessing best-practice professional services, most rely on 'ad hoc' interpreters – individuals employed by interpreting agencies who typically lack formal qualifications or specialised training. These interpreters, often from refugee or migrant communities themselves, differ from both fully qualified professional interpreters and informal community volunteers. They occupy a middle ground, being paid for their work but lacking comprehensive training in medical terminology, ethical boundaries, and interpreting techniques (Mayo et al. 2016).

The prevalence of this ad hoc interpreting stems from practical challenges identified in Mayo et al.'s 2016 study: difficulties locating qualified professionals, extended waiting times, and technical challenges with professional services. MacFarlane et al. (2009) further demonstrate the significant risks of relying on undertrained interpreters. Their research in Irish primary care settings with refugee and asylum-seeking patients revealed that miscommunication and diagnostic errors often stem from interpreters' limited medical knowledge and unclear role boundaries. Service users frequently had to 'patch together' meaning from fragmented interpretations when working with interpreters who had limited English proficiency themselves.

Despite these challenges, these semi-professional interpreters fulfil a crucial role, particularly where fully qualified services are scarce. MacFarlane et al. (2009) found that many service users valued having interpreters from their own communities present for emotional support and cultural mediation, even while acknowledging the limitations of their training. Their cultural knowledge and community connections facilitated trust and understanding beyond simple language translation.

However, it is important to recognise that this arrangement does not suit all refugee adolescents. In my own clinical work, I have found that some prefer not to have interpreters from their own communities, especially when discussing sensitive or personal issues. These adolescents may feel that their stories could circulate within their tight-knit communities, potentially leading to stigma or breaches of confidentiality. Research by Rohlof et al. (2009) supports this, finding that some refugees preferred interpreters from outside their communities due to concerns about moral judgement and cultural attitudes. In such cases, the presence of a community interpreter, even in a professional capacity, might inhibit open communication about topics like mental health, sexual experiences, or family conflicts.

Given this complex landscape, where ad hoc interpreting remains the primary form of language support for refugee adolescents, attention must focus on improving quality and safety within existing constraints. This requires sustained attention to several interconnected factors:

- Developing proper training and support systems for ad hoc interpreters;
- Establishing clear protocols around confidentiality and role boundaries;
- Ensuring fair payment and professional recognition;
- Creating integrated approaches that combine community and professional services; and
- Securing organisational commitment to language access as a quality and safety priority.

In the following sections, the experiences of Mira, Hassan, and Aran illustrate how semi-professional interpreters work across different settings, demonstrating both the challenges and possibilities of interpreted support. Their journeys help us understand how to maximise the effectiveness of interpreting work through paying careful attention to core principles, session set-up, communication strategies, power dynamics, and the therapeutic relationship.

Core Principles for Interpreted Communication

Having outlined the landscape of ad hoc interpreting for refugee adolescents, it is crucial to consider the fundamental principles that guide effective interpreted communication across all contexts:

- Directly address the young person and family members, avoiding indirect speech through the interpreter;
- Use clear, concise sentences with natural pauses that allow for accurate interpretation;
- Employ plain language that avoids idioms, professional jargon, and complex metaphors;
- Conduct regular understanding checks, particularly around key decisions and complex concepts;
- Pay attention to non-verbal communication while remaining mindful of cultural variations;
- Allow sufficient time for accurate interpretation of important points; and
- Remain flexible in rephrasing or explaining concepts differently when necessary.

These principles create conditions for meaningful dialogue that extend beyond simple language translation. They apply across all settings – from educational and healthcare environments to therapeutic contexts – helping to establish the foundation for genuine engagement and understanding. While these core principles provide the foundation for effective interpreting communication, their practical implementation begins with thoughtful preparation and set-up of the interpreting environment.

Setting Up Interpreting Sessions

The preparation and set-up of interpreting sessions requires careful attention to both physical arrangements and preliminary discussions. The physical set-up and positioning of participants shape communication dynamics. When Aran first met with his school support team, the interpreter was seated beside staff members across a large desk, creating an unintended barrier. Both Aran and his father gave only brief responses, looking primarily at the interpreter rather than engaging with staff. Recognising the impact of this arrangement on communication, the team rearranged the seating into an open triangle formation with the interpreter positioned equidistant and slightly set back. This thoughtful adjustment, combined with a clear discussion about the confidentiality of the sessions, created a foundation for Aran to gradually disclose his experiences of bullying.

Successful interpreted sessions rely on two crucial relationships that require attention before the actual meeting. First, professionals and interpreters need dedicated time before sessions to establish their working partnership. This preliminary meeting creates space to share essential background information about the young person, clarify everyone's roles and expectations, discuss relevant cultural considerations, and agree on protocols for managing distress or difficulties. Equally important is groundwork with the young person and their family. This involves taking time to explain how interpreting will work, discussing confidentiality arrangements, and understanding their preferences for interaction style.

The value of thorough preparation was evident in Hassan's early experiences in group psychotherapy. While Hassan and his interpreter shared Arabic as a common language, initial sessions were disrupted by differences between Iraqi and Sudanese Arabic dialects. These unanticipated linguistic variations led to confusion and withdrawal during the early meetings. Recognising these challenges, the psychotherapy team adapted their approach. They began scheduling brief meetings before each group session where Hassan and the interpreter could clarify any confusion from the previous week and prepare for upcoming topics. They also developed a running glossary of terms that caused confusion, with agreed-upon translations that worked for both parties. These interventions markedly improved communication flow and Hassan's engagement in subsequent sessions.

In Mira's expressive arts psychotherapy, careful preparation helped establish safety from the outset. Her therapist and interpreter met before the initial session to discuss trauma-informed interpreting approaches and establish protocols for managing stress, including agreed signals for breaks (such as a discreet hand gesture) and regular check-ins about comfort levels (like engaging with a simple 1–5 scale for stress levels). This preparation time allowed the interpreter to raise potential cultural considerations around discussing trauma and enabled both professionals to agree on how they would work together to support Mira's healing journey.

This initial investment in the set-up of sessions can help mitigate challenges while maximising the potential benefits of cultural connection and trust building. By thoughtfully considering who speaks to whom and how these interactions are structured, professionals can create conditions for effective interpreted sessions.

Practical Communication Strategies

Once sessions begin, success depends on how communication is managed moment by moment. A fundamental principle is how speech is directed within sessions. Professionals should always address the young person and their family members directly, not the interpreter. Phrases like: 'Ask him or her how that makes them feel' should be avoided in favour of direct address such as 'What thoughts are going through your mind right now?' This maintains the primacy of the therapeutic or supportive relationship while allowing the interpreter to facilitate communication without becoming the focus.

Each young person's story demonstrates how small adjustments in the communication approach can significantly impact engagement and understanding. In Mira's psychotherapy sessions, the therapist developed a rhythm of speaking in short, clear sentences with natural pauses, allowing the interpreter to maintain the emotional resonance of Mira's narrative while ensuring accurate translation. The therapist maintained direct eye contact with Mira, asking 'How did you feel when that happened?' rather than directing questions through the interpreter. This direct engagement strengthened their therapeutic connection even within the interpreted setting.

Hassan's experience highlighted the importance of regular comprehension checks, particularly given the dialect differences. The psychotherapist established a practice of periodically summarising key points and explicitly inviting clarification: 'I want to make sure I've understood correctly.' This approach normalised the process of seeking clarity while respecting Hassan's agency in the communication process. Professional jargon and complex metaphors were carefully avoided or unpacked collaboratively when they arose. The psychotherapist noticed that technical terms around emotions and mental health concepts often needed particular attention, and she worked with the interpreter to find culturally meaningful ways to convey these ideas.

In Aran's ongoing school support meetings to address the bullying situation, attention to non-verbal communication proved crucial. Over a series of weekly meetings with his head of year and pastoral team, the staff observed how the engagement of both Aran and his father evolved. Their body language showed increasing comfort and trust as they worked together to develop and monitor an intervention plan. More direct eye contact emerged naturally, and their postures became more relaxed as they participated in discussions about school safety measures and peer support strategies. However, the team remained mindful that interpretations of body language might vary culturally, avoiding assumptions about what different gestures or expressions might mean.

These case examples demonstrate different facets of effective communication: the careful pacing and rhythm from the work with Mira, regular comprehension checks in the sessions with Hassan, and cultural awareness of non-verbal cues in the support for Aran. When professionals thoughtfully manage both the technical and relational aspects of interpreted communication, young people and their families can more fully participate in their support journey.

Power Dynamics and Cultural Considerations

While effective communication strategies are fundamental, their implementation occurs within complex webs of power and cultural dynamics that require careful attention. Sessions with interpreters inherently involve intricate power relationships that need skilful management. Research by Gartley and Due (2017) found that clients often develop stronger initial connections with interpreters who share their cultural background – a dynamic that can either facilitate or complicate therapeutic work. This interplay of power, culture, and relationship emerged distinctly in each young person's journey.

For Mira, sharing a cultural background with her female interpreter initially provided comfort when discussing her difficult journey to safety. The shared understanding of Syrian cultural norms around trauma and emotional expression helped create safety in the sessions. However, this connection became complex when the interpreter became visibly emotional during Mira's trauma narrative, reminding her of her own daughter. When Mira sought additional contact with the interpreter between sessions, her need for cultural connection was validated and redirected to appropriate community resources.

Hassan's experience highlighted how power dynamics can manifest through language itself. As an unaccompanied minor navigating a new country, he was already in a vulnerable position. When linguistic differences between Iraqi and Sudanese Arabic surfaced, Hassan initially became withdrawn, opting to check translations on his phone instead of voicing his confusion. This hesitancy reflected both cultural attitudes towards authority and the disempowering experience of struggling with what was supposed to be a shared language. The psychotherapist's choice to openly acknowledge these differences and establish a collaborative protocol for clarifying meaning helped shift the power dynamic, enabling Hassan to actively participate in ensuring accurate communication.

Aran's case illustrates how power dynamics extend beyond the session room into broader community contexts. His reluctance to tell his father about school bullying reflected complex layers of family and community dynamics. The interpreter, while sharing Kurdish cultural understanding, needed to maintain neutrality while facilitating these sensitive family discussions. The school team's decision to explicitly address confidentiality helped create safety for Aran to speak freely despite these community interconnections.

Research underscores that interpreters can serve as valuable cultural bridges when power dynamics are thoughtfully managed (Almommani 2024). While maintaining appropriate boundaries, they can help professionals understand cultural attitudes towards authority, gender, mental health, and help-seeking behaviours. This requires moving beyond viewing interpreters as cultural experts to instead engaging collaboratively around each young person's unique cultural framework and lived experience.

Therapeutic Alliance and Managing Emotional Content

These power dynamics are inextricably linked to the development of therapeutic relationships, which take on additional complexity when working through an interpreter. While traditional therapeutic frameworks focus on dyadic relationships, research by Miller et al. (2005) found that skilled interpreters can actively enhance therapeutic engagement when thoughtfully integrated. This triadic dynamic manifests differently across settings, requiring careful attention to both emotional and relational elements.

In clinical settings, as seen in Mira's expressive arts psychotherapy, the interpreter's role extends beyond simple translation to creating emotional safety through cultural understanding. The therapist's acknowledgment of cultural resonance, while maintaining clear clinical focus, helped transform potential complications into therapeutic strengths.

Group settings present unique challenges, as demonstrated in Hassan's case. The early confusion around dialectal differences could have fractured therapeutic trust. However, the psychotherapist's choice to openly acknowledge these challenges and establish collaborative protocols transformed potential barriers into opportunities for connection. The interpreter's role expanded to include cultural mediation alongside emotional support, enhancing rather than diminishing group cohesion.

Even in educational settings where therapy is not the primary focus, therapeutic alliance remains crucial. In Aran's school support, the careful attention to creating an equitable environment enabled him to gradually share his experience of bullying. This thoughtful structuring of the support space, combined with a clear discussion of confidentiality, demonstrates how interpreters can help create emotional safety across different contexts.

The experiences of these adolescent refugees show that therapeutic alliance in interpreted work succeeds when all participants understand their roles while remaining responsive to emerging needs. Rather than viewing interpreters as potential obstacles to therapeutic connection, their thoughtful integration can deepen and enrich the therapeutic process. The success of these therapeutic relationships relies heavily on careful attention to professional boundaries.

Professional Boundaries and Supporting Wellbeing

Professional boundaries take on particular importance when working with refugee adolescents across languages and cultures, requiring careful navigation of multiple relationships and roles. Each young person's situation demonstrates how boundaries must be both clear and culturally responsive while maintaining focus on their specific developmental needs.

For Mira, boundary management in expressive arts therapy required careful attention. When her interpreter became emotional during trauma narratives, the therapist recognised an opportunity to model healthy professional boundaries while acknowledging human connection. Through regular post-session debriefing with a senior clinician, the interpreter could process her responses appropriately while maintaining professional containment. When Mira sought direct contact with her interpreter between sessions, the therapist validated her need for cultural connection while maintaining clear professional boundaries.

Hassan's group work highlighted how boundaries operate within broader therapeutic systems. The emergence of dialect differences required both interpreters and therapists to establish flexible working boundaries that allowed for linguistic clarification without disrupting group process. This balance of professional distance with necessary adaptability demonstrated how boundaries can be both clear and responsive to young people's needs.

Aran's school-based support illustrates how boundaries function within community contexts, which is particularly important for adolescents navigating multiple social systems. The interpreter maintained professional neutrality while facilitating sensitive conversations between Aran, his father, and school staff – no small feat within a small refugee community where roles often overlap. This delicate balance required clear protocols around confidentiality and role boundaries.

Conclusions

The journeys of Mira, Hassan, and Aran illuminate the complex realities of interpreting work with refugee adolescents. Their experiences demonstrate how effective support extends far beyond simple language translation, requiring attention to multiple ecological systems, from immediate therapeutic relationships to broader community contexts. While the reality of ad hoc interpreting brings inherent challenges, thoughtful preparation and clear frameworks can help maximise its potential benefits.

Mira's expressive arts psychotherapy illustrates how cultural understanding and professional boundaries intersect in therapeutic work. Her case demonstrates the delicate balance required when interpreters serve as cultural bridges while maintaining appropriate professional distance. Hassan's experience highlights how potential barriers, whether linguistic or cultural, can become opportunities for deeper engagement when power dynamics are thoughtfully managed. Aran's school-based support shows how seemingly practical considerations, from seating arrangements to confidentiality protocols, profoundly impact young people's ability to engage across different settings.

These narratives underscore several key principles for effective interpreting work with refugee adolescents. First, careful preparation and set-up create foundations for meaningful engagement. Second, attention to power dynamics and cultural considerations shapes how young people access and experience support. Third, strong therapeutic alliances can develop through interpreters when roles and boundaries are clearly defined. Finally, interpreters can serve as valuable cultural bridges when their role is thoughtfully integrated within broader support systems.

Together, these insights point to the importance of moving beyond technical approaches to embrace the complexity of interpreting work. When professionals maintain focus on adolescent needs while working thoughtfully across languages and cultures, they can create spaces where refugee young people feel truly heard, understood, and supported in their recovery and development.

References

Almommani, O. 2024. 'Navigating the gray zone: When interpreters become mediators and communication facilitators'. *Journal of Language Teaching and Research*: 1372–1380. doi:10.17507/jltr.1504.35

Bronfenbrenner, U. 1979. *The ecology of human development.* Harvard University Press.

Fennig, M and Denov, M. 2021. 'Interpreters working in mental health settings with refugees: An interdisciplinary scoping review'. *American Journal of Orthopsychiatry*, *91*(1): 50–65.

Gartley, T and Due, C. 2017. 'The interpreter is not an invisible being: A thematic analysis of the impact of interpreters in mental health service provision with refugee clients'. *Australian Psychologist, 52*(1): 31–40.

Henriques, A. 2019. *Guidelines on working with young refugees and migrants: Fostering cross-sectoral co-operation.* Council of Europe.

Hunt, X and Swartz, L. 2017. 'Psychotherapy with a language interpreter: Considerations and cautions for practice'. *South Africa Journal of Psychology, 47*(1): 97–109.

MacFarlane, A, Dzebisova, Z, Karapish, D, Kovacevic, B, Ogbebor, F and Okonkwo, E. 2009. 'Arranging and negotiating the use of informal interpreters in general practice consultations: Experiences of refugees and asylum seekers in the West of Ireland'. *Social Science and Medicine, 69*: 210–214. doi:10.1016/j.socscimed.2009.04.022

Mayo, R, Parker, V, Sherrill, W, Coltman, K, Hudson, M, Nichols, C, . . . Pribonic, A. 2016. 'Cutting corners: Provider perceptions of interpretation services and factors related to use of an ad hoc interpreter'. *Hispanic Health Care International, 14*(2): 73–80.

Miller, K, Martell, Z, Pazdirek, L, Caruth, M and Lopez, D. 2005. 'The role of interpreters in psychotherapy with refugees: An exploratory study'. *American Journal of Orthopsychiatry, 75*(1): 27–39. doi:10.1037/0002-9432.75.1.27

Rohlof, H, Knipscheer, J and Kleber, R. 2009. 'Use of the cultural formulation with refugees'. *Transcultural Psychiatry, 46*: 487–505. doi:10.1177/1363461509344306

Chapter 14

Self-Care through the Expressive Arts

Introduction

As practitioners and caregivers supporting refugee adolescents in their healing process, we face multiple challenges. We need to build meaningful connections, manage healthy boundaries, and bridge cultural and linguistic differences in our work. Regardless of our specific roles as support providers, maintaining this balance requires sustained attention and care. These intense demands make it essential for us to nurture our own wellbeing through intentional self-care practices (Bent-Goodley 2018).

Like the refugee adolescents we support, creative and body-based approaches will help us to process our experiences and stay grounded (van der Kolk 2014). Without such practices, providers of support risk experiencing well-documented stress responses, including vicarious trauma (a profound shift in worldview and beliefs about safety), compassion fatigue (diminished capacity for emotional engagement), and burnout (physical, emotional, and mental exhaustion) (Pryce et al. 2007; Shepherd and Newell 2020). As already discussed in Chapters 5 and 6 and illustrated throughout the case studies, the expressive arts, including movement, visual art, music and writing, activate neural pathways beyond those used in verbal expression alone, offering rich opportunities to release the physical and emotional tension that can build up when holding space for trauma narratives while supporting our own emotional regulation and wellbeing.

Drawing from extensive experience of working systemically with refugee adolescents and their support networks, I explore how such stressors manifest and can be recognised early through mindful awareness. The following narratives are composites which synthesise the experiences, challenges, and coping strategies observed across many professionals in the field, and offer confidential, representative accounts.

Laura, a residential care worker supporting unaccompanied minors, identified subtle changes in her emotional and physical capacity, showing early indicators of burnout through physical fatigue and emotional detachment during demanding night shifts. In the classroom setting, experienced teacher Conor recognised early signs of compassion fatigue as his emotional reserves became gradually depleted

DOI: 10.4324/9781003430032-15

while supporting adolescent refugees. Miriam, through her close engagement with trauma narratives in her psychotherapy work with this population, noticed subtle shifts in her worldview and beliefs about safety, signalling the first indications of vicarious trauma.

By prioritising our own wellbeing through creative self-care, we not only sustain our professional capacity but also model healthy coping for the young people we support. When we nurture our own capacity for resilience through creative expression, we strengthen our ability to create and maintain the healing spaces that are central to this work. Drawing upon the experiences of Laura, Conor, and Miriam, this chapter explores the professional impact of working with refugee adolescents, establishes fundamental principles of arts-based self-care, and presents practical strategies for incorporating these approaches into daily practice, both individually and collaboratively.

Expressive Arts in Practice: Learning from Practitioner Experiences

The expressive arts offer distinct benefits in addressing the challenges of practitioners and caregivers outlined above. Creative modalities provide pathways for ongoing processing rather than crisis intervention, helping professionals maintain boundaries, work through emotions as they arise, and continuously refresh their perspectives. The value of these approaches is illustrated through the experiences of our three practitioners.

Laura's story from the residential care setting reveals how burnout can have physiological and psychological impacts. She identified subtle changes in her emotional capacity across her shifts, initially taking longer to recover between intense interactions with the unaccompanied minors in her care. The particular demands of providing round-the-clock emotional support, manifested in headaches and physical tension, alongside emotional exhaustion. This became more pronounced during transitions such as when young people had recently arrived, when they were processing asylum decisions, or when they were preparing to move on.

Recognising these patterns, Laura developed specific strategies which integrated expressive arts into her daily practice. These included brief guided mindful breathing practices during shift changes where staff would stand together for two minutes, breathing deeply and slowly as a group while focusing on transitioning mindfully between work and home. Initially, colleagues were sceptical of these practices, but after Laura provided brief psychoeducation on the importance of deep breathing for regulating the nervous system (see Chapters 8 and 15), they agreed to participate, and the benefits quickly became apparent. Staff finishing their shifts reported feeling more grounded and better able to transition to home, while those beginning work felt more present and attuned to the needs of the young people. Laura also found that colouring in simple mandalas during quiet moments provided effective grounding and energy restoration between intense interactions. Sometimes other staff members would join her in this activity.

Conor first noticed signs of compassion fatigue when he found himself emotionally drained after providing support to students whose stress levels had intensified following escalating violence in their home countries. As his students struggled to remain regulated and maintain focus during these challenging periods, he recognised that his growing sense of detachment could impact both his teaching and their wellbeing. He began incorporating creative and body-based practices to look after his own wellbeing which included mindful diaphragmatic breathing between classes, regular quiet times for processing difficult moments, and using music intentionally at the beginning and end of the day. These tools proved essential for his emotional restoration and recovery.

In her therapeutic work with adolescent refugees, Miriam experienced the gradual development of vicarious trauma, which began to affect her way of seeing things beyond the therapy room. The trauma narratives of the young people she supported stayed with her after sessions, while a heightened awareness of potential threats began to affect her personal life. When sleep disruption and persistent mental reviewing of sessions signalled deepening vicarious trauma, she recognised the need to create stronger boundaries between work and home. She established deliberate transition rituals between sessions, using brief art journaling that combined writing with visual expression, a practice described by Hadar (2021) as creating a visual diary that integrates both artistic and written elements to process experiences.

These practitioner experiences demonstrate how creative and body-based practices such as mindful breathing, mandala colouring, music, and art can be effectively integrated into different professional contexts to address the specific challenges of supporting refugee adolescents. Their stories illustrate the importance of recognising early signs of burnout, compassion fatigue, and vicarious trauma while highlighting how personalised arts-based strategies can sustain wellbeing and professional continuity. Through Laura's identification of the early signs of burnout, Conor's management of compassion fatigue, and Miriam's navigation of vicarious trauma, we see how the expressive arts can provide essential tools for maintaining both professional effectiveness and personal balance.

Core Principles of Arts-Based Self-Care

Five key 'good practice' principles emerged from the practitioners' experiences described in this chapter: inclusivity, regular practice, supportive environments, integration, and playful exploration. Inclusivity welcomes all creative abilities emphasising process over product. Regular creative engagement builds emotional resilience which is vital when supporting trauma-impacted displaced adolescents. (Alayarian 2007). Supportive environments enable practitioners to engage in expressive activities without judgement, creating safe spaces to process sensitive content. Integration weaves creative practices naturally into daily routines, ensuring sustainability. Playful exploration encourages spontaneous discovery and emotional release through creative expression, allowing practitioners to find approaches that resonate with their individual needs. Each practitioner's response to workplace challenges demonstrates these principles in action.

Laura's evening practice of crocheting after her shifts effectively integrates creative self-care into her daily routine while establishing clear work-home boundaries. The repetitive, tactile nature of working with wool during her evening wind-down time provides both a calming ritual and tangible outcomes, both of which may often be lacking in emotional support work with adolescent refugees.

Making music became Conor's pathway to self-care, particularly through his evening guitar practice, where he embraced the principles of regular practice and playful exploration. His after-work ritual helps him to process the emotional weight of supporting adolescent refugees in crisis, as the rhythmic patterns and melodic creation provided a restorative space away from classroom demands. Through experimenting with different melodies and rhythms, he discovered how this musical approach helped release accumulated tension and restore his capacity for emotional presence after challenging days in the classroom.

Miriam's evening visual art practice demonstrates the interplay of safe spaces and regular engagement. Each evening after work, she engages in creating visual art to process the events of the day. This creative routine helps maintain professional boundaries while honouring the emotional weight of her work, showing how multiple creative pathways allow practitioners to match their expression to varying emotional needs.

These self-care practices demonstrate how the five core principles identified by the author work together to create sustainable approaches to professional wellbeing. Through engaging multiple sensory pathways – tactile, auditory, and visual – practitioners process complex emotional experiences while maintaining healthy boundaries. The interplay of these principles creates a robust framework: inclusivity opens the door to creative expression, regular practice deepens its impact, safe spaces allow for authentic engagement, integration sustains the practice, and playful exploration ensures that these approaches remain dynamic and enriching over time. Together these principles establish a strong foundation for maintaining practitioner wellbeing while supporting trauma-impacted displaced adolescents.

Expressive Arts Modalities: Deepening Practice

Building on this foundation for practitioner wellbeing, I now explore how specific arts modalities embody these principles. Each approach offers unique benefits: visual arts facilitate expression through colour and form (Wertheim-Cahen 1998), movement brings awareness into the body (La Torre 2008), drama creates space for exploring professional challenges (Zografou 2014), music integrates sensory experience (Simhon et al. 2019), and writing encourages narrative exploration (Bolton and Shuttle 2011). A personalised blend of these modalities creates a balanced self-care practice that can adapt to changing needs.

Visual arts offer accessible ways to process clinical experiences. Quick sketching between sessions transforms abstract emotional experiences into concrete visual narratives, while different materials support specific needs: pastels offer gentle processing when overwhelmed and watercolours facilitate emotional flow (Horovitz 2017; Penzes et al. 2014). Activities such as collage-making help practitioners identify patterns in their work, especially valuable when supporting refugee adolescents with complex trauma responses (see Chapters 9 and 10).

A central theme throughout this book, relevant to both practitioners and those they support, is the fundamental role of the body in trauma processing and heal-ing, as emphasised by contemporary trauma research (see Chapter 9). This under-standing is supported by a number of seminal works in the field. Van der Kolk's (2014) influential research demonstrates how trauma becomes embedded within the physical body, necessitating body-based (somatic) interventions for healing. Levine (2010) observes that trauma healing occurs through the discharge of 'frozen energy' that becomes trapped in the nervous system during overwhelming events when the natural fight–flight–freeze is interrupted before completion. Ogden and Fisher's (2015) sensorimotor approach emphasises that trauma recovery must engage the body through mindful awareness and movement to reestablish healthy regulation.

The Capacitar programme, meaning 'to empower' in Spanish, equips practition-ers and those engaging in therapy with a comprehensive framework for trauma healing that operationalises these theoretical frameworks through body-based practices accessible to all (Rebmann Condon and Mathes Cane 2011). Through extensive practitioner field work across multiple countries, the programme has developed emergency response tools for wellbeing, which are available in 41 lan-guages. The breathing and body-based practices outlined in these kits offer both practitioners and those they support concrete tools for healing that align with con-temporary trauma theory while remaining culturally adaptable and accessible with-out needing specialised resources. Practitioners can implement simple yet effective techniques such as finger-to-thumb touches for nervous system regulation, gentle wrist rotations for tension release, and conscious postural adjustments for ground-ing (Mathes Cane and Revtyak 2016).

Complementing the somatic approaches discussed earlier, practitioners can integrate mindful movement practices that demonstrate measurable benefits for trauma recovery. For example, Gotink et al. (2016) found that guiding individ-uals through mindful walking at a measured pace while attending to physical sensations, breath, and surroundings reduces stress and anxiety while building emotional resilience.

These mindful movement practices demonstrate how practitioners can embody the core principle of trauma research in their daily work: that attention to physi-cal sensation supports trauma resolution and emotional regulation. While this somatic awareness benefits all therapeutic work, it becomes particularly valuable when supporting refugee adolescents through displacement trauma, where practi-tioners often carry the weight of witnessing profound loss and disruption. These practices offer grounding for both practitioner and adolescent during therapeutic encounters that can stir deep emotional responses. For a comprehensive collection of these techniques and detailed guidance on their implementation, please refer to the Toolkit in Chapter 15.

Writing techniques can help contain and process the complex emotional experiences encountered in professional practice (Bolton 2011; Pennebaker and Chung 2011). While reflective journaling offers a foundation for daily processing, practitioners may choose different writing forms depending on their specific needs. When confronting challenging themes in their work, poetry offers a space for metaphorical engagement, allowing for difficult material to be approached through symbolic language (Baraitser 2014). During intense periods of clinical work, haiku, the Japanese three-line poetry form, can be particularly useful for distilling overwhelming experiences into manageable pieces, creating containment through its structured brevity (Stephenson and Rosen 2015).

To understand patterns in professional practice, narrative writing helps identify recurring themes and responses, supporting professional development through the construction of coherent stories (Bolton 2006). This narrative approach becomes especially valuable when supporting refugee adolescents who may be relocated suddenly without opportunity for proper closure. In these situations, unsent letters offer a contained way to process abrupt endings while honouring the emotional complexity of interrupted relationships.

Music and sound practices provide immediate access to emotional regulation throughout the workday. Research shows that even brief musical interventions can significantly reduce workplace stress and improve cognitive function (Thaut and Hoemberg 2014). Practitioners can develop personal libraries of sound resources: calming nature sounds for brief reset moments, rhythmic pieces for energy restoration, or melodic compositions for emotional processing. As Porges (2011) demonstrates, simple humming between sessions helps regulate the nervous system through vagal stimulation, activating the vagus nerve system that acts as a counterbalance to the fight or flight system and can trigger a relaxation response in our body. He also advocates gently tapping sequences for grounding, which can be incorporated into different activities. The effectiveness of these techniques lies in their flexibility and adaptability to individual needs and workplace contexts.

Whether in a private office, quiet hallway, or staff room, these practices can be seamlessly integrated into daily routines: a two-minute sketch while writing case notes, a walking meditation between sessions, or a calming playlist for the commute home. Group practices like opening meetings with collective breathing or ending supervision with shared creative reflection help create environments where self-care is valued and normalised. Rather than adhering to any single method, this approach draws on multiple perspectives to support sustainable practice through embodied awareness and regular creative engagement while maintaining safe spaces for exploration.

Integrating Creative Self-Care into Professional Practice

The natural rhythm and sustainability of embedding expressive arts approaches into daily practice require thoughtful attention. Just as the refugee adolescents we support need consistent, reliable spaces for processing their experiences, practitioners need to establish rhythms to embed creative self-care. Whether starting a morning shift or beginning night work, these transition points offer natural opportunities for creative and embodied engagement. These rituals at the beginning of shifts help practitioners to prepare emotionally for holding space for young people's trauma narratives, while end-of-shift practices support the vital boundary between professional and personal life. Laura's practice of creating mandalas during quiet moments in her night shifts, combined with evening crocheting, demonstrates how different creative modalities can frame the working day, while Conor's use of music marks clear transitions between teaching and home life.

The intensity of trauma-informed work with refugee adolescents means that practitioners need moments to replenish their emotional reserves throughout the day. Brief practices like Miriam's quick sketching between therapy sessions or Conor's mindful movement between classes help process each interaction before moving to the next, leaving space for each new encounter while maintaining professional presence. These brief but intentional moments of creative engagement allow practitioners to ground themselves between intense emotional encounters.

Group settings also provide valuable opportunities for collective creative care (Argyle and Winship 2015). Whether through shared art-making in team meetings, group breathing exercises, movement practices, or reflective groups, collective creative practices strengthen team cohesion while providing contained spaces for processing the unique challenges of refugee trauma work (Boyles et al. 2023). Professional supervision particularly benefits from these creative approaches, with visual mapping, conscious breathing, movement exploration and arts-based reflection capturing nuances of practice that are difficult to express through verbal discussion (Bradley et al. 2024). Such creative supervision deepens both personal and professional development, strengthening practitioner's capacities for sustained engagement in trauma-informed work with refugee adolescents (Lahad 2000).

Creating a sustainable practice requires acknowledging and addressing common barriers such as time constraints and initial discomfort with creative expression. Starting small, perhaps with just two minutes of mindful breathing or a quick sketch between sessions, allows these practices to become manageable parts of daily routines. Setting realistic goals means recognising that self-care, like any skill, develops gradually through consistent engagement rather than making dramatic changes.

Conclusions

Supporting refugee adolescents through their healing journeys benefits from practitioners maintaining their own emotional wellbeing through consistent creative engagement. The experiences of Laura, Conor, and Miriam demonstrate how integrating expressive arts into daily practice, whether through visual art, movement, music, writing, or any of the other many creative modalities available to practitioners, helps process the emotional weight of this work while staying present and regulated.

These creative self-care practices are most effective when practitioners naturally incorporate them into their daily routines, customise them to fit their personal preferences and work environment, and operate within a team culture that actively supports such practices. When practitioners nurture their own resilience through creative expression, they not only sustain their capacity to support young people's healing but also model healthy ways of processing difficult experiences.

When practitioners prioritise their creative self-care, the benefits extend directly to the refugee adolescents they support. By maintaining their emotional regulation and presence, practitioners model healthy coping strategies that young people can observe and internalise. This 'parallel process' demonstrates that managing difficult emotions is both possible and valuable. Additionally, practitioners who engage in regular creative self-care preserve their capacity for attunement and empathic connection, essential qualities when working with trauma-impacted youth. Rather than viewing self-care as separate from the care of those they support, this integrated approach recognises that practitioner wellbeing and adolescent healing are fundamentally interconnected. Through their own creative engagement, practitioners embody the very resilience they hope to nurture in the refugee adolescents they support.

For the practical implementation of these and other expressive arts approaches, readers are encouraged to explore the activity locator provided in Chapter 15. While designed with the refugee adolescents we are working with in mind, this toolkit offers valuable self-care techniques that can benefit practitioners across various helping professions and contexts.

References

Alayarian, A. 2007. 'Trauma, resilience and creativity'. In A Alayarian, *Resilience, suffering and creativity: The work of the refugee therapy centre,* 1–15. Karnac Book Ltd.

Argyle, E and Winship, G. 2015. 'Creative practice in a group setting'. *Mental Health and Social Inclusion, 19*(3): 141–147.

Baraitser, M. 2014. *Reading and expressive writing with traumatised children, young refugees and asylum seekers: Unpack my heart with words.* Jessica Kingsley Publishers.

Bent-Goodley, T. 2018. 'Being intentional about self-care for social workers'. *Social Work, 63*(1): 5–6. doi:10.1093/sw/swx058

Bolton, G. 2006. 'Narrative writing: Reflective enquiry into professional practice'. *Educational Action Research, 14*(2): 203–218.

Bolton, G. 2011. *Write yourself: Creative writing and personal Development.* Jessica Kingsley Publishers.

Bolton, G and Shuttle, P. 2011. *Write yourself: Creative writing and personal development (Writing for therapy or personal development).* Jessica Kingsley Publishers.

Boyles, J, Ewart-Biggs, R, Horn, R and Lamb, K. 2023. *Groupwork with refugees and survivors of human rights abuses: The power of togetherness.* Routledge.

Bradley, L, Mendoza, K, Hollingsworth, L, Johnson, P, Duffey, T and Daniels, J. 2024. 'Creative supervision: Ten techniques to enhance supervision'. *Journal of Creativity in Mental Health*: 262–274. doi:10.1080/15401383.2023.2176391

Gotink, R, Hermans, K, Geschwind, N, De Nooij, R, De Groot, W and Speckens, A. 2016. 'Mindfulness and mood stimulate each other in an upward spiral: A mindful walking intervention using experience sampling'. *Mindfulness*, 7: 1114–1122. doi:10.1007/s12671-016-0550-8

Hadar, R. 2021. *Layers of meaning: Elements of visual journaling.* Stackpole Books.

Horovitz, E. 2017. *A guide to art therapy materials, methods and applications: A practical step-by-step approach.* Routledge.

La Torre, M.-A. 2008. 'The role of body movement in psychotherapy'. *Perspectives in Psychiatric Care, 44*(2): 127–130.

Lahad, M. 2000. *Creative supervision.* Jessica Kingsley Publishers.

Levine, P. 2010. *In an unspoken voice: How the body releases trauma and restores goodness.* North Atlantic Books.

Mathes Cane, P and Revtyak, K. 2016. *Capacitar practices of self-care and trauma healing for refugees and those who walk with them.* Capacitar.

Ogden, P and Fisher, J. 2015 *Sensorimotor psychotherapy: Interventions for trauma and attachment.* W. W.Norton and Company.

Pennebaker, J.W and Chung, C.K. 2011. 'Expressive writing: Connections to physical and mental health'. In H.S. Friedman, *Oxford handbook of health psychology*, 417-437. Oxford University Press.

Penzes, I, van Hooren, S, Dokter, D, Smeijsters, H and Hutschemaekers, G. 2014. 'Material interaction in art therapy assessment'. *The Arts in Psychotherapy, 41*: 484–492.

Porges, S. 2011. *The polyvagal theory: Neurophysiological foundations of emotions, attachment, communication and self-regulation.* W.W.Norton and Company.

Pryce, J, Shackelford, K and Pryce, D. 2007. *Secondary traumatic stress and the child welfare professional.* Lyceum Books.

Rebmann Condon, J and Mathes Cane, P. 2011. *Capacitar: Healing trauma, empowering wellness: A multicultural popular education approach to transforming Trauma.* Capacitar International and Trocaire.

Shepherd, M and Newell, J. 2020. 'Stress and health in social workers: Implications for self-care practice'. *Best Practices in Mental Health, 16*(1): 46–65.

Simhon, V, Elefant, C and Orkibi, H. 2019. 'Associations between music and the sensory system'. *The Arts in Psychotherapy, 64*: 26–33.

Stephenson, K and Rosen, D. 2015. 'Haiku and healing: An empirical study of poetry writing as therapeutic and creative intervention'. *Empirical Studies of the Arts, 33*(1): 36–60. doi:10.1177/0276237415569981

Thaut, M and Hoemberg, V. 2014. *Handbook of neurologic music therapy.* Oxford University Press.

van der Kolk, B. 2014. *The body keeps the score: Brain, mind and body in the healing of trauma.* Penguin Books.

Wertheim-Cahen, T. 1998. 'Art therapy with asylum seekers: Humanitarian relief'. In D. Dokter, *Arts therapists, refugees and migrants: reaching across borders,* 41–62. Jessica Kingsley Publishers.

Zografou, L. 2014. 'Four elements: Group supervision and playback theater'. In A Chesner and L Zografou, *Creative supervision across modalities: Theory and applications for therapists, counsellors and other helping professionals,* 59–71 Jessica Kingsley Publishers.

Chapter 15

Activity Locator

Finding Expressive Arts Tools by Need and Chapter

Introduction

This activity locator serves as a navigational guide to help practitioners quickly find and implement appropriate expressive arts and breathwork techniques based on specific adolescent refugee needs. While previous chapters have explored theoretical frameworks and provided detailed case studies, this chapter acts as a comprehensive reference system to locate relevant activities throughout the book.

The locator is organised around the five core needs consistently identified in my clinical work with refugee adolescents and reflected in the case study chapters:

- Managing stress and anxiety
- Validating feelings
- Supporting sleep
- Building social connections
- Coping with loss.

These core needs require flexible, culturally sensitive approaches that can be adapted across different settings and professional roles.

This chapter consists solely of reference tables organised by these core needs, providing a comprehensive system to locate relevant activities throughout the book. Each core need table details the chapter numbers/page numbers, activity names, and brief descriptions to facilitate the quick identification of appropriate tools. To further support implementation, downloadable resource cards for all activities are available online to accompany this book. These cards provide portable, easy-to-reference summaries of key techniques that practitioners can use in various settings.

Using the Toolkit Effectively

Before using any activity in this toolkit and in previous chapters, practitioners should consider the following guidelines to ensure that practice is safe, ethical, and culturally responsive:

DOI: 10.4324/9781003430032-16

Preparation and Safety

1. Ensure that participants have sufficient regulatory capacity for the planned activity by assessing current distress levels before starting the activity.
2. Ensure appropriate space and privacy for the activities, creating an environment where participants feel secure expressing themselves.
3. Check the cultural appropriateness of the planned activities, considering cultural backgrounds and potential sensitivities.
4. Have grounding techniques readily available in case participants become triggered during the activity.
5. Begin with basic regulation activities such as simple breathing exercises or gentle movement to establish safety.

Cultural Considerations

1. Familiarise yourself with the cultural backgrounds and contexts of participants and be culturally curious.
2. Respect cultural practices in relation to the expression of body awareness.
3. Ensure activities are developmentally appropriate.
4. Select metaphors and language that are culturally appropriate.
5. Recognise that activities may need adjustment to align with participants' cultural values and preferences.

Professional Boundaries

1. Work within your qualifications and expertise.
2. Establish clear boundaries with participants regarding time limits, confidentiality, and disclosure obligations.
3. Maintain appropriate referral networks for issues beyond your scope of practice.
4. Seek supervision when needed.
5. Regularly evaluate effectiveness and adjust approaches accordingly.

Conclusions

This Activity Locator provides a systematic way to navigate the expressive arts and breathwork techniques presented throughout this book, enabling practitioners to quickly identify appropriate activities based on the specific needs of refugee adolescents. By organising these resources according to core therapeutic needs, this chapter facilitates sufficient preparation and programme planning across various practice settings. The tables serve as a planning tool for developing tailored support programmes, while the downloadable resource cards available online offer

Comprehensive Table of Activities by Therapeutic Purpose

Managing Stress and Anxiety

Activity	Approach	Chapter Reference	For Use by	Key Features
7/11 Breathing	Body-based	Chapter 8	All practitioners	Breathing in for count of 7, out for 11; focuses on longer exhale for parasympathetic activation
Diaphragmatic Breathing	Body-based	Chapters 8, 10, 11	All practitioners	Deep belly breathing focusing on stomach expansion rather than chest
Progressive Muscle Relaxation	Body-based	Chapter 10	All practitioners	Systematic tension and release of muscle groups with body mapping using colours
Butterfly Hug	Body-based	Chapter 10	All practitioners	Self-administered bilateral stimulation by crossing arms and alternately tapping upper arms
Bilateral Drawing	Arts	Chapter 5	All practitioners	Drawing with both hands simultaneously for grounding and integration
Mandala Colouring	Arts	Chapters 8, 10	All practitioners	Colouring circular geometric patterns for meditation and focus
Safe Space Visualisation	Mind-body	Chapter 9	All practitioners	Creating detailed multisensory mental sanctuary as an anchor for grounding
Mindful Awareness of Senses	Mind-body	Chapter 10	All practitioners	Focused attention on sensory experiences in present moment
Grounding Movements	Body-based	Chapters 9, 12	All practitioners	Gentle neck rolls, shoulder rotations, and ankle circles to release tension
Finger-to-Thumb Touches	Body-based	Chapter 14	All practitioners	Touching each finger to thumb in sequence for nervous system regulation
Wrist Rotations	Body-based	Chapter 14	All practitioners	Gentle circular movements of wrists for tension release
Mindful Walking	Body-based	Chapter 14	All practitioners	Measured walking pace with attention to physical sensations, breath, and surroundings
Humming	Sound-body	Chapter 14	All practitioners	Simple humming to stimulate vagal tone and trigger relaxation response

Activity	Type	Chapter	Practitioners	Description
Gentle Tapping Sequences	Body-based	Chapter 14	All practitioners	Rhythmic tapping on body for grounding and regulation
Natural Objects as Grounding Tools	Symbolic	Chapters 9, 12	All practitioners	Using stones, shells, pinecones as transitional objects for grounding
Stone Decoration	Arts-Symbolic	Chapter 8	All practitioners	Decorating stones with meaningful symbols or quotes
Singing Bowl	Sound-Symbolic	Chapter 12	All practitioners	Using singing bowl for opening/closing rituals and grounding
Rhythm Work	Music-Movement	Chapter 5	All practitioners	Using rhythmic movements and drumming for regulation
Calming Playlists	Music	Chapters 10, 14	All practitioners	Curated music collections for different emotional needs
Nature Sounds	Sound	Chapter 14	All practitioners	Using recorded natural sounds for grounding
Rhythm-Based Regulation	Music	Chapter 5	All practitioners	Using steady rhythms to regulate nervous system
Mental Health Toolbox	Multiple	Chapter 8	All practitioners	Personalised collection of coping strategies and resources
Group Breathing Ritual	Body-based	Chapters 12, 14	All practitioners	Collective breathing practice to begin/end sessions
Worry Time	Cognitive	Chapter 10	All practitioners	Designated time earlier in the day to process concerns
Clay Work for Trauma	Arts	Chapter 11	Psychotherapists	Tactile processing of trauma memories through clay sculpting
Quick Sketching	Arts	Chapter 14	Psychotherapists	Brief drawing between sessions to process experiences
Stretching Sequences	Movement	Chapters 12, 14	All practitioners	Gentle stretching to release physical tension

Validating Feelings

Activity	Approach	Chapter Reference	For Use by	Key Features
Collaging	Arts	Chapters 5, 9	All practitioners	Creating layered visual expressions using magazine images and other materials
Inside-Outside Mask	Arts	Chapter 5	Psychotherapists	Creating masks showing external presentation and internal feelings
Art Journaling	Arts	Chapter 14	All practitioners	Combining visual art and writing to process experiences
Symbol Cards	Symbolic	Chapter 11	Psychotherapists	Using cards with various images to facilitate expression
Sand Tray Work	Symbolic	Chapter 11	Psychotherapists	Creating scenes in sand with miniature objects to represent experiences
Movement Mapping	Movement	Chapter 12	Psychotherapists	Exploring emotional responses through physical movement
Sound Stories	Music	Chapter 12	Psychotherapists	Using instruments to express experiences non-verbally
Personal Soundtrack	Music	Chapter 11	Psychotherapists	Creating playlist representing identity and journey
Group Soundscape	Music	Chapter 12	Psychotherapists	Collaborative creation of sound environment
Expressive Writing	Writing	Chapters 5, 14	All practitioners	Free-form writing to process emotions and experiences
Haiku Writing	Writing	Chapter 14	All practitioners	Creating three-line poems to distill experiences
Unsent Letters	Writing	Chapter 14	All practitioners	Writing letters (not to be sent) to process relationships
Poetry Writing	Writing	Chapters 5, 14	All practitioners	Using poetic forms to express complex emotions
Witnessing Circle	Relational	Chapter 12	Psychotherapists	Structured sharing of experiences with attentive listening
Body Mapping	Body-based	Chapters 8, 10	All practitioners	Visual representation of physical sensations on body outline drawings
Transformative Sculpting	Arts	Chapter 11	Psychotherapists	Reshaping clay to transform representations of difficult memories
Embodied Storytelling	Movement	Chapter 11	Psychotherapists	Using movement to access and integrate physical memories
Dream–Sense–Memory Approach	Sensory	Chapter 10	Psychotherapists	Present-tense recounting of dreams with focus on sensory elements
'I Am' Poems	Writing	Chapter 11	All practitioners	Identity-based creative writing using repetitive structure

Supporting Sleep

Activity	Approach	Chapter Reference	For Use by	Key Features
Worry Dolls	Symbolic	Chapter 10	All practitioners	Crafting small figures to symbolically transfer worries before sleep
Dream Landscape Visualisation	Mind-body	Chapter 10	All practitioners	Detailed imaginary peaceful place for sleep transition
Sleep Hygiene Practices	Educational	Chapter 10	All practitioners	Structured routines and environmental adjustments for better sleep
Sleep Playlist Creation	Music	Chapter 10	All practitioners	Personalised collection of calming sounds for sleep
Nocturnal Journaling	Writing	Chapter 10	Psychotherapists	Documenting dreams, sleep experiences, and sensory details
Dream Processing	Psychological	Chapter 10	Psychotherapists	Exploring meanings and patterns in dream content
20-Minute Rule	Behavioural	Chapter 10	All practitioners	Getting up after 20 minutes of sleeplessness for quiet activity
Evening Wind-Down	Multiple	Chapter 10	All practitioners	Structured transition activities before sleep
Mindful Colouring	Arts-mindfulness	Chapters 8, 10	All practitioners	Focused attention on colouring process for meditative effect
Progressive Muscle Relaxation	Body-based	Chapter 10	All practitioners	Systematic tension and release of muscle groups with body mapping
Guided Imagery	Mind-body	Chapter 5	All practitioners	Structured visualisation combined with gentle movement
Cultural Comforters	Cultural	Chapter 8	All practitioners	Personal objects with cultural significance that provide comfort

Building Social Connections

Activity	Approach	Chapter Reference	For Use by	Key Features
Eco-mapping	Arts	Chapter 11	All practitioners	Visual representation of social supports and relationships
Fabric Narratives	Arts	Chapter 12	Psychotherapists	Using textiles to create visual maps of relationships
Tree of Life	Narrative Arts	Chapter 8	All practitioners	Using tree metaphor to explore roots (origins), trunk (strengths), branches (hopes)
Visual Resource Mapping	Arts	Chapter 11	All practitioners	Creating visual representations of community resources and support networks
Team Support Map	Arts	Chapter 11	All practitioners	Visual mapping of support services organised like a football pitch
Team Tactics in Motion	Movement-Symbolic	Chapter 11	All practitioners	Physical positioning in space to represent support network
String Connections	Symbolic	Chapter 11	All practitioners	Using coloured string to represent connections between supports
Invisible Toolkit	Digital	Chapter 11	All practitioners	Digital visual guide of support networks stored in phone
Collective Tapestry	Arts	Chapter 12	Psychotherapists	Group creation of connected fabric pieces representing shared journey
Shared Art Making	Arts	Chapters 11, 12, 14	All practitioners	Collaborative creation of visual expressions
Group Movement	Movement	Chapters 12, 14	All practitioners	Synchronised or responsive movement activities
Collective Meaning-Making	Multiple	Chapter 12	Psychotherapists	Group process of creating shared narrative from individual experiences
Cultural Bridging Activities	Cultural	Chapter 11	All practitioners	Practices that connect home and host cultures
Sand Art	Arts	Chapter 9	All practitioners	Using coloured sand and glue to create patterns and expressions
Staff Transition Rituals	Multiple	Chapter 14	All practitioners	Structured practices for shift changes in residential settings

Coping with Loss

Activity	Approach	Chapter Reference	For Use by	Key Features
Memory Holders	Arts	Chapter 12	Psychotherapists	Creating containers (boxes, etc.) for processing memories
Matryoshka Dolls	Symbolic	Chapter 11	Psychotherapists	Using nested dolls to explore layered aspects of identity and experiences
Memory Envelopes	Writing-Symbolic	Chapter 12	Psychotherapists	Creating sealed envelopes containing written memories
Fabric Movement	Arts-Movement	Chapter 12	Psychotherapists	Exploring relationships through movement with fabric pieces
Unsent Letters	Writing	Chapter 14	All practitioners	Writing letters (not to be sent) to process relationships
Art Timeline	Arts	Chapter 11	Psychotherapists	Visual representation of life journey using Matryoshka dolls
Personal Flag Creation	Arts	Chapter 11	Psychotherapists	Designing a personal flag representing different aspects of identity
Self-Landscape	Arts	Chapter 9	Psychotherapists	Creating three-dimensional representation of identity
Identity Mapping	Multiple	Chapter 11	Psychotherapists	Exploring evolving sense of self across cultures
Cultural Symbol Integration	Cultural	Chapters 8, 11	All practitioners	Incorporating meaningful cultural symbols into creative work
Faith-Based Resources	Spiritual	Chapter 8	All practitioners	Using religious texts, prayer mats, or other spiritual items
Bilingual Resources	Linguistic	Chapters 9, 13	All practitioners	Creating materials in both native language and host country language

portable summaries that can be readily accessed before and during sessions in class-rooms, community centres, clinical settings, and residential facilities. Together, these resources aim to enhance practitioners' capacity to respond effectively to the complex needs of adolescent refugees through culturally responsive, evidence-informed, expressive arts approaches.

Conclusions

In these final reflections, we return to the core challenges faced by adolescent refugees – navigating the dual transitions of forced displacement and adolescent development while carrying the weight of traumatic experiences. Throughout these chapters, we have explored how the expressive arts offer unique pathways for supporting these young people, creating opportunities for healing, connection, and growth that transcend language barriers and cultural differences.

The opening chapters of this book establish the essential foundations upon which our expressive arts approaches are built. From Bronfenbrenner's ecological systems framework that contextualises adolescent refugee experiences, to the neurobiological understanding of how trauma manifests in the body, these concepts inform every approach described. Our examination of culturally sensitive language for mental health, combined with trauma-informed principles for creating safety, provides the necessary conditions for meaningful engagement. These theoretical underpinnings, together with a comprehensive exploration of the unique therapeutic benefits of the expressive arts, create a robust framework that supports the diverse applications demonstrated throughout the case studies.

The case studies presented throughout this book illustrate the remarkable versatility of creative approaches. We have witnessed Daahir developing his mental health toolkit, Nabeel reconnecting with frozen emotions, Anastasija navigating nighttime distress through creative tools, Omar building community through football, and Ovie processing grief in a group setting. Each narrative demonstrates how expressive arts can be thoughtfully adapted to address specific needs while honouring individual journeys, cultural backgrounds, and developmental stages.

A central theme emerging across these cases is the power of non-verbal expression. When words fail, whether due to language differences, the impact of trauma on verbal processing, or cultural variations in emotional expression – the expressive arts provide alternative languages. Through drawing, movement, music, drama, and other creative modalities, refugee adolescents can express that which might otherwise remain unspoken, gradually integrating fragmented experiences into more coherent narratives of identity and belonging.

DOI: 10.4324/9781003430032-17

The ecological systems framework that underpins this book reminds us that supporting refugee adolescents requires attention to multiple interconnected environments. The creative interventions described throughout these chapters address needs across these systems, from helping individuals regulate their emotional responses and process traumatic memories, to fostering connections within peer groups, to building bridges between home and host cultures. This multi-layered approach acknowledges the complex interplay between individual healing and broader social integration.

We have seen how these creative approaches can be implemented across diverse professional contexts. For teachers, youth workers, and residential care staff, the expressive arts offer accessible tools for building safety, providing psychoeducation, and bearing witness to young people's experiences. For psychotherapists and counsellors, these modalities provide powerful vehicles for deeper trauma processing and identity development. The clear distinction between approaches appropriate for all practitioners and those requiring specialist training ensures that professionals can implement these techniques ethically within their scope of practice.

Working with interpreters, as explored in Chapter 13, adds another dimension to this practice. The thoughtful integration of interpreters into expressive arts work creates possibilities for deeper cultural understanding and more nuanced therapeutic engagement. Rather than viewing interpretation as a barrier, we have seen how it can become an opportunity for richer communication when approached with cultural sensitivity and clear professional boundaries.

The self-care practices outlined in Chapter 14 remind us that supporting traumatised young people requires sustained attention to the wellbeing of practitioners. The expressive arts offer a valuable resource not only for our work with refugee adolescents, but also for processing our own emotional responses to this demanding yet rewarding field. By nurturing our capacity for creativity and presence, we strengthen our ability to create safe, supportive spaces for the young people we support.

The Activity Locator in Chapter 15 provides a practical bridge between theory and implementation. By organising techniques according to common needs such as managing stress and anxiety, validating feelings, supporting sleep, building social connections, and coping with loss, this resource enables practitioners to quickly find relevant approaches for specific situations. This practical focus reflects the book's commitment to translating theoretical understanding into meaningful support for refugee adolescents.

For instance, a school counsellor working with a recently arrived refugee student showing signs of anxiety might quickly consult the 'Managing Stress and Anxiety' table to identify appropriate techniques based on their setting and training. They could locate the 'Safe Space Visualisation' activity from Chapter 9, implement it during a support session, and later introduce the student to 'Mandala

Colouring' as a take-home practice. When noticing the student's sleep difficulties, they might return to the locator to find appropriate interventions under 'Supporting Sleep' and coordinate with the student's residential care team for consistent use of these practices across settings.

Looking towards the future, the principles outlined in this book offer possibilities for broader applications. The principles of trauma-informed expressive arts work can inform institutional policies, educational curricula, and community integration programmes. By recognising the value of creative expression in healing and connection, we can create more responsive systems for supporting refugee adolescents across various contexts.

Throughout these chapters, we have emphasised the importance of cultural humility – approaching each young person with curiosity, respect, and openness to learning. The expressive arts, with their emphasis on personal meaning-making and self-directed expression, naturally align with this stance through their emphasis on personal meaning-making and self-directed expression. Rather than imposing predetermined interpretations or expectations, these approaches invite refugee adolescents to define their own meanings and cultivate their own pathways towards healing.

Perhaps most importantly, creative approaches help us to recognise and nurture the profound resilience that characterises so many refugee adolescents. Despite experiencing displacement, loss, and trauma, these young people demonstrate a remarkable capacity for adaptation, connection, and growth. Creative approaches help uncover and strengthen these capacities, shifting focus from deficits to resources, from damage to possibility.

As practitioners supporting refugee adolescents, we strive to become trusted witnesses to their journeys of healing and integration. The expressive arts give us tools to accompany them respectfully, creating spaces where their voices can be heard, their experiences honoured, and their identities affirmed. In these creative encounters, transformation becomes possible – not as something we impose upon young people, but as something we cultivate together through shared exploration and mutual respect.

The road ahead for refugee adolescents remains challenging. Political, social, and economic barriers continue to complicate their integration and wellbeing. Yet within these constraints, the expressive arts offer spaces of possibility – moments where young people can reclaim agency, rebuild connections, and reimagine futures beyond trauma and displacement. By continuing to develop and refine these approaches, we contribute to more compassionate, effective support for adolescent refugees worldwide.

I hope this book invites ongoing exploration, adaptation, and innovation rather than serving as a definitive statement. The field of expressive arts with refugee populations continues to evolve, shaped by new research, emerging practices, and, most importantly, the wisdom of the young people themselves. I invite you, as practitioners, to apply these approaches in your own contexts, to document your findings, and to share your innovations with the wider community. By remaining attentive to the experiences of refugee adolescents and responsive to their needs, together we can continue to develop practices that truly honour their journeys and support them to thrive in new contexts.

Index

Note: Page numbers in **bold** reference tables; page numbers in *italics* reference figures.

For Product Safety Concerns and Information please contact our EU
representative GPSR@taylorandfrancis.com
Taylor & Francis Verlag GmbH, Kaufingerstraße 24, 80331 München, Germany

www.ingramcontent.com/pod-product-compliance
Lightning Source LLC
Chambersburg PA
CBHW052000270326
41929CB00015B/2733